To Lena, my wife and companion for half a century

A JOURNEY OF FAITH : AN AUTOBIOGRAPHY Copyright ● 1993
Centre for Mennonite Brethren Studies
1-169 Riverton Ave.,
Winnipeg, MB R2L 2E5
Canada

Published simultaneously by Kindred Press, Winnipeg, MB, Canada R2L 2E5 and Kindred Press, Hillsboro, USA 67063

Printed in Canada by The Christian Press, Winnipeg.

Canadian Cataloguing in Publication Data

Ewert, David 1922–

A journey of faith : an autobiography

ISBN 1-895432-20-0

1. Ewert, David 1922-   2. Mennonites - Canada - Biography.
3. Educators - Canada - Biography.
I. Centre for Mennonite Brethren Studies. II. Title.
BX8143.E93A3 1993   289.7'092   C93-098087-5

A Journey of Faith

An Autobiography

by

David Ewert

Publisher's Foreword

One of the mandates of the Centre for Mennonite Brethren Srudies is to promote research, writing and publication of materials that contribute to an understanding of Mennonite Brethren history, theology and identity in Canada. David Ewert has been a significant actor on Mennonite Brethren stage during the past generation, not only in Canada but also in the United States and, to some extent, in Europe and other continents. He has published extensively, especially on topics relating to biblical studies and theology. His most significant contributions have been in the area of education and preaching. For many years he was on the faculty of the Mennonite Brethren Bible College and for six years he was the President. He also served at other Mennonite and Mennonite Brethren institutions, including the Mennonite Brethren Biblical Seminary in Fresno, California. Throughout his career weekends were usually devoted to the preaching ministry. In addition, Ewert served on many Conference boards and committees and gave theological direction on many issues.

Ewert's rich career of teaching and preaching has left a profound impact on the church and on many individuals, particularily on those who were his students. He was a leader during an important transitional period for Mennonite Brethren. During the early period of his ministry he served with many leaders who had gained most of their educational background and experience in Russia and who were not very fluent in the English language. Ewert became fluent in English and received all of his theological education in North America. His roots were nevertheless closely linked to the culture of the previous generation, even as he taught a new generation of Canadian MBs who were attuned to North American culture and values. Some viewed him as an innovator who had become much too "liberal." For example, his rejection of dispensationalism and his acceptance of the Revised

Standard Version of the Bible made him suspect in the eyes of many. In time, others viewed him as too conservative on certain issues, particularly on such issues as women in ministry.

This autobiography gives us insights into the nature of the man, the nature of the church and the nature of the world which formed the backdrop to Ewert's career. Many readers will wish that Ewert would have been more personal and openly reflective, but that might have involved asking something which was contrary to his nature. Ewert, like many Mennonites of his generation, was not much given to baring his soul to others. Nevertheless, there is much to be gleaned "between the lines" in this autobiography, and our knowledge of this period of our history and the concerns and values which preoccupied the church will be enhanced by this volume.

The Centre wishes to acknowledge the help of several readers, especially Sarah Klassen and Harry Loewen, and the work of Alf Redekopp and Joel Wohlgemuth in the final preparation of the manuscript.

Abe Dueck
Director
Centre for Mennonite Brethren Studies

CONTENTS

PREFACE

A puritan writer, John Flavel, made the observation that "the providence of God is like Hebrew words--it can only be read backwards." The following pages are an attempt to do just that.

Wiser people than I have suggested that autobiographies ought not to be written too late in life. Some people in old age have perfect recall but can no longer distinguish between insignificant details and the rather more important aspects of life. Details are, of course, not unimportant. Indeed those who have a sharp eye for detail are often the most interesting story-tellers. However, there is nothing quite so irritating as a very short story which has been made into a full-length novel.

Whether seventy is an appropriate age at which to review one's past, I am not prepared to say. It may well be that if I waited another fifteen years I would see some things through different eyes. Be that as it may, what follows is a rehearsal of the seventy years of my life which God has graciously given me. The book is divided into chapters, not only for the sake of convenience, but also because it represents only some chapters from my journey thus far.

One cannot help but ask whether it is not a bit presumptuous and perhaps even narcissistic to let one's life pass in review in the presence of family, friends and, perhaps, even strangers. Is my life more important than that of others? The answer to that question is obviously, "No." We are all equally precious in the sight of God. Besides, there is an interesting story hidden in every life--and some of these untold stories would surely be more interesting than mine. However, I have been helped greatly on my Christian way by reading the life-stories of others. Autobiographies and biographies have, in fact, been favourite books of mine for some time.

I always encouraged our children to read the lives of men and women. Often they can be a great inspiration to us and help us shape our ideals. Also, they always represent a slice of human history and help to broaden our horizons. On one occasion, when one of our daughters, then in her teens, felt I was putting unnecessary restrictions upon her, she complained: "All you want us to do is to go to church and read biographies."

One dilemma a raconteur cannot avoid is what to include and what to leave out. How much self-revelation is appropriate when one writes for a wider audience? Reticence seems to be a rare quality these days in which it is the rage to "let it all hang out." I always find it rather embarrassing when people feel the urge to share intimate details of their life with the public. As I see it, there is an inner sanctum in every person which should be guarded against invasion and over-exposure. Some experiences are so sacred they become trivialized and even profaned when they are made public. By virtue of my upbringing and my personality I have tended perhaps to err on the side of reticence.

Hopefully, however, enough has been said in the following pages to allow fellow-travellers to see the grace of God in my life and to encourage them along the way. If it is not presumptuous, I would dare to hope that some readers will do what the Judean churches did in Paul's day: "They glorified God because of me.
I would like to thank Dr. Abe Dueck, of the Centre for Mennonite Brethren Studies, for seeing this manuscript through the press.

David Ewert

1

Land of my Birth

My family roots are in the former Soviet Union. That's where my cradle stood. As early as 1789 Mennonites from Prussia (now Poland) began to move into the Ukraine. They came in response to Catherine the Great's invitation and to her rather liberal promises of land and freedom. As the original settlements, Chortitza and Molotschna, grew and became overcrowded, new lands were acquired and daughter colonies established. One of these was Memrik.

Memrik was colonized by Mennonites in 1884. Some 30,000 acres of fertile farm-land were purchased from two Russian noblemen, and ten villages were established. The Volshja River, a tributary of the Samara, which spills its waters into the mighty Dnieper, flowed in serpentine fashion through the southern parts of Memrik. The land was mostly unbroken steppe. Among the first settlers of Memrik were my forebears.

About forty families established the village of Waldeck, which lay somewhat to the west of the Volshja River. The name "Waldeck" was chosen because it bordered on vast woodlands. Most of the inhabitants of Waldeck engaged in agriculture and the raising of cattle. At the end of the village's main street stood a factory for the production of farm implements and, typical of all Mennonite villages in South Russia, Waldeck had its own flour mill.

As was the custom at that time, the individual houses on either side of the village street were connected with the barn and the sheds. Behind the buildings lay the gardens and the orchards. Surrounding the village were the communal pasture lands and the beautiful woodlands. Beyond the grazing areas, the farms of the villagers stretched in every direction. At the centre of the village stood the school which also served as the church.

All the Mennonite villagers spoke a form of Low German in everyday life, but in school and church High German was the language of discourse. The Russian Mennonites, like their Anabaptist forebears, held to the concept of a believers' church. They had rejected infant baptism and, as a consequence, had suffered terribly at the hand of the state churches. However, the spiritual fervour and the missionary zeal which had characterized the Anabaptist movement in the sixteenth century had been largely lost in the following centuries and there was a crying need for revival. About the middle of the nineteenth century, winds of renewal blew across the Mennonite communities in Russia, leading to a re-examination of the New Testament concept of the church and a renewed emphasis on conversion and a personal knowledge of Christ. This led to the founding of the Mennonite Brethren Church in 1860--a church to which my parents belonged after their conversion and baptism.

My father, David Ewert, was born in 1894 and spent the first seven years of his life in the village of Waldeck. When he had finished his first year of school his parents decided to move to another village of the Memrick colony, namely Alexanderhof. This village lay on the eastern side of the Volshja River and was within walking distance of the Russian village of Galizenovka. Thirty *versts* from Alexanderhof lay the large Russian town of Yuzovka, where Mennonite farmers sold much of their fruit and other farm produce. Their grain, however, was shipped to Shelanaja, a railway station on the Catherine Line, from where it was transported to markets in Russia and western Europe.

My mother, whose maiden name was Margaret Wiebe, was born in 1900 in the village of Waldeck, where my father's cradle had also stood. Shortly after her birth the Wiebe family moved to Samara, near the Volga, where her father worked as a locksmith for a French factory owner. After several other moves the family returned to Waldeck where mother spent her youth. By then, however, the Ewert family had moved to Alexanderhof, and whereas the two villages were only four *versts* apart, my parents did not get to know each other until later in life.

Since the Czarist government had given the Mennonites the privilege of establishing their own educational system, both my father and mother received their elementary education under Mennonite teachers. Besides drilling their students in the three R's (reading, 'riting and 'rithmetic), Mennonite schools added a fourth, namely "religion." Village school teachers also often functioned as preachers of the church, and that was true of my father's teacher as well. In any case, Mennonite children all received basic religious instruction in school.

My father's school years were happy and carefree. There was fishing and swimming in the Volshja in summer and skating in the winter. The woods in the distance invited adventure-loving boys, and the village greens were perfect for playing ball. Of course summer holidays also meant working in the barn, the orchard and the fields, but school-years for both father and mother were uneventful. There were some dark clouds on the political horizon, such as the war with Japan and the demand by some Russian leaders for representative government, but those were concerns to adults, not to children.

At age fourteen, my father's school days were over. Memrik had no high school (Zentralschule), and dad's parents were too poor to send him to another colony for further schooling. The next several years he spent on the farm, helping his parents. There were nine children in the family, seven brothers and two sisters. Father's elder brother, Heinrich, had married Justina Wiebe (my mother's elder sister), and that is how father got to know the girl who was later to become his wife. Mother spent her teenage years in her parental home in Waldeck. Here she developed her culinary skills and became an excellent seamstress.

Father was working as a clerk in a store located in a neighbouring Russian village when the news that Russia had declared war on Germany sent shock waves through the Mennonite colonies. With thousands of other Mennonite men, father, as a conscientious objector to war, immediately volunteered for medical service in the Russian Red Cross as an alternative to the bearing of arms. From 1914 until the end of the First World War, he cared for the wounded on hospital trains that moved back and forth from the Russo-German front to the interior. The entire experience was a rude awakening for a boy who had known only the sheltered life of a Mennonite village. In later years, whenever we as children wanted dad, who was quite taciturn, to tell us a story, the war years always provided an ample store.

The joy of returning home after the war quickly changed to sorrow as the Bolshevik Revolution plunged the country into utter chaos. Among other things it unleashed the fury of the Machno bandits who terrorized the Mennonite villages, robbing, raping, burning and killing. The period between November 1918, when the German troops left the Ukraine, and the fall of 1920, was a time of anarchy, and many Mennonites lost their lives in that reign of terror. Mother was seventeen when she was captured on one occasion by a band of Machno's men, and her escape was nothing less than miraculous.

As in the case of the apocalyptic horsemen of the Revelation, war was followed by revolution; revolution brought disease and famine and death in its train. One of dad's younger brothers had been forcibly inducted into the Red Army. Here he contracted typhus, and before he had recovered he brought this deadly disease into the parental home. Within a month my paternal grandparents and four of father's brothers, none of whom I ever learned to know, were carried to their graves.

Father's brother, Heinrich, who had married my mother's older sister, also lay dying of typhus. This brought my mother, who was then in her later teens, to Alexanderhof. She came to help her sister Justina care for her suffering husband and her two small boys. My father, with several other members of the Ewert family, lay delirious with typhus fever. She then took it upon herself also to care for them. Humming a cheerful tune, she came again and again to tend to the needs of the sick and the dying, exposing herself to this contagious disease. My father vowed then that should God restore his health he would marry that girl.

God in his mercy did spare his life. After he had recovered from his bout with typhus, God began to move deeply in my father's life, convicting him of his need for a personal commitment to Christ as Saviour and Lord. He had already memorized the catechism and was prepared to be baptized in the Mennonite Church in which he had been brought up, but he hesitated because he knew that he had not been saved.

Through the preaching of Mennonite Brethren ministers, the singing of gospel songs in their home Bible studies which he had attended, and the personal witness of a brother-in-law, my father put his trust in the Saviour and was baptized upon his confession of faith in the Mennonite Brethren Church in Alexanderhof. Mother also had made a personal commitment to Christ, and much against the wishes of her parents, who belonged to the Mennonite Church as well, she was baptized in the cold river late in the year and was received into the Mennonite Brethren Church in Waldeck.

One day, when dad was twenty-six, he made his way from Alexanderhof to Waldeck where Margaret Wiebe, who was then twenty years old, lived. After much prayer he had made the decision to ask her parents for permission to marry their daughter. Even though dating was not in vogue in those days, young people still fell in love with each other, and my parents were no exception. Mother Wiebe thought Margaret was still too young, but she offered only moderate resistance. Permission having been granted by mother's parents, the wedding date was set. They were married in Waldeck, in October, 1920. For more than sixty-eight years, well past their golden wedding anniversary, they remained faithful to the vows they made on that day (Father passed away when he was 94).

After the wedding, dad took mother to live with him in his

parental home in Alexanderhof. A brother and a sister, with whom dad had shared the family home and farm after typhus wiped out almost the entire family, married about the same time. After dividing up the property, my parents lived alone in the house in which dad had lived since the age of seven.

In 1921 their first child was born. They named him John, after dad's brother who had been a minister of the gospel and who had also died of typhus. The times were still badly out of joint politically and the economy was in shambles. The armies that had moved back and forth over the Ukraine had requisitioned all the grain and most of the draft horses. As a result the farmers had no seed grain and no horses to do the field work. My parents now faced the awful spectre of famine. John was seven months old when his distended stomach began to show the marks of malnutrition. A neighbour lady who had received some rice from America one day brought the little fellow a cupful. Such little acts of kindness took on enormous significance in those days. The 1922 harvest was very meagre--just a bit of wheat, corn and sunflowers. The family lived mostly on small potatoes that year. Then on a cold winter's day, December 5, 1922, I was born.

By now not only had the food supply dwindled to almost nothing, but there was no cloth for clothing either. Father had two shirts left, and so for the first three months of my life, mother wrapped me in one of dad's shirts. In February, 1923, dad was finally able to press some oil from the sunflowers they had harvested. He sold this in the Russian town of Yusovka and bought some cloth for their two infant sons. In the spring of 1923 a Bulgarian family rented our land, and since they had nowhere to live, they moved in with us. They had grown vegetables along the river the previous summer and we were able to purchase a few cabbage heads from them. These Bulgarians took a liking to my brother and me and occasionally treated us to *chalwa*. Every bit of food was appreciated in those days. Understandably my parents always retained a high regard for daily bread and were very critical of wastefulness.

By the end of the year 1923 the economy seemed to improve somewhat and the bare necessities of life were becoming available once more. The Russian cooperative in Galizonovko, where dad had earlier worked as a clerk, began to function again, and he was asked to be the manager. Galizonovko was within walking distance from Alexanderhof and so, after letting out their land for rent, dad accepted the position.

However, the hopes for a brighter future were mixed with foreboding as Stalin gained his iron grip on the Soviet Union. Communist authorities made it very clear that religion had no place in the new society they were about to create. All religious instruction in the schools was forbidden, and many of the Mennonite teachers lost their jobs. Moreover, the Mennonites, who had a long tradition of hard work and private enterprise, found it hard to accept the planned collectivization of their farms by the new regime. Rumours of a mass exodus of Mennonites began to spread. No one could predict the future. There were those who foresaw better days ahead; others decided to leave the country while it was still possible. It was a hard decision to make, but my parents, after much prayer and consultation with friends and relatives, came to the conviction that if they could get an exit visa they would emigrate to Canada.

2

Lost Fatherland

Following the imperial Decree of 1870, which threatened to make military service obligatory, a great many Mennonites left Russia and settled in the United States and Canada. Single individuals and smaller groups continued to emigrate to North America in the following decades. After the Bolshevik Revolution, however, it appeared as if a mass exodus of Mennonites was about to take place.

A Study Commission left for North America in 1920 with the intention of informing Mennonites in America of the plight of their brothers in Soviet Russia, and also to investigate the possibilities of immigration and settlement in the United States and Canada. One result of the Commission's visit was the organization of the Mennonite Central Committee in Elkhart, Indiana, for the purpose of bringing famine relief to many starving Mennonites in Soviet Russia. Also, the visit of the Commission gave birth to the Mennonite Board of Colonization under the leadership of David Toews, Rosthern, Saskatchewan. This Board was able to persuade the Canadian government to allow Mennonite settlers from Russia to enter Canada.

In Soviet Russia the leader of the Association of Citizens of Dutch Extraction (most Mennonites who had come to the Ukraine from Prussia had their roots in the Netherlands) was B.B. Janz. The obstacles that had to be overcome both on the Canadian as well as on the Russian side were horrendous. Nevertheless, about 18,000 Mennonites were able to leave the Soviet Union between 1923 and 1927 and make their journey to Canada.

My mother's parents, the Abram Wiebes, together with several of their unmarried daughters, had decided to emigrate to Canada. This encouraged my parents also to seek permission to leave the Soviet Union. (My father's family had been almost totally wiped out by typhus.) At a preliminary medical examination by a Russian doctor it was discovered that my father had a trace of trachoma--an eye disease that was to keep many Mennonite families from leaving Russia. Although my parents were willing to remain in Russia if it should be God's will, my father had his eyes treated during the winter of 1925-26, and to his delight they responded to medication and he was declared fit.

In March, 1926, a third child, Margaret, was born into our family. Spring was in the air. Economically the future looked a bit brighter once again. The following summer brought a reasonably good harvest. It seemed as if the Memrik colony was coming to life once more. Then came the word that our family was to appear before a British doctor. Dr. Drury had been appointed by Canadian authorities to examine all those who applied for immigration to Canada. Without his certification entrance visas to Canada were not granted.

Mother's parents, the Wiebes, were confident that they and their unmarried daughters would receive permission to emigrate, and had sold their property and were sitting on their travel bags, as it were. To their great dismay the entire family was rejected because two of the Wiebe girls had signs of trachoma. Since family units were not broken up, my maternal grandparents with their daughters had to stay in the Soviet Union. It was a crushing disappointment. Several years later they were all sent to Siberia and today those still alive live scattered in Asiatic Russia.

Since my father's eyes had shown signs of trachoma earlier as well, he was quite certain now that they too would be rejected by Dr. Drury. However, to their great surprise, they were given a clean bill of health. My brother John had a red eye and screamed when the doctor examined it. Dr. Drury gave him a whack on his seat and said he wanted to see the little fellow once more when we got to Moscow. In any case, a medical examination of a few minutes had determined the future of our family--and also of my life. My father often wondered whether it wasn't his calloused hands, which the doctor had looked at, that had tipped the scales in his favour. Canada wanted workers, and clearly my father was one. How inscrutable are God's ways!

After the medical examination, father had to appear before a representative of the Canadian Pacific Railway Company to arrange for tickets. When asked whether he could pay the fare he was taken aback, for he did not have the money. The CPR was willing to settle for half cash with the other half to be paid back once the family had settled in Canada. But the cash had to be there the next day. Moreover, mother's widowed sister, Justina, and her two little boys, had also passed the medical tests, and my parents "adopted" them as part of our family.

Dad hurried home to see how he could scrape up enough money to pay the half-fare the next morning. After several futile attempts and after much prayer, his brother Gerhard lent him the money until dad could liquidate his property--something next to impossible after 1926. The next morning he was on his way to Nordheim once again to pay for our tickets. Then he discovered that the visas would cost 200 rubles per family member. Although he did not know where the money would come from, he applied for the visas and in a month word came from Yuzovka that the visas had arrived. Dad went to town once again to pick up the visas and stayed with a Jewish friend for the night. When this man heard that we were leaving the Soviet Union, he gave dad a fork and a knife as a parting gift. They were on our table regularly for many years. At the bazaar in Yuzovka dad met a Russian friend who pled with him not to make the dangerous voyage across the stormy Atlantic.

But the decision had been made; there was no retreat now. In a month we were to leave. Dad found a buyer for our house. He sold the grain he had just harvested. All household articles had to go. Some were hard to release because of the precious memories associated with them. What was left was auctioned off. Many Russians from neighbouring villages came, not to buy things, but to press the hand of David Davidowich, as my father was known among them.

Rumour had it that if roving bandits got wind of an auction sale held in one of the Mennonite villages, they were bound to strike in the hope of making a profitable raid. As a measure of precaution our family members stayed in different homes for the next few days. Finally the day came when we, together with Aunt Justina and her two little boys, were to leave for Moscow.

The departure from Alexanderhof was a devastating experience emotionally for my parents. In a sense it was like a funeral, for we would never see any of our relatives again. In Canada, Aunt Justina settled in a different province and so we as children grew up without grandparents, aunts or uncles. We didn't notice the complete absence of an extended family as we grew up, but in retrospect I can see this was a great loss.

With the words of the Traveller's Psalm ringing in their ears ("The Lord will keep your going out and your coming in from this time and for evermore"), my parents packed our few belongings and prepared to leave for the train station. Father's sister Anna and her husband took us by wagon to Shelanaja. For the last time we drove through father's native village, Alexanderhof. Four *versts* down the road we passed through Waldeck, where mother wanted to say goodbye to friends and relatives.

It was October 16, 1926. Five other families from Memrik were at the station waiting for the train to take them to Moscow. Only thirty families emigrated from Memrik to Canada prior to 1926. A few more left via Moscow in 1929. A great many were sent to Siberia. The remaining population was eventually organized into collective farms, which had their headquarters in the former Mennonite Brethren Church of Kotlyarevo. With the outbreak of the Second World War all remaining Mennonite men were deported to Asiatic Russia.

Finally the train arrived. We boarded, taking with us a small bundle of clothes and bedding, and a bag of roasted buns and a ham for the long journey on the train. The whistle blew and we were on our way. John was five years old, I was almost four, and Margaret was eight months. Mother carried the baby, and dad looked after the baggage. Aunt Justina had herself and her two boys to look after.

After a few hours we had to change trains. We detrained at Singelnikowo and as we entered the station John slipped on the pavement and wrenched his ankle so badly that he could not walk. But the train to Moscow was about to leave and after two days and two nights on the train the ankle had rested sufficiently so that he could walk again.

My dad knew Moscow well, for he had come to this great city numerous times when he served on hospital trains during the war. Dr. Drury was now in Moscow and we had to get final medical clearance from him before we were allowed to proceed further. John's eye was better by now and so without difficulty we got permission to leave for Latvia. Dad exchanged his few remaining Russian rubles for American dollars and, after waiting for several days for the train to Riga, the CPR sent trucks to pick up the passengers bound for that city.

By now the weather had turned bitterly cold. Strong winds blew and snow began to fall. However, we were happy to be on the train that was to take us to the Russian border. Upon arrival at the border town of Sebesch, confusion reigned supreme. All the passengers had to leave the train and every parcel and bit of baggage had to be opened for inspection, leaving us with a jolly mess and in a sombre mood.

After the excitement and confusion of the border inspection we were happy to be back in the train once more. Finally we passed through the Red Gate and said farewell to Russia for good. My parents had learned not only to love their Russian homeland but also the Russian people. It was not easy for them to break all those emotional ties. However, they were happy when the Russian trainmen were replaced by Latvian officials after they had crossed the border. They felt much more relaxed when these rather more polished and gracious Latvian gentlemen entered the train.

We arrived in Riga on October 23, 1926. Riga was another city where dad had often unloaded wounded soldiers from his hospital train during the war. In fact the very barracks in which the wounded had been hospitalized during the war were now to be our living quarters until we boarded ship. All our clothes and baggage were thoroughly disinfected in Riga for fear that we might be carriers of some disease.

The morning after we arrived in Riga the medical authorities came to examine the children and to our great consternation it was discovered that I had contracted chicken pox. Our family was immediately quarantined and I was put in an isolation ward in the hospital. Our travel companions who had come with us from Memrik now left by steamer for England, but we had to stay behind. It was a severe test for our family, but my parents were learning step by step to put their life into God's hands and to trust him for guidance.

Whereas my memories of the long trip to Canada are somewhat vague, I do remember the feeling of dereliction when I was put into isolation. Dad stayed with me for long days. Mother, with John and Margaret, lived in the barracks. In the hospital they served us buttered bread and tea and, having lived some time on rather meagre fare, I thought this was a great delicacy. To this day when I drink tea and eat buttered bread, I am reminded of Riga. We were delayed two weeks in Riga. While waiting there, an entire train of Mennonite emigrants from Siberia arrived. These were to be our travel companions on the way to London.

The day of our departure from Riga finally came and so we boarded the good ship Boltara to sail through the Wilhelmskanal on to the stormy North Sea. Once we were on board we were given good food and encouraged to eat well. The ship's crew knew what they were talking about, for once we got to the high seas very few of the adults could stand the sight of food. John and I managed quite well, although on occasion as we slid back and forth in the ship's hallways, we got a bit queasy. The voyage across the North Sea in November was unusually rough. From the crest of the wave we plunged again and again into the trough, and it took five days to sail from Riga to London. How relieved we were when our feet could touch solid ground once more!

In London the buses stood ready for us. The CPR had arranged that we spend the first night in London. The following day we were taken by train to Southampton. Here we were put up in army barracks--still intact from the war. The bunks in the barracks were rather uncomfortable. Besides, it was winter and the buildings had no heat. Our hope was that this stop-over would be of short duration.

The first thing we had to do when we arrived in Southampton was to take a bath. As dad emerged from his bath he saw to his dismay that an attendant was making off with John who was screaming his head off. The medical authorities had noticed something on his body that made them suspicious. Fortunately, after a thorough examination, he was declared well. Aunt Justina was not so fortunate. Her older boy, Henry, contracted the chicken pox and he was not allowed to remain in the barracks. Instead he was taken away without his mother to an isolation ward in the hospital. Since none of us spoke a word of English it took a long time before Aunt Justina found out where her boy was. Even so she was not allowed to see him and when they returned him to his mother several weeks later he was so traumatized by the quarantine that he had lost his ability to speak. All he did was sit in the corner of the room and stare. When Henry had recovered, the young boy, Jacob, got the chicken pox. As a result Aunt Justina with her two boys stayed behind in Southampton, while our family made its way to Liverpool and then on to Canada.

3

Canada

When our train from Southampton arrived in Liverpool, the steamer Montclary stood ready in the harbour. Before boarding this huge liner all of us had to pass another dreaded medical examination. We always feared these inspections, for immigrants were often detained for months in England because of minor illnesses. However, the checkup just before we crossed the bridge on to the vessel seemed to be quite routine and soon we were in our assigned cabins.

Again the passengers were advised to eat well before the journey over the stormy Atlantic. The crew members of the Boltara had spoken both German and Russian and so there had been no language problems, but the crew of the Montclary spoke English only--a language none of us understood. There was actually little need to understand, for all we had to do was to eat and to sleep--neither of which was all that easy once our ship began to rock and roll on the high waves of the Atlantic.

The first day went quite well. We spent a lot of time on the deck. John and I were completely taken in by all the new things we got to see: the huge masts, the big chimney belching black smoke, the sharp-looking sailors in their uniforms and the thousands of sea gulls who attended our way and skillfully picked up morsels of food we threw on the water for them. The most exciting moment for us boys was the sound of the dining hall bell. Not only did they serve delicious meals, but we got apples, oranges and all kinds of other goodies. Margaret cried a lot on the voyage across the Atlantic because of lack of nourishment. My parents did not know that they were also permitted to get food for babies from the ship's kitchen. A little knowledge of English would have helped.

Once we were on the high seas my parents got so sea-sick

that they had to stay away from the dining hall altogether. No one suffered as much as mother. It was very discouraging, and our parents thanked God at the end of each day that he had brought them through. The voyage was to last ten days. What helped our parents to survive were the leftover buns and the ham they had taken with them from Russia. Somehow their stomachs could take these better than the rich food in the ship's dining hall. In their distress, the question of whether they should have left Russia or not often came up. In the wee hours of those long sleepless nights when the mighty waves beat against the Montclary and the fog horn sounded so plaintively, the night of the soul at times seemed darker than the blackness of the ocean.

However, the day came when the waves got smaller, the sea gulls forsook us, and rumour had it that we were nearing land. The ship began to glide more gently as the storm subsided and the sea-sick passengers took new courage. On the last day of the voyage we were able to go to the dining hall without incident. Mother had lain on her cabin bed so long without proper nourishment that she could not walk without father's help. Suddenly the good news burst upon us: "Land in sight!" Sure enough, in the distance one could see the dim outline of Canada's eastern seaboard. Soon the tugboats arrived to pull our steamer into the harbour of Quebec. It was November 12, 1926.

Before we left the ship we were given another good meal and so we stood ready to cross the bridge to our new homeland. As the passengers disembarked they were given English New Testaments. That seemed incredible! The Red Cross nurses were very helpful with the small children. They gave Margaret small toys and good food. John and I revelled in our new freedom after the many hours in cramped quarters. My parents breathed a sigh of relief that at long last they were in Canada--land of the free.

But now what? Canada was big. Where should they go? The Mennonite Board of Colonization had sent several representatives to Quebec to assist the immigrants with travel arrangements. A special train stood ready, bound for Winnipeg. In Winnipeg immigrant families were re-directed to the destination of their choice.

Many of our fellow-travellers had relatives waiting for them, but we didn't know a soul in Canada and didn't really know where to go. We were "displaced persons," as immigrants after World War II were called (Malcolm Muggeridge referred to it as one of the cruelest expressions ever invented). Again and again we were asked where we wanted to go. Finally it was decided that we would go on to Herbert, Saskatchewan. Mother remembered that in the 1870's an uncle by the name of Heinrich Penner had emigrated to America. This uncle died in the meantime, but his widow, as mother recalled, lived in Herbert. However, we had never seen the Penners nor did we know whether Mrs. Penner was still alive or whether she would acknowledge us as relatives. Never did our family feel so homeless and forlorn as on that long train ride from Quebec City to Herbert, Saskatchewan.

Moreover, as the train snaked its way around Lake Superior, the terrain looked so inhospitable that father wondered how anyone could eke out an existence on such rocky soil. As our train left Winnipeg and headed for the open prairies, which now lay covered with a blanket of snow, my parents almost lost heart. The little farms that dotted the landscape looked so lonely in contrast to the well-kept villages of the Ukraine.

We had no idea what kind of "city" Herbert was. In Russia our parents somehow got the notion that only the wealthy could afford to turn over their lands to managers and to move to the city. Could that be the case with the Penners too? How shocked we were when the conductor came through the train and announced, "Herbert, next stop." We peered through the window but couldn't see the "city." In a matter of minutes the train ground to a halt and our family, with a little bundle of bedding and clothing, stood on the platform of the train station. Now we could see Herbert. A few rows of small houses, a school, several churches and a few grain elevators. How disappointing! Herbert was smaller than the village of Alexanderhof!

The whistle blew, the train began to move, and we were left standing under the open sky. It was late November and the weather had turned bitterly cold. We were not properly dressed for a Saskatchewan winter and I began to cry bitterly because of the cold. Suddenly two men appeared and greeted us warmly. They spoke our Low German; that we could understand.

Now the questioning began. Who were we? Where were we from? Did we know anyone in Herbert? Dad asked if there might be a Mrs. Penner in Herbert. Evidently there was more than one Mrs. Penner and so after some consultation they suggested we try a Mrs. Penner whose children lived "north" of Herbert. Horrors, thought my father, if it's so frightfully cold in Herbert, what must it be like in the north (in Russia the word "north" had acquired a sinister ring). To his great relief he discovered later that " north of Herbert" meant Main Centre--a little hamlet some twenty miles from Herbert.

It was agreed that we go to Mrs. Penner, an old widow who lived in a little two-room Shenn (a lean-to). Mother carried Margaret, dad our baggage, and Mr. Wiebe, one of the men who had come to meet us at the station, took John and me by the hand, and off we went.

Soon we stood before the door of the little cottage. Could it really be that a long lost relative should live in this hovel? Mr. Wiebe knocked on the screen door. An old lady opened the inner door just a crack to keep the cold out and to see who was there. Mr. Wiebe addressed her in Low German, "Taunte, ech hav die Jast jebrocht" (Lady, I have brought you visitors). As she stood in the doorway, shivering with cold, she wanted to know who we were. She could tell we were new-comers to Canada by the way we were dressed. But what was our name, and where were we from? Finally she looked at mother and said, "If you are the daughter of Abram Wiebes of Memrik, then come in." And so, for the first time we stepped into a private dwelling in Canada.

A big stove radiated pleasant heat. How glad we were to get out of the cold. But where would we sleep? There were only two rooms. Well, the five of us would all sleep in one room and Mrs. Penner in the other. It was evening and we were hungry and tired. Mother helped with the supper and soon our growling stomachs were satisfied. However, before they could go to bed, my parents had to satisfy Mrs. Penner's curiosity about life in the Soviet Union and about her many relatives she had left behind many years ago.

After a night's rest dad was raring to go. He wanted to work, earn our daily bread, and build a home for the family. But he was told that there were no jobs available during the winter months and that we should be content to live with other people at least until spring. This was a terrific blow to dad's independent spirit. The very thought of being dependent on other people's charity was quite abhorrent to my parents. However, there was no way out, and our parents never forgot the kindness people showed them when they came to Canada with nothing but a huge debt to the CPR--a debt they couldn't pay back until several years later.

Mrs. Penner had several children living in Main Centre. Shortly after our arrival Mr. Dietrich Klassen, her son-in-law, came to Herbert with a bobsled to get a load of coal and he stopped in to see his mother-in-law and her strange guests. The Klassens had already lived in Canada for a generation and owned a sizeable farm. Klassen invited dad to come down and see a Canadian farm. After helping Mr. Klassen load his coal from a railroad car, he was off to Main Centre. Because he was so poorly clothed, dad walked behind the sled almost the entire distance to keep from freezing.

The Klassens had six children and lived in a rather spacious farm-house. They seemed to be well-to-do. They even drove a motor car. Mrs. Klassen was a friendly lady and welcomed dad kindly. Supper was ready and dad's eyes popped as he saw all the appetizing food on the table. For fear of breaking Canadian rules of etiquette he took only very small helpings and left the table still hungry.

Mr. Henry Penner, a son of the widow in Herbert, who also lived in Main Centre, came to meet dad at the Klassens and suggested that our family come and live with them, since they had more room than their widowed mother in Herbert. The next day, Mr. Penner came to get us and we moved in with his family. Mother helped in the house, and dad on the farm-yard--cleaning the barn, watering the cattle and whatever else needed to be done in winter. The Penners were kind to us, but we were very crowded. Mr. Dietrich Klassen then suggested that we had better come to their house. Since we had no earthly possessions, moving was no great problem.

Again my parents tried to make themselves useful. Besides doing the work in the barn, father took the Klassen children to school every day by horse and buggy. Mother helped in the house, and she and Mrs. Klassen became good friends.

On a neighbouring farm stood a vacant house and it was suggested that perhaps we should make it livable and move into it. Obviously we could not stay with the Klassens for any length of time. The prospect of living alone as a family was very pleasant. Our only worry was what we would eat, for we had no money. Our parents had many anxious moments in those first weeks in Canada, but they claimed the promise of Jesus that he would never leave us nor forsake us. Help came in the nick of time.

Mrs. Henry Penner was expecting a child after Christmas, and since Main Centre had no hospital, the Penners decided to spend the month of January in Herbert. As a result, they offered our family their farm-house and the necessary provisions if we would take care of their two teenage children during the time of their absence. It was an answer to prayer, and the experience turned out to be quite enjoyable.

Soon, however, winter would be over. What then? One day Mr. Dietrich Klassen came by with his sleigh and invited dad to go with him to Rush Lake, where Klassen had a sister who worked for a wealthy farmer. Mr. Gehman owned several sections of land and hired labourers every year to help him with his huge farming operation. The two-storey house, the big barn with a silo, the many granaries, and the machine-shed impressed my father very much.

Mr. Gehman spoke a broken German and bluntly told my dad that he had vowed never to hire a Russian. Also, he wanted a hired man who wouldn't ask for holidays (Sunday, of course, was an exception). "Can you handle a binder?" he asked. After a lengthy interrogation he said, "Dave, I will hire you temporarily for February and March." He promised to pay thirty-five dollars per month and also offered us a small house, with one bedroom and a kitchen, that stood on his yard.

Penners returned from Herbert with their new born babe at the end of January and we moved to Rush Lake. Friends gave us a table, a few chairs and a stove. Our new boss had put two beds into our living quarters, as well as some coal for the stove and flour for baking. My parents didn't believe what was happening to them. It was just too good to be true. After months of knocking about, it was such a relief to have an ordered life again, including family devotions.

Father worked from early till late--milking cows, feeding and watering horses, cleaning barns, and so forth. He tried hard to please Mr. Gehman and when the two months of probation were over, Gehman promised him a summer job, with sixty dollars per month. Gehman also hired a certain Mr. Ulmer, a recent immigrant from Germany. Both men worked from dawn to dusk. Gehman turned out to be a real slave driver. When seeding began the days became incredibly long. Then came the summer fallowing and the haying and, before long, the harvest. Dad sat on the binder from five in the morning till ten at night. Gehman had told dad when he hired him, "Dave, your time belongs entirely to me." He meant every word!

Mother worked hard too. Besides taking care of the family,

she planted a garden, raised chickens, sewed clothes for us and, during the harvest, helped with the milking. We children had a glorious time. Margaret was walking by now and the three of us found plenty of interesting things on the farm to entertain ourselves. John would be six in August and the concern for the schooling and the spiritual welfare of their children weighed heavily on my parents' minds. Gehman had by now discovered dad's worth and wanted him to sign a contract promising to work for him for many years. However, my parents could not see a future for themselves and their children at the Gehmans, and decided to leave Saskatchewan.

4

The Poor Man's Land

A Christian family, the John Klassens, had befriended us and invited us to their place for Sunday dinner. Gehman allowed us to use his horse and buggy. Hermann Neufeld, father of the editor of the *Mennonitische Rundschau,* published in Winnipeg, was visiting churches in Saskatchewan. The Klassens wanted us to meet him and so they invited us as well. When Neufeld heard that we had come from Memrik he asked us with surprise: "How could you ever leave that beautiful country?" The parents remembered Mr. Neufeld from Russia, where he served as itinerant minister. Although he lived in the Old Colony he had preached frequently at harvest festivals in Memrik. There was then no end of reminiscing about the good old days.

Rather incidentally Neufeld asked whether we subscribed to the *Rundschau.* My parents did not even know there was such a paper. Neufeld promised that he would see to it that we received this publication. True to his word, the *Rundschau* came. What a treat for my parents, who had nothing to read! They did, of course, read their German Bible faithfully.

The *Rundschau* carried news items about the various settlements in Canada where Mennonite immigrants from Russia were now to be found. Several articles reported on a new development in Risor, Ontario, not far from Kapuskasing. These articles were written by a certain Mr. Hildebrand and bore the title, "The Poor Man's Land." They described how a man without money could make a living by cutting lumber for the paper company. One could buy a tract of forest for a modest price and sell the lumber.

Dad's summer contract with Gehman was running out and his boss wanted him to promise to stay for a few more years. After much prayer, however, my parents made the decision to move to

Northern Ontario. Gehman was very disappointed and thought his entire farming operation would now go to ruin. Nevertheless, he promised dad that a job would be waiting for him should he ever decide to return.

It was a hard decision to make, but our parents wanted so much to be on their own. Also, the reports indicated that Risor had a Christian community that offered spiritual resources to the settlers.

Once again it was winter. We had been in Canada one whole year. Gehman paid father his wages but, miser that he was, gave him much less than he had promised. Dad said nothing.

Tickets for the family were purchased and on December 1, 1927 friends took us to Herbert. From here we were to begin the long train ride back to Ontario. The household belongings which we had accumulated in the course of the year (many of them gifts of friends) were sent by freight. Before we departed, we dropped in at Mrs. Penner's once more--the dear old lady who took us in when we arrived from the Soviet Union a year ago. Friends from Main Centre had come to the station to see us off. The train arrived and once again we were on our way into the unknown. The ticket agent had told dad that the train did not stop at Risor and had given us tickets only to Mateis, the nearest stop. How we would get from Mateis to Risor no one knew.

The trainmen seemed to take a special interest in us children and after travelling for several days and nights the conductor did the unusual: he stopped the passenger train at Risor and let us off. But there was no station there, and as the train left we found ourselves standing in the deep snow in the dead of winter, wondering where to turn. Herbert at least had a station, but Risor was a whistle stop. A wagon box stood beside the tracks. When freight was sent to Risor it was deposited here and people who lived in the forest would come to pick it up.

Some distance along the track where the train had stopped lived Wilhelm Rempels. They had noticed the passenger stop, and as they looked along the tracks they saw several tiny specks in the bright snow. Immediately they hitched a team of horses to their sleigh and came to get us. They took us in for the night very kindly. Mr. Rempel drew a rough sketch of the settlement on a piece of paper to show us where other Mennonite families lived. Next morning, following this crude map, dad went to see the Gerhard Siemens and Jacob Petkaus. Both of these couples were about the same age as my parents and both had children our age. Besides, they were Mennonite Brethren. Our paths were to cross again when all of us lived in Grassy Lake, Alberta. The friendship born in a time of need proved lasting and strong.

But where would we live? We couldn't stay at the Rempels. The Rempels, however, had married children who lived deep in the forest, and this young couple was kind enough to invite us to live with them until our log cabin was ready.

As the sleigh slid over the soft snow, on our way to these kind people, the deathly silence of the forest was broken only by the sound of axes and saws. Here and there one could see a log cabin, half-hidden in the forest. Also, we could see the boundaries of the homesteads marked on the spruce trees.

Finally we arrived at the home of our gracious hosts. The next day dad and Mr. Siemens, who had come to Risor with his family only recently as well, went to stake out their homesteads. Then they decided to help each other build loghouses for their families.

The walls of our house were already up when dad met a bachelor, John Bergen, who wanted to sell his homestead, together with its log house. Dad bought the property for a pittance and we moved into our own house. It had only two rooms and an attached shed. The cracks between the logs were filled with moss on the outside and papered with heavy grey paper on the inside. It had a peaked roof, covered with tar paper.

Bergen had decided to leave Ontario and so he threw a big wood-burning range, a table and a few smaller items into the bargain. Our few household utensils which we had shipped by freight from Herbert eventually arrived also.

With the family finally settled, dad signed a contract with the pulp and paper company and began to fell trees, cut them into four-foot lengths and pile them up in cords. This lumber had to be hauled out of the forest while the winter snows lasted, for there were no roads for wheeled vehicles. Any lumber that was left after the snow disappeared was held over for next year. Since we could not afford horses or sleigh, we had to pay for the hauling of the wood. Although dad began work only in December, he was still able to cut a great many cords of lumber. A company agent then came by and measured the logs and paid six dollars and fifty cents for a cord.

My parents soon discovered that most of the Mennonite families in Risor belonged to the General Conference Mennonite Church, and since the lines between Mennonite Brethren and General Conference were still drawn rather clearly at the time, they, together with several other Mennonite Brethren families, began to meet in homes for Sunday School, Bible study and prayer. Since they had no minister among them, they sang and prayed a lot. Every now and then we did attend the church of the General Conference, but that meant walking through many miles of forest, and my sister had to be carried all the way. I have no recollections of the services, but I do recall how frightened I was as a five-year old when on our way to church a monstrous moose came crashing through the trees of the forest.

Although there was a small store in the area, we ordered most of our groceries in bulk from Eatons in Toronto. Canned milk, rolled oats, sugar and rice were sent to Risor and deposited in the wagon box beside the railroad, where teamsters would pick up these shipments and pass them on to the settlers.

Dad worked in the forest five days a week. On Saturdays he cut fire-wood. Since the weather was frightfully cold, our stove, which was kept burning day and night, consumed a great amount of wood. We soon discovered that if we used green poplar instead of spruce the fire lasted longer. Birch was also plentiful and so there was no lack of fuel. Sunday, of course, was a day of rest and worship.

At the beginning of May the sap began to rise and the trees became supple. Now the logs had to be peeled. The peeled logs were also piled in cords, but had to wait for the winter snows before they could be hauled away. Peeled logs yielded a somewhat higher price.

When we arrived in December, Mr. Rempel had said that he wished it were always winter. That had puzzled my parents. But with the coming of spring they understood. Swarms of mosquitoes and black flies began to harass us and made our lives almost unbearable. We just did not know how to defend ourselves against this plague. We wore nets of cheese-cloth over our heads, but still our ears were swollen from the bites. Mother hung cheese-cloth over our beds, or otherwise we could not have slept. Dad usually mixed lard with coal-oil and put a heavy mixture of this concoction over his face so that he could work, but it wasn't very effective. Occasionally mother helped him with the peeling of the bark from the logs and she would wrap her legs with paper and put her stockings over it to keep the pesky creatures from tormenting her.

One day at the railway during the summer lull, dad met Mr. Siemens who told him in his Low German brogue, "Ech sie saut von Risor" (I've had enough of Risor). He probably echoed the feelings of many Mennonite families at Risor. Surely there must be other ways of making a living than to be condemned to such a lonely and tedious life in the forest!

About that time the government offered free tickets to men who were willing to travel to the prairie provinces to help farmers bring in the harvest. Mr. Hildebrand, whose articles in the *Rundschau* had been the occasion for our move to Risor, encouraged dad to join him for the trip to the harvest fields in the west. Interestingly, just at that time dad had a letter from Jacob Martens of Main Centre, a man with whom he had served on hospital trains during the war, asking him to come and help him bring in his harvest. After consulting with the family, dad left for

Saskatchewan. Mr. Hildebrand chose Alberta.

Dad worked in Saskatchewan for a full two months--the minimum length of time to be eligible for a free ticket--and earned 200 dollars. After bringing in the harvest at Marten's, Mr. Gehman of Rush Lake begged dad to stay on and help him also. Gehman now offered dad money if he would buy the neighbour's farm. It was a ploy to bind dad to himself and dad politely declined. Back in Risor, mother spent lonely months with us in the forest. One night when we were fast asleep dad came home. When we woke up in the morning we had a grand surprise. Little Margaret was now jabbering incessantly and wanted to know who the man was and why he had come. She had completely forgotten her daddy.

Mr. Hildebrand, too, returned. He had made a downpayment on a farm in Grassy Lake, Alberta. One more winter in the forest and he was moving his family to southern Alberta. Our parents had also come to the conviction that there was no future for them in Risor. John began to go to school, but since there were no means of transportation and the snow was deep, he had to drop out.

Dad made up his mind that he would fell as many spruce trees as possible that last winter and then move to the west in spring. As November drew to a close our parents were preparing for an addition to our family. On December 4, 1928, my brother Abe was born--not in a hospital, of course, but in our loghouse. There was no doctor in the area and often our parents wondered what we would do if any of us should become ill. Fortunately our family enjoyed good health.

An accident that left me with a permanent scar on the left side of my forehead occurred one day in our shed. A neighbour's boy had come over to play. John and I just then wanted to play outside, but he insisted we play inside. In a fit of anger he grabbed a hammer that happened to lie in our shed and struck me on my head. He then quickly made off for home. I was left with a deep gash. The wound had almost healed when our family visited the neighbours. When Mrs. Matties noticed the scab on my head she asked what had happened and the truth came out, much to the discomfiture of her son who was given a good trouncing.

The spring of 1929 arrived and our family, together with the Siemens, boarded the train for western Canada. All the cords of wood of the previous summer and past winter had been hauled to the railway. Financially we had not done too badly. We sold some articles of furniture before we left, but no one wanted to buy our homestead, even though there was a lot of lumber left. So we left everything behind and made our way to Winnipeg.

5

Sunny Alberta

Upon our arrival in Winnipeg, we rented temporary quarters, while dad and Mr. Siemens looked for farms. At the land offices of the CPR they were told that north of Calgary, Alberta, the company had farms for sale. The company required twenty-five dollars to indicate seriousness of intent and promised to help them when they arrived in Calgary. So they left the mothers with the children in Winnipeg and travelled alone to Calgary to see what they could find.

When they arrived at the CPR offices in Calgary they met two Mennonite land agents who worked for the CPR. These men immediately phoned Abram Klassen of Acme, about 60 miles northeast of Calgary, who was on hand when dad and Mr. Siemens arrived at the train station. He put them up for the night and next day they travelled by car looking for farms. Several were available, but all of them far from the Mennonite community at Linden. Farmers belonging to the Holdeman Church had settled in Linden as early as 1902. By now Mennonites from various backgrounds lived in the area, although it was not until 1930 that a Mennonite Brethren Church was established. Until 1948 it was affiliated with the Evangelical Mennonite Brethren Conference.

Spring had arrived in Alberta and the farmers were getting ready to put in their crops. Obviously it was too late to buy a farm, acquire horses and implements and seed grain. What should they do? They would look for jobs and wire the families in Winnipeg to take the train to Acme. Mr. Siemens got a job with Mr. Toews, and dad with Mr. Baerg. Toews had several farms and on one of them stood a vacant house. It was a rather dilapidated two-storey building but he offered it to us without any rental charge. Telegrams were sent to Winnipeg and we got ready to leave for

Alberta.

While dad was away in Alberta I had a rather traumatic experience in Winnipeg. We often went to the corner of the street to watch the street cars go by. On one such occasion when I had gone alone, I turned to go home, but instead of turning right I turned left. Suddenly I was struck by the strangeness of the surroundings. I was lost. I ran as fast as my legs would carry me, but I didn't know where I was going. I got more and more frightened and began to cry. I came to a large body of water, which must have been the Red River. Suddenly a lady on the street grabbed my hand and took me with her. Before long we entered a huge building, at least so it seemed to me. We were at police headquarters. The policemen tried to calm me down, but I screamed and constantly pointed to the window. I wanted to tell them to let me out, but I spoke only German. They did everything they could to shut me up: they took me to the washroom and they threatened me with a long whip, but with little success. Finally the door swung open and there stood my mother. Although I was only six at the time, the experience stands out vividly in my memory. I have always had at least an inkling of what it means when the Bible speaks of people without Christ being "lost." Later in life when I taught in Winnipeg I often wondered where we had stayed during those weeks of waiting and where it was that I had lost my way.

After changing trains in Calgary we were on our way to Acme. Here two anxious fathers were awaiting their families. Together with the Siemens family we moved into the vacant ramshackle farm house. Living together in such close quarters was not easy. Siemens had five children; we were four. There was a lot of quarrelling, not to mention the incredible amount of mischief we were able to get ourselves into.

The country school at Linden was overcrowded and so John, who had attended school off and on at Risor, was not able to finish his first year of school. Since I was only a year younger and would begin school in September, John and I were to be in the same grade throughout our public school years.

Dad worked for Mr. Baerg all summer. After the seeding was done, Mr. Siemens decided to move to Grassy Lake where he was able to purchase a farm. Our parents enjoyed their stay at Linden. If there had been a farm available in the Linden community our family might have settled there permanently.

Linden had not had a crop failure in twenty-five years. However, that summer one night in July a heavy frost struck and ruined the crops. Since there would be no harvest that year, Mr. Baerg could not afford to employ dad any longer and so he would have to look elsewhere for work. Just then a letter arrived from Mr. Hildebrand, whom my parents knew so well from Risor, asking dad to come to Grassy Lake and help him with the harvest. He had purchased a farm just a year ago and now had 300 acres of ripening wheat.

This meant moving again. Dad hired Mr. Toews, on whose property we had been living, to take us and our belongings to Grassy Lake with his truck. Mother, Margaret and the baby sat in the cab; dad, John and I sat at the back on top of our household things. The trip took one long day. Hildebrands took us in for the night. Next day we moved into a granary which stood across the road from their house. Hildebrand had already begun to cut wheat and so mother was left alone to set up house, since dad began immediately next day to stook the sheaves of grain.

Several miles away lived the Peter Neufelds. Neufeld farmed several sections of land and employed as many as twenty labourers in harvest season. These all had to be fed, and so Mr. Neufeld came over one day and asked whether mother would be willing to move to his place with the children and do the cooking for his crew. Since every bit of extra income was welcomed in those days, we moved to the Neufelds. Saturday nights Mr. Neufeld would bring us home so we could spend Sunday together as a family. Church services were held in a local school at the time and we always attended. A Mennonite Brethren Church had been established just recently.

It was the beginning of September, 1929, and time for school to begin. We were still at Neufelds. They too had school children. Together with them, John and I began to attend the Deer Park School. Jake, one of the older Neufeld boys, took us to school with horse and buggy. Every day he scared us half to death by driving in and out of the ditches beside the road. School was exciting, even though I knew next to no English. Mother prepared a lunch for each of us. On the first day of school I ate my lunch at the first recess, thinking it was already noon. Unfortunately I had nothing to eat when twelve o'clock came round.

Once the harvest was over we moved back to our granary at Hildebrand's. This put us into a different school district and so John and I had to switch to the Flickinger School--a one-room country school within walking distance from where we lived.

About sixty miles west of Grassy Lake, on the CPR line that runs from Medicine Hat to Lethbridge, lay the little town of Coaldale. At the turn of the century Mormon families from Utah had come to this area to help in the construction of an irrigation system that was to provide water for half a million acres in the southwestern parts of the province. This made it possible to grow sugar beets and other row crops. A number of Mennonite immigrant families from the Soviet Union had already been attracted to Coaldale where the CPR had farms for sale.

The sugar beet harvest always followed the grain harvest and so, after dad had helped Mr. Hildebrand bring in his harvest, he went to Coaldale to work for Mr. Franzen in the beet harvest. One day he met Mr. Peter Regehr, who had been a teacher in Memrik and who like other teachers from Russia now made his living by farming. On the side, however, Mr. Regehr worked for the CPR as land agent. He promised dad he would keep his eyes open for a farm, should one become available.

After the beet harvest in Coaldale dad came back to Grassy Lake. Mr. David Penner, who that fall had harvested 20,000 bushels of wheat, asked him to work for him during the winter months. Penner's wheat was stored in granaries and needed to be transported to the elevators in Grassy Lake, 18 miles away. Penner purchased a new Dodge truck and week upon week dad shovelled grain by hand from granary into truck. Dad and Mr. Penner became good friends and the Penners showed us many kindnesses. Sometimes dad rode to the elevator with Mr. Penner and read the *Rundschau* to him on the way.

My parents enjoyed the Christian fellowship in this community. However, farms were difficult to come by, unless one had a sizeable sum of money. Even though the soil was fertile, it was all dryland, and during the "dirty thirties" the farmers in this district suffered repeatedly from crop failures. At the time, however, the community prospered.

We had now been in Canada three and a half years and still had no farm. Dad had always had work, but the wages in those years were low and so the savings were obviously very limited. One evening towards the end of the winter he went to Peter Dicks for a Bible study. Mr. Dick had just returned from Coaldale with a message from Peter Regehr. Dad was to be in Lethbridge next morning; the CPR was about to sell several irrigation farms. It was getting closer to spring and our parents were very anxious to establish a more permanent home.

The town of Grassy Lake was about twenty miles from Hildebrands. After consulting with mother, dad decided to walk through the night in order to catch the early train to Lethbridge. Part of the way he walked across the open fields, still covered with a crust of snow which always broke through as he trudged along. He got to Grassy Lake just in time to flag the train down with a lantern which he found on the platform. The conductor sold him a ticket and by morning he was in Lethbridge. When he got to the land office of the CPR a number of men had already gathered and were making applications for farms. Dad also quickly completed his application, and an agent of the company took him to the

Readymade School District, about sixteen miles east of Lethbridge, where a 160-acre irrigation farm was for sale. The conditions were that we grow sugar beets and annually return one third of our entire crop to the CPR to cover the mortgage.

From 1910 to 1912 the CPR had sent colonization agents to England and northern Europe to entice immigrants to settle on their newly obtained lands in Alberta. The company owned a huge tract of land comprising the Readymade School District. There were, originally, seventeen farms of 160 acres of irrigation land. The barns and houses which were built on these farms in preparation for the coming of the settlers were all of a similar style and gave the district the name "Readymade." The first farms in this district were sold in 1913. After World War I, veterans from England took up farming in this district. Some of the English settlers who came to this area were not very adept at farming, and by the early 1920s many of them became discouraged and left. By now the CPR was happy to have immigrants from Eastern Europe settle on its lands, and this is how some of our Mennonite people also found a home in Readymade. However, by the time we arrived on the scene, most of the farms had been taken by Czechs, Poles, Hungarians and Ukrainians.

The farm which dad bought that morning was only half a mile from the Readymade School. The price of the farm was 11,000 dollars. Only a small downpayment was required. This was to be our home for fifteen years. The farmyard had a house, a garage and a barn, and was surrounded by several rows of trees--willows, poplars, maples and caraganas. A creek ran diagonally through our quarter section. Along the creek was pastureland; the rest was under cultivation. There was a well with a pump on the yard, but with irrigation we really did not need wells. In the distance we could see the Rocky Mountains silhouetted against the sky. Eight miles from our farm was the town of Coaldale with its post office, stores and other businesses. Our address for the next decade and a half was to be Box 64, Coaldale, Alberta.

It was March, 1930, and the snow was fast disappearing. The conversation in our family turned frequently to Coaldale. Preparations were made for the move. Dad bought second-hand farm implements from Mennonite farmers in Grassy Lake who were acquiring bigger machines as their land holdings increased. From C.A. De Fehr, Winnipeg, he purchased a seeder-plow. He also bought five horses and a wagon.

Mr. David Penner, for whom dad had worked most of the winter, offered to move our family with all our belongings to Coaldale. Pigs, chickens and even some farm implements, together with our household goods, were loaded on to Penner's big Dodge truck, and off we went.

The journey of sixty miles was made without incident and upon arrival the men carried the furniture into the house, put the pigs and chickens in the barn, got mother and the children settled, and then dad returned to Grassy Lake with Mr. Penner. Early next morning he hitched his horses to a wagon, loaded the cow onto it and said farewell to Grassy Lake. It was a slow and tedious journey to Coaldale with horse and wagon. However, by midnight he pulled onto our yard. Finally we had a home. From age six until I left home at twenty-one, my life was intimately bound up with the farm, the Readymade School, and the Coaldale Mennonite Brethren Church.

6

The Coaldale Community

Our parents could hardly believe what was happening to them. For almost four years now they had been on the move. Finally they had a place they could call home. As they reflected on God's goodness to them they could not help but offer praise and thanksgiving to God. Eventually a dozen other Mennonite families were able to purchase farms in the Readymade area. All of them were recent immigrants from the Soviet Union and most of them belonged to the Mennonite Brethren Church. Across the road from us lived the John Esaus, a half mile south lived the Wienses, and across the road from them the Stobbes. A half mile north of us lived the John Voths, and a half mile farther north the Henry Koops. A mile to the west of us lived John Goosens and Nick Hamms; a mile to the east lived the Jacob Fasts and the John Ungers. Almost every family had children our age.

Coaldale has an interesting climate. Summers can be very hot and winters always have some severe cold spells. However, the Chinook winds that blow from the mountains can create radical changes in the weather overnight. On one occasion our neighbour borrowed our bobsled to get a load of coal from the mines in Lethbridge. On the way home the Chinook began to blow and before long the snow was gone. He had to leave the sleigh beside the road, come home to get a wagon, load the coal and the sleigh onto the wagon and complete his trip on a muddy road. One man claimed the Chinook had caught up with him so fast that the front runners were still on the snow when the back runners of the sleigh were already in mud. In spring we often had dust storms and in winter we could expect an occasional blizzard. When our neighbours, the Esaus, moved to British Columbia, Mr. Esau enjoyed the lovely climate but he missed the wind. It had evidently become second nature to him.

When we bought our farm, dad had to promise that he would raise sugar beets.   Growing beets in those days was no picnic. Almost all the work had to be done by hand: the thinning, the hoeing, the cleaning, the topping, and the loading.   The beets were hauled to the railroad at Tempest, where they were weighed and loaded onto open railroad cars and shipped to the sugar factory.

The CPR had promised to build a "beet dump," as they were called, closer to where we lived, but they did not follow through on this promise and so we were eventually free to discontinue growing beets.   Dad then decided to raise potatoes.   For us children that changed very little.   While earlier we had to help with the beet work, now we had to hoe and spray and pick potatoes.   We dug a huge root-cellar on our yard and after the harvest was completed, dad would spend many weeks during the winter picking over and bagging potatoes for market.   We would often help after school and on Saturdays.

We also kept a number of pigs, chickens, turkeys and ducks.   In the dugout behind our barn the ducks enjoyed their natural habitat. They were often in our way during the summer months when we claimed the pond as a swimming hole.   When we began to farm, the CPR offered us a cow (on credit) for every acre of beets we planted.   This helped to build up a herd of cows and for many years we shipped our milk to the Coaldale Cheese Factory.   Fortunately we always had plenty of pasture for our cows.   Our only problem was that they repeatedly broke through the fences and got into the grain fields.   John, who was always tinkering with gadgets, got the bright idea that we electrify one of the wires of the two-mile long fence.   It worked.   Even our fierce bull decided to observe the rules after that.

Cattle need feed, and so we always had a big field of alfalfa, which yielded up to three crops in one season.   We shared a John Deere mower with Henry Koops, but had our own rake.   The rest of the work was done by hand.   Normally dad did all the heavy work himself, until we were big enough to pitch hay.

To begin with we farmed with horses, but in time we changed over to mules--stupid and stubborn beasts, but very tough. I took great interest in horses and one day dad bought me a black beauty from the Blood Indian Reserve near Lethbridge and gave it to me as a present. It was a well-trained saddle horse and a fast runner. Unfortunately one day Blacky, as I named him, walked on to the thin ice of the pond out in our pastureland and broke through. No one was there to help and he drowned in the icy waters together with another one of our work horses. It was a very sad day for me when I suffered the loss of my saddle-horse. John was more mechanically inclined and got a bicycle instead of a horse.

After farming with horses and mules for a number of years we were ready to buy our first tractor. It was harvest season and dad was very busy. He had purchased an Oliver rubber-tired tractor in Lethbridge and took John and me to town to drive it home, while he returned to his harvest work. I was fourteen at the time and quite old enough to handle a tractor. After all, John and I had already spent several summers sitting on horse-drawn implements, cultivating our fields. We proudly drove our new tractor out of the city. Several miles outside the city it was my turn to drive and as my brother got out of the hammock seat he must have stepped on one of the differential brakes, for in a split second the tractor flipped over on its back into the ditch. I was pinned under the left fender; John was jammed between the seat and the bent steering wheel. Several days earlier we had laughed our heads off when Mr. Henry Koop overturned his tractor, and now we lay under ours.

After the initial shock I noticed that I could still move my legs. The weight of the tractor lay on the engine, not on the wheel. Finally I was able to wiggle out from under the fender, badly bruised, but no bones broken. My first thought was: John. With a lot of twisting, shoving and pulling, I was able to get him out. We sat down beside the ditch and looked at our crushed tractor. That we had both been miraculously saved from death did not register with us at the moment. Our greatest worry was what dad would say.

Cars began to stop at the scene of the accident. We wished they would go away. Finally the John Deere agent from Coaldale came by. When he saw that we had bought an Oliver tractor he was angry. Nevertheless, he took us to Lethbridge in his car. The Oliver people sent out a wrecker to bring back the tractor and then an agent took John and me home in his car. I waited in the car until John had told dad. I was too embarrassed. We didn't let on how badly we were hurt and lay awake in bed for a long time that night. Dad came in late from the field. He did not know that we were still awake and we overheard him say to mother, "I'm only glad nothing happened to the boys." I will never forget those words. We were worth more to him than all his machines. Of course we knew that, but this comment drove the truth home.

As for machines, we acquired the necessary implements one by one. To begin with, however, all the Mennonite farmers were poor and so they often owned implements jointly, using them in turn. We and Henry Koops went together on several implements and for many years also operated a threshing outfit jointly. Until we bought our own tractor we supplied the threshing machine and Mr. Koop the tractor. Each of us supplied two teams of horses and hayracks. At age fourteen I began to pitch bundles.

To own farm implements jointly with a neighbour was not a problem, since we did not need them exactly at the same time. More problematic for me was my father's willingness to lend our implements to any neighbour who wanted to borrow them. Dad knew the Sermon on the Mount and refused to listen to our protestations when we saw neighbours using our machines (and sometimes breaking them). He was far too generous, we thought.

John and I spent much of our summer holidays working on the fields--summer fallowing, picking rocks, hoeing and spraying potatoes, haying, and so forth. Dad was busy with irrigating. Some Saturday nights we would take off and go to the irrigation dam near Chin, about four miles away, and fish. We made dippers of chicken-fence wire and fastened them to long poles and caught white-fish, jacks and suckers, as we called them. Irrigation canals, of course, also provided us with excellent places to swim, and we spent many summer hours in the water.

For several years we had no car and did all our driving with horse and wagon or buggy. One day, in 1934, dad surprised us when he came home with a Model T Ford. Although I was only twelve, I quickly learned to drive it (without a license, of course). Several years later we moved up to the Model A Ford. We had entered the twentieth century, it seemed. Now we could venture out beyond Coaldale. Almost every year we went to Grassy Lake for their missions and harvest festival. On one occasion we travelled as far as Main Centre, where the Canadian Conference met--my first introduction to a wider church community. Also, one summer our family went on a two-day outing to Waterton Lakes National Park, which was about a hundred miles from where we lived--considered a great distance in those days. We climbed mountains, boated and swam. On the way home we met the John Dicks, who drove a Model T pickup. They had engine trouble. What could be done? We cut a long piece of barbed wire from the fence, tied the pickup to our car and pulled the Dicks for almost a hundred miles. We admired father's generosity. What we did not like was that he made us boys sit in Dick's pickup, and Mrs. Dick and her girls came into our car. That was going a bit too far, we thought.

Our family was not yet complete when we moved to Coaldale. Another sister, Elizabeth, was born in 1931, and a fourth son, Henry, was added in 1934. As our family increased, dad hired a carpenter to build a stairway to our attic. After that, John, Abe and I always slept upstairs.

In most respects, I suppose, we were a typical Mennonite immigrant family. At home we spoke Low German, in church it was High German, and in school it was English. Dad regularly led the family in Scripture reading and prayer at the breakfast table. At that time it was still a sign that you were Mennonite Brethren if you stood (or knelt) for prayers (in the church which they had left, people also sat for prayers).

Sunday and the church's sacred festivals were always strictly observed. It became a question of conscience whether irrigation water could be run onto one's fields on Sunday or not, or whether it was permissible to clean the cowshed on Sunday (no questions about milking). Fortunately our parents did allow us to play on Sundays--after church, of course.

We lived very simply and frugally. Mother usually got us boys a pair of coveralls at the beginning of the school year and these we wore every day except Sunday. We needed no shirts. Of course mother washed them occasionally, but since we had no washing machine to begin with, and everything had to be done by hand on a scrubbing board, washing was kept to a minimum. I recall how proud I was when I got my first Sunday suit.

Our house had no electricity or running water. Since irrigation water was plentiful, cistern was dug next to our house and filled with "ditch water" for our daily needs. We dug a huge round hole in the ground and plastered the walls and the floor with cement. When we were about four feet in the ground a skunk inadvertently wandered across our yard at night and fell into the hole. Since guns were strictly taboo on our farm, we had to ask Mr. Koop to come and shoot it. The smell was unbearable. Mrs. Herman Stobbe came over just then, and since she had a bad cold and couldn't smell a thing, she offered to throw the dead beast out of the cistern with a pitch-fork. Once the cistern was completed we filled it with water from an irrigation ditch and that usually lasted us through the winter. We drew the water with pail and rope.

In the earlier years we had only small coal-oil lamps, but we didn't do much reading anyway, so we managed quite well. Finally we were able to get an Aladdin lamp and, eventually, a gas lamp with mantles. Mr. Nick Hamm bought it for us in Lethbridge. Dad and he put on new mantles and lit the lamp. The flame frightened them and both of them blew for all they were worth and extinguished the flame (and also blew away the mantles). But we learned.

Besides the kitchen range we had a coal heater in the living room to keep us warm in winter. However, we usually let the fires go out during the night and in the mornings the water in the kitchen sometimes turned to ice and our floors (we had no basement) were so frightfully cold that we would stand on chairs to dress. Dad usually got up early to do chores and mother would light the fires and get the porridge ready for breakfast. To have cornflakes on Sunday was always a treat. Vegetables were stored in a root cellar (mother always planted a big garden). Hogs and chickens were butchered to supply us with meat. It was always exciting when the Jacob Stobbe family joined us annually for the big day when we butchered one or two hogs.

Wood for fuel was not available, but Lethbridge had several coal mines and as the need arose we would get a wagonload of coal from the valley of the Old Man River. The road down to the mines was rather steep and in winter it could be icy. We were always glad when our mules managed to pull our load to the top of the hill.

Life on the farm was very routine and often quite tedious. There was next to nothing to read. We still didn't have a radio to listen to (that was considered worldly), so when we didn't work we had to find other things with which to occupy ourselves. Fortunately the Esaus, who lived across the road from us, had a number of boys, and so we always had enough players for baseball or hockey. The highlight of the week was Sunday, when we could go to church and meet friends. One Sunday it had rained so hard dad thought the roads were too muddy to go to church. I reminded him that if this were a weekday and the milk needed to be shipped, we would certainly go. It hurt, and soon we slithered to church through the gumbo in our Model A Ford. I had touched a very sensitive nerve in my dad, who was deeply devoted to Christ and the church. How cruel children can be!

7

Coaldale Mennonite Brethren

The first Mennonites to settle in Coaldale were the Klaas Enns family. Having recently come from the Soviet Union, Klaas Enns with his wife and seven children first came to Stirling, Alberta, in 1925, to work in the sugar beet industry. The wages were better than expected and so he wrote to his brothers and other immigrants to come to Stirling. Before long 19 families came to work in the beet fields. In November of the same year ten men went to work in Coaldale, after completing the beet harvest in Stirling. They worked for Mr. Lathrop, a CPR agent, who offered to sell them his farm. They agreed to buy the farm for 53,000 dollars without a downpayment on condition they grow 150 acres of beets annually to pay the mortgage.

Almost overnight Coaldale became the attraction for Mennonite immigrants. Dr. T. Herzer, of the Canada Colonization Association, came from Winnipeg to inform the Coaldale Mennonites that the CPR was willing to sell another sixteen farms without downpayment on condition that each farmer grow at least ten acres of beets on every eighty acres of land. Where the farm had no buildings the company was willing to advance 400 dollars for the construction of a modest house. This proved very attractive and by the end of 1926 at least forty families had settled around the town of Coaldale. Others followed in spring. The majority of the new immigrants were Mennonite Brethren.

The first Mennonite Brethren church was organized in 1926 with Klaas Enns as temporary leader. To begin with they met in houses or in the hay loft of the big barn on the Lathrop farm. In 1928 the first church building was erected, but with immigrants continuing to come, it had to be enlarged in 1929 and again in 1932. By 1939 it became necessary to build an even larger structure, seating about 800 people. The time would come when the Coaldale congregation had over 600 members (making it one of the largest churches in the Canadian Conference of Mennonite Brethren at that time). B.B. Janz, who had done so much to get the Mennonites out of Russia, became the leader of the church in 1929 and held that position for a great many years. As many as twelve ordained ministers helped him with the spiritual nurture of the congregation.

The Mennonite Brethren Church was well established in Coaldale when our family moved on to a farm nine miles from this church. Since those of us who lived in the Readymade District did not have cars and the round trip to church was eighteen miles with horses and wagon, it was decided to have Sunday morning services in homes. Once a month, on communion Sunday, we all went to Coaldale. This was not particularly pleasing to B.B. Janz, who would have wanted all of us in Coaldale every Sunday, but he finally accepted the situation.

As time went on, about ten Readymade families banded together and bought a vacant house which was moved onto our front yard (since our farm happened to be centrally located) and that became our meeting house for some time. Mr. John Unger, who lived a mile from us, was an ordained minister and he often preached on Sundays. Later, Mr. Isaac Janzen and his family moved into our district and he did much of the preaching. For some time we were the only family with a telephone and so my dad was asked to assume the responsibility of inviting ministers to serve us on Sunday.

Herman Hamm organized a choir which sang regularly at our Sunday morning services. Ministers from the Coaldale M.B. Church, Bible School teachers, and visiting missionaries often preached on Sundays. What John and I did not like about having the church on our yard was that we automatically became its janitors (without pay, of course). Also, it bothered us that frequently our yard was a total mess after a morning service, because church goers came with horse and buggy, leaving us to clean up the left-over hay and the manure.

After several years the little meeting house became too small and a bigger building was erected on the same location on our front yard. This meant that we usually had guests for Sunday dinner, something we as children enjoyed very much, but it must have been a bit burdensome for mother, although we never heard her complain. As a teenager I helped in the construction of this building.

I have many fond memories of this chapel on our yard. We heard some very good sermons in which the Word of God became alive. For a number of years I sang in the choir and participated in youth work. Since our congregation was too small to have a graded Sunday school, where some attention was paid to age differences, Sunday school left much to be desired. Coaldale had a reasonably good Sunday school for children (adults had a two-hour church service), but since we went there only one Sunday a month I never felt at home there, although I enjoyed meeting young people with whom I did not also go to public school. The trip to Coaldale was always a big undertaking, especially in winter when we froze half to death riding on a wagon.

When I was sixteen I enrolled in the Coaldale Bible School. During the three years that I attended this school I regularly went to the Coaldale Mennonite Brethren Church and got to know most of its members. Later I was to teach in this Bible school for four years and again we fellowshipped regularly in the Coaldale congregation. Moreover, after we had acquired a motor car, we attended many services in the Coaldale Mennonite Brethren Church other than on communion Sunday. Coaldale often invited visiting speakers such as A.H. Unruh (Winkler), Jacob Thiessen (Vancouver), D.D. Derksen (Boissevain), Jacob Reimer (Greendale), J.B. Toews (Reedley), Aaron Toews (Namaka), and others. We never missed such special meetings.

Coaldale was blessed with a number of good preachers. The

leading minister B.B. Janz, seldom preached, but he decided who would preach from Sunday to Sunday. We had no bulletins in those days and we never knew when we came to church who would be the speakers. Fortunately we always had two sermons so if the one fell flat one could always hope that the next one would be better. While the children had Sunday school from 10:00 to 11:00, we adults had a prayer meeting, usually led by a lay brother, and a sermon. Bible school students got their first chance to give a brief meditation in these prayer meetings. After several hymns (we sang from the *Dreiband* and mostly by memory) we had the first sermon. Often a younger speaker would be asked to give the first sermon while the children had Sunday school. This gave aspiring preachers a wonderful opportunity to test themselves, and it is not surprising that scores of ministers in the Canadian Conference received their call to the ministry through the Coaldale Mennonite Brethren Church.

After the prayer meeting and the first sermon we sang hymns while the children came in and filled row upon row of seats in the front of the large auditorium. The choir sang at the beginning of the ten o'clock service, then again at eleven o'clock, and at the conclusion of the morning service. The second service began with announcements, singing and the main sermon. Often B.B. Janz, who was a strong leader but not a very good preacher, closed the service in prayer. His prayers were usually inordinately long. On one occasion, when my brother John timed him, he prayed for a full ten minutes.

We were always glad when one of the Bible school teachers preached on Sunday morning. Preachers such as Abram Schierling, B.W. Sawatzky, J.H. Quiring, J.A. Toews, Jacob Franz, and others, were always a delight to listen to. Since they had taken homiletics they structured their sermons a bit more carefully. Sometimes I wrote their outlines down and eventually I bought a loose-leaf in which I filed these away. As I got older and a message from God's Word struck me in a particular way I would try to retain as much of the sermon as possible in my memory and when alone on the field I would rehearse it and preach it to myself (or to the birds).

Other than the Bible school teachers, who had had some formal theological training, most of our preachers were self-taught men of God. Considering their very limited training and resources, I marvel now when I recall how well they preached. The older J.A. Toews (father of J.B. Toews) had a gift of pouring the balm of Gilead on wounded souls; A.P. Willms was something of a mystic and a poet and allowed his imagination to wander somewhat freely at times. Jacob Siemens, who became the leader of the church after B.B. Janz resigned, had trained in Wiedenest, Germany, and could speak quite powerfully; if only he had kept to the gospel rather than constantly denouncing the worldliness of the members (pity the women who came to church wearing short-sleeved dresses!). Jacob Dueck also preached well, except that he always had a hoarse throat. Henry Kornelson's favourite topic was eschatology. Rarely did he preach a sermon that did not hold out hope for the people of God in the millennium. He was an intelligent man and could express himself well. However, because his sermons lacked organization, I could never remember any of them. For a number of years John Unger, in his meek and mild manner, also participated in the preaching ministry. Abram Brauer, brother-in-law of B.B. Janz, always moved us deeply and emotionally with his evangelistic fervour. Somewhat younger than the ones just mentioned was David Pankratz, who served for years in the executive of the Canadian Conference. He had a great gift of communication and could preach powerful messages. With the exception of men such as Alexander Neuman and Henry Nikkel and the Bible school teachers, who were fluent in both German and English, all our ministers preached in German. Only on special occasions, such as weddings, funerals and mission festivals, did we hear sermons in English.

Weddings were always great occasions. As a rule the entire congregation was invited and attended. Three sermons, two in

German and one in English (in case an English speaking neighbour should be present) were standard. Weddings were usually held on Sunday afternoons when everyone was free to come. The long service was always followed by coffee and *Zwieback* (buns) in the lower auditorium of the church. Also, we attended every funeral, even if it meant missing school. The Mennonite Brethren Church had a cemetery behind the church and the burial services were always attended by the entire congregation. As a teenager I participated at times in digging the grave when someone in our community died. A surprisingly high number of deaths among children and young people took place when I was a boy. Young boys operated farm machinery at an early age and there were many serious accidents and even deaths. A twelve-year-old girl who was in my class at school was killed when the horse she was riding reared up and fell on top of her. Since we worked with horses, I myself was involved in several potentially dangerous runaways.

Through the influence of my parents and the serious preaching of God's Word from Sunday to Sunday, the Spirit of God began very early in my life to convict me of my sinful condition and of my need for a Saviour. Conversion was high on the agenda in the sermons I heard in my childhood, and I knew there must come a time where I would have to confess with my mouth that Jesus Christ is Lord. Also, the Second Coming of Christ was often the subject of sermons and at times I was frightened at the thought that I might be left behind when the Lord came. From earliest childhood I loved Jesus, and the thought of rejecting him never really crossed my mind. But what must I do to be saved? No one ever talked to me about it--neither parents, nor preachers, nor friends. It was generally held at the time that a person had to go through a period of struggle, of darkness, of repentance, in preparation for a kind of Damascus-Road experience. In my distress and in my fear that I would be like one of the foolish maidens when the Bridegroom came, I prayed fervently to God to forgive my sins and accept me as his child, but I found no peace. One night I dreamt the Lord had come and when I awoke I was so terrified that I jumped out of bed and went to my parents' bedroom to check if they were still there. To my great relief they were, and since they were too devoted to Christ to be left behind, I thought, I knew that he had not yet come.

When I was about twelve I lay awake in bed one night, as I often did, praying to God to be gracious and not to condemn me for all my sins (the childhood variety--disobedience, quarrelling, mischief, and the like). John, with whom I shared a double-bed for many years, was also restless. Although we did everything else together, we kept our inner struggles to ourselves. All of a sudden he got out of bed, went into the living room and told my parents that he wanted to be saved. Like a flash I bolted out of bed and told my parents that I too wanted to be converted. I don't remember anything dad told us, only that both mother and dad prayed with us. A flood of joy and peace entered my troubled soul. I had believed with my heart a long time; now I had confessed with my mouth, and the deep assurance that I belonged to God came into my soul. Sleep was long in coming that night.

There were no radical changes in my life after my conversion. Through my upbringing I had adopted a kind of Christian life style long before I confessed Christ as Saviour and had quite unconsciously accepted many Christian values. My understanding of the Christian life was, however, very elementary, and the practice of it left even more to be desired.

8

Readymade School

Readymade got its first school in 1918. This one-room school served the community until 1927 when the increasing enrollment called for a new two-room building. High school grades were now added. The children were taken to and from school with horse-drawn vans. In 1935 another classroom and an auditorium, which served as gymnasium, were added. After a number of Mennonites had moved into the district, Mr. Henry Kornelson, who knew English better than the rest, was elected to the school board, and in this way the concerns of the Mennonite families in matters of education, discipline and social behaviour were represented in the board.

John and I began grade one in the fall of 1929. For a few months we attended the Deer Park School, in Grassy Lake, and then for the winter months transferred to the Flickenger School. In the spring of 1930 we came to Readymade. Three different schools in my first year! John should have been in the second grade according to his age and our teacher must have thought that was where he belonged. Since I was in the same grade with him, she put me into grade two as well, so I finished grade two at the end of my first year of school. Our teacher, Miss Parker, must have thought our English was good enough to get along with the second year students, for we knew next to no English until we enrolled in grade one.

Readymade school began promptly at 9:00, but since we lived only half a mile from the school we did not need to rush in the mornings. We always walked. Mother usually prepared sandwiches spread with syrup for lunch. Rogers Golden Syrup could always be found in our pantry, and often when we came home from school after four o'clock we would sneak into the pantry and have a few more slices of bread with syrup. We rarely had any fruit in the 1930s. If we ever had apples, they were considered such a luxury that only half an apple was allowed for lunch.

At school the noon hour was the most important part of the day for me--not because I was so hungry, but because we could play. Some of us regularly gulped down our sandwiches as quickly as possible in order not to lose time for games. Until 1935, when the school got a gymnasium, we played outside year round. On very cold or on rainy days we played in the basement of the school. We swang, played marbles in spring, and soccer and baseball during the autumn and summer months. When it snowed we played snowball and that usually got us into trouble with the principal, Mr. Roycroft, who would make us stay in at recess for weeks as punishment for playing snowball too close to the school. Also, he got very upset when he rang the bell and we did not drop everything that very second and run for school.

I have only pleasant memories of my teachers in the lower grades: Miss Parker, Miss Cole, Miss Bulmer. They were all very fine women, I thought, and until I got into Mr. Roycroft's room my school days were quite uneventful. Unfortunately we did not have a library in our country school and so I read very little during my public school years. I don't recall ever doing homework either. Since we had up to six grades in one room, with only one teacher for the room, the others worked on assignments while the teacher instructed one of the grades. At times this became rather tedious, especially after one had looked at all the pictures in the geography textbook a hundred times.

In everyday life, as in church life, the Mennonites kept very much to themselves. It was hard for our parents to relate to non-Mennonite neighbours because they knew so little English. Besides, in the Ukraine they had always lived separated from the Russian people, and they found it somewhat awkward now to live in the midst of people of different nationalities. Moreover, our ministers were very strong in their emphasis on separation from the world, and that was understood to mean that one did not associate freely with non-Christians. In school that was different. Here we played, studied and quarrelled with children of other nationalities (most of them Slavic). Children from English families usually thought of themselves as several cuts higher on the social scale than immigrant children, and consequently we were often subject to abuse, both verbal and physical. Our parents often warned us against forming close friendships with non-Mennonite classmates. In this regard they were short-sighted, even though they meant well. It is, of course, a very common attitude of immigrant parents who are afraid of losing their traditions and values.

Once I passed into grade seven I had the principal, Mr. Roycroft, as teacher. By now, an extra class-room had been added and we had a large gymnasium. Mr. Roycroft was an Irishman, about sixty years old, who ran Readymade School very much along European models. Mr. Hamilton, chairman of the school board, was also Irish, and supported the principal in all that he did. The Mennonite parents liked him because of his strict discipline--the kind they had known in the Mennonite schools of Russia. One of his guiding principles was the proverb "spare the rod and spoil the child." He used the strap and the yard-stick rather liberally. Strapping was done in the presence of the entire class. One day the entire grade eight got the strap because they had not done their arithmetic as well as they should have. During writing periods he walked up and down the aisle with the strap in his hand, and if our writing was not up to par we got it on the hand.

On Ascension Day we had to go to school as usual. On our farm stood the little chapel where Mennonite Brethren families would be gathering for a service that day in the afternoon (at that time it was considered to be in very bad taste if a Mennonite farmer worked on the field on Ascension Day). So it occurred to several of us boys that we might be able to escape the boredom of school by sneaking off to church in the afternoon. After all, no one could fault us for an interest in things religious. Just as we left the school gate Mr. Roycroft saw us and rang the bell. We paid no attention but ran off to church. Next day we faced an angry principal, who assured us that he had nothing against church, but that our behaviour was absolutely intolerable and he wanted to make sure we wouldn't forget that.

Mr. Roycroft was a teacher from head to toe. He had little use for anything but study. He lived in the teacherage on the school yard with his family, and in the evenings, after the lessons for the next day had been prepared, we often watched him walking up and down the road reciting poetry. Had he been able to control his temper in the classroom, we might have responded more positively to his efforts to give us a good education. We could usually tell in the morning by the way he started school when he was in a bad mood. On those bad days we did not say the Lord's Prayer. And if we did not immediately take out our books and begin to work we could expect anything--a blow with the fist, expulsion for the day, or the cancellation of recess. One morning I decided to go to school somewhat earlier in order to shoot baskets. When Mr. Roycroft saw me he called me in and I had to do arithmetic until school was called at nine.

Frequently about five minutes before noon, when we could hardly wait to be dismissed, he wrote a long sentence on the board and all the grades together had to analyze the sentence grammatically. If we answered a question poorly he might say (as he often did), "You have a head and so has a pin." Then again, if we surprised him upon a rare occasion with a flash of insight, he might say, "When the king hands out medals I shall see that you get one." If we misbehaved he might denounce us vehemently as the "biggest blackguard of the school," and in his anger he often handed out unjust punishment, such as staying in at recess for a month.

Mr. Roycroft meant well, but because he made no effort to come even a little closer to his students, and because of his manner of punishing them, he received rather less appreciation from many of his students than perhaps he deserved. Late in life, we were told, he committed his life to Christ. We wondered how that might have affected his temper. Largely because of the support he received from the Mennonite families who were represented on the school board by Mr. Kornelson, Mr. Roycroft taught at Readymade for many years. I had him until I finished grade nine. Several years later I heard that he had gone to northern Alberta to teach and I wrote him a letter apologizing for all the trouble I had caused him. He responded with a very friendly letter. What amazed me was that he had kept track of all "his boys," as he called us--proud of those who had made out well. Only later in life did I realize that in spite of the limitations of curriculum, staff and library, Mr. Roycroft had taught us the three R's every bit as well as they are taught today.

When I entered grade ten we had a new teacher, Mr. Jackson. Rumour had it that he was a Christian, and I have no reason to doubt it, although he never talked about it in school. He was a very fine person and I had the impression he wanted to be friends with his students. However, most of us had learned by then to view our teacher as the enemy, and we must have been hard to win. Although he had a better formal education, Mr. Jackson came straight out of university and had little experience in teaching, and so grade ten was a disaster for me in many respects.

What made grade ten a bit more interesting was the arrival of the Poetker family from Meadow Lake, Saskatchewan. Their older children, Helen, Henry and Paul, had not had opportunity to go to high school in Saskatchewan and now came to take their grades eleven and twelve. They were several years older than the rest of us and took their studies more seriously. Helen found it hard to endure the nonsense of us younger students, Paul took an interest in our spiritual life, and with Henry we argued endlessly. He went on to spend his life in India as a missionary.

Since the language of the church was German, our parents were very concerned that we become fluent in that language so that we might enter more fully into our spiritual heritage. Indeed, this heritage, it was thought, was so closely tied up with the German language that some stated without reservation, "If we lose the German, we lose the faith." Hardly had we settled in Readymade when Mennonite families arranged for German classes to be taught either on Wednesday nights or all day on Saturday (mostly the latter).

Mr. Bernard Dick, an excellent teacher from the Ukraine who, like many of his fellow-teachers, now farmed in Coaldale, offered his services. On the yard of the John Dicks (his brother) a small school-house was erected and so we had to go to German school. We were still rather young, but with horse and wagon (or buggy) we travelled the six miles round trip every week of the winter months. Sometimes our teacher helped us hitch the horses. On one occasion the barbed wire gate was still closed as we approached German school and we couldn't get the mules to stop in time and so they walked into the gate and tore it to pieces and cut themselves badly. Mr. John Dick did not appreciate in the least what had happened to his gate. At other times we had difficulty controlling our horses who had stood out in the cold so long and we often got ourselves into potentially dangerous situations.

If we didn't learn as much German as we might have, it was not Mr. Dick's fault. He taught with great enthusiasm. He introduced us to German poetry, hymnody and folk songs. He taught us German grammar and composition. Although I took a number of German classes later in Bible school and still later at the university, Mr. Bernard Dick gets much of the credit for having laid the foundation for my knowledge of German.

Wednesday nights at German school were reasonably bearable, but when we had to attend German school all day Saturday, after five days in public school, we came to class with little enthusiasm. But, like or not, Mr. John Unger, a neighbour of ours who had also been a teacher in Russia, was engaged to teach us German in the little church building that stood on our yard. Mr. Unger was a very different kind of person than Mr. Dick. Discipline was difficult to maintain at "Saturday School," as we called it, and I contributed my share to this problem. Somehow the students had the impression that in German school they did not need to toe the line as they did in public school. Nevertheless, we did pick up a lot of German. Mr. Unger later taught German in Bible school where I had him once again as teacher of the German language. When I entered the University of British Columbia, in 1947, I enrolled in a German Literature course. After Dr. Cowie had heard me translate from German into English, she suggested that I no longer come to class and waste my time. All I needed to do was to write the exams. In fact Dr. Cowie then asked me to tutor a fourth year student at UBC who had finished all his work for his degree but could not graduate because he couldn't pass his German. In retrospect I am grateful to parents and German-school teachers for making us bear what we thought at the time was a rather heavy yoke. Not only did my proficiency in German prove invaluable in the study of theology, but it also opened many doors of service in the kingdom of God.

Saturday school came to an end with the spring weather, for then Mr. Unger, who was a farmer like the rest of us, had to pay attention to his farm. Before the term closed, however, we had to prepare for a closing program in which we demonstrated to our parents what we had learned. Every pupil had to be involved. Reams of poetry had to be recited, dramas were presented, dialogues, songs, readings, and so forth. I was never a conscientious student in German school, but I took great delight in dramas and recitations.

Saturday school closing was not the only event at which we developed our gifts of communication. The monthly *Jugendvereine* (youth programs) provided ample opportunity for group singing, the reciting of poems, dialogues and the like. On one occasion John and I had learned a long *Zwiegespräch* (dialogue), and as we carried on before the large Coaldale congregation we forgot some of our lines but we made up our own and carried on in a manner that no one realized what was happening. We did not often hear words of praise from our parents (people at that time thought such comments led to pride). However, on this occasion dad had in fact been impressed, and let us know. Reciting poems of twenty stanzas was not usual for young people in those days. For our Christmas programs our German school teachers usually gave us long pieces to memorize and I recall standing on a chair at home and rehearsing my lines with the proper intonation.

One regret, among others, which I have as I think of my childhood and youth is that we had so little to read. The two papers that came into our home were the *Rundschau* and the *Family Herald*--neither of which held much attraction for us as children. Readymade School had no library and Lethbridge was too far away. Even if we had been able to borrow books from a public library, my parents would have been somewhat apprehensive about such reading. Mr. Dietrich Matties of Coaldale had a large collection of German books and occasionally we stopped at his house to borrow a few, but they were mostly German war stories, such as *Richthofen, Der Rote Kampfflieger* or *Pieter Maritzburg*--a huge volume on the Boer War in South Africa. When the Second World War broke out dad was sorry he had allowed us to read so many war stories.

From age six to fifteen my life was concerned with school, farm and church. Life on the farm after school hours mercifully was not all work. Across the road from us lived the John Esaus and we spent a great many evenings playing ball on our front yard, until Mr. Esau whistled and the boys had to hurry home. In winter, with the many ponds around, we had glorious times playing ice hockey. In summer we spent endless hours swimming in ponds and irrigation ditches.

Most of the Mennonite children in our community dropped out of school after grade eight and helped their parents on the beet fields and in the home. I was fifteen years of age and found grade ten insufferably boring, and so I decided I had enough. Farming was getting more interesting. Days without end I sat on the tractor during the summer months working the fields and dreaming about the future. I loved farming. Although earlier I had always wanted to be a cowboy, now I was certain I would be a farmer.

9

Coaldale Bible School

After enduring a tenth year in public school, I was greatly relieved that I could stay home and work on the farm. My brother John also quit school. Although we had cows, pigs, chickens and horses to take care of, and although we raised wheat, oats, barley and flax (not to mention the despised potatoes), there was not enough work to keep dad and the two of us busy the year round. Time was often heavy on our hands during this year at home. About the only break in the routine was an occasional trip with our Federal truck to the sugar factory in Picture Butte, where we got beet pulp to feed the cows. Dad thought of buying more land and getting his sons started in farming, but hesitated.

I did a lot of daydreaming that year. And, because I wasn't accomplishing anything, I developed a bad image of myself. I felt like a good-for-nothing. Since many of our friends had also dropped out of school, we frequently visited them in the evenings, in an effort to fill up the many empty hours.

My spiritual life, too, left much to be desired. Although I prayed frequently, I did not study the Scriptures for myself and devotional reading material was not available. The one book which I did read was the German version of Bunyan's *Pilgrim's Progress.*

Until I was fifteen we had no radio. It was not that we could not have afforded one, but the church still frowned on this modern instrument of communication. Those members of the church who purchased radios were considered *avant garde* and not very spiritual. It was feared that the radio would bring "the world" right into the living room. My brother John, who was always tinkering with gadgets, outwitted the parents by rigging up a crystal set with ear-phones. Before long, however, all the members of the Coaldale church had radios. Our radio, of course, was strictly controlled by the parents, and besides the daily news I do not remember listening to anything other than a few religious broadcasts. Early in the morning came the Sunrise Gospel Hour from Calgary. More important to me was the Victory Broadcast from Prairie Bible Institute in Three Hills. I always drank in Mr. Maxwell's messages. At that time it did not even occur to me that I would have Mr. Maxwell as my teacher some day. On Sunday evenings came the Old Fashioned Revival Hour of Charles E. Fuller, from Pasadena, California, with its marvellous quartet and Rudy Atwood at the piano. It was a program we rarely missed and it was in some respects the high point of my week. Fuller, with his simple gospel messages, and Maxwell, with his emphasis on the deeper Christian life and on mission, contributed significantly to the nurture of my spiritual life in those rather vacuous early teenage years.

Since we had nothing to read, I was almost desperate at times to keep myself occupied. I bought a guitar and learned to chord. Soon I was able to accompany myself as I sang hymns, sometimes for hours at a time. Memorizing came easily to me and so I decided to memorize all the stanzas of a great many German hymns from the *Dreiband.* Most of them I remember to this day. With English hymns, which I learned to sing later in life, the matter is quite different; I am always glad if I can sing at least the first stanza for memory. The messages of the hymns I learned in those days often moved me very deeply as I sang them--especially those that expressed *Sehnsucht.*

By chance I learned of a Christian organization that offered a free English Bible to anyone who memorized 300 Bible verses. I committed them to memory in short order, had my sister verify that I had indeed learned them, and got my first English Bible with soft India paper. I had already received a German New Testament. Mr. Schroeder, colporteur of the Canadian Bible Society, was travelling through Southern Alberta with his Bible van. My parents put him up for the night. Next day my dad presented me with a German New Testament. I was so overwhelmed that I went into the hayloft and with tears pressed it to my heart and thanked God for giving me such a treasure.

After spending a monotonous year on the farm, I began to think seriously of doing something more interesting the following year. I was sixteen and could not imagine myself puttering around on the farm for another year. It was autumn and our parents encouraged both John and me to consider enrolling in the Coaldale Bible School. It was an attractive alternative to another winter on the farm. Yes, I would go; John decided to join me. However, since I was only sixteen and the minimum age for admission was seventeen, dad asked the Bible School Board to make an exception, explaining that I would be seventeen in December. They graciously bent the rules and allowed me to apply.

The whole matter got more serious when I received the application form. One question I found downright amusing: "Are you in love?" It was generally assumed at that time that if a person was in love he or she could not pay attention to studies. Moreover, for one's girl or boyfriend to be in Bible school at the same time was strictly forbidden, for that created discipline problems (boys were not allowed to visit girls and vice versa). Dating, incidentally, was taboo in the Mennonite Brethren community of Coaldale. My sister, Margaret, on one occasion rode in a car together with some other boys and girls and came close to being excommunicated from the church. As for myself, I had taken an interest in several girls in our community as I grew up, but what did it mean to be in love? I recall when I was twelve I was greatly attracted to a girl in my class at school, but she was tragically killed in an accident--an event that made a deep impression on our community. Another girl in my class showed great interest in me and one day gave me a beautiful pen-and-pencil set. I kept it in my desk at school for some time, for I did not dare take it home: that would have created a scene. I didn't have the heart to return the gift to her and so one day I asked her older brother if he would tactfully intervene and give the set back to his sister.

But now, how should I answer the question, "Are you in love?" One fellow-student wrote, "Somewhat!" However, I thought I had every good reason to write an unequivocal, "No!"

The question that led to considerable soul searching was "Are you saved?" What should I write? Yes or No? Had I not accepted Christ as my Saviour when I was about twelve? Yes, indeed; but we heard so much about holy living in church, and as I thought of my many faults and imperfections, I began to harbour doubts about the genuineness of my conversion. What made the question even more complicated was the next one: "When were you saved?" I thought they wanted the exact date, and that I had forgotten; I had never marked it on the calendar. Surely I would be rejected! But then I said to myself that even though I had forgotten the date, and even though I was so imperfect, I belonged to Christ; and so I wrote, Yes! That decision, as I think of it now, set the sails for my life's voyage.

I recognized the profound significance of my "Yes" when I discovered that my brother John, who must have had similar questions, had written "No!" It seemed as if for the first time our lives were on two different tracks. After a few weeks of Bible school he wanted to quit. We persuaded him to stick with it for at least the year, but his heart was not in it. His tragic death at age twenty-one was so painful for us largely because we were left wondering where he had stood in his relationship to Christ whom he had confessed as Lord the same evening I was saved.

Our family had always attended the opening convocations of the Coaldale Bible School, and often as a boy I wondered whether I might some day be among that "sacred throng" that devoted a year or more to the study of the Scriptures and related subjects. In the fall of 1939 I, with fifty other freshmen, enrolled in the first year of a three-year program of studies at the Coaldale Bible School.

This school had its beginnings in 1929, when Mr. Abram Schierling began teaching young people in the home of the David Klassens (brother-in-law to C.A. DeFehr, Winnipeg). Mr. Schierling was an eccentric in many respects, but had an outstanding gift of teaching and had a profound grasp of the Scriptures. He had already taught in the Herbert Bible School and was called to Coaldale from there. In 1930 the church took over the cost and the governance of the Bible school. Other teachers were added, among them J.A. Toews, the father of the well-known J.B. Toews. Students came from all over Alberta and even Saskatchewan-- particularly from Fairholm and Glenbush, where the German language was still held in high regard.

When the Coaldale Mennonite Brethren Church took charge of the infant school, it was moved from the Klassen home to the church building. In 1934 a school building was erected next to the church and the student body continued to increase. By 1936 the school offered a three-year course of training in a great variety of subjects. It was also in that year that Mr. B.W. Sawatzky, who was to serve as principal for many years, and J.H. Quiring were appointed as instructors. They were new to the community. I attended the opening convocation. Although I was only fourteen at the time, I have never forgotten the text and the sermon Mr. Sawatzky preached that evening: *"O Herr hilf, O Herr lass wohl gelingen"* ("O Lord, we beseech thee, give us success," Ps. 118:25). He had me completely memorized.

The year I entered Bible school there were only three faculty members: B.W. Sawatzky, J.H. Quiring and John Unger. Of the fifty students in our first year class only two had completed high school. Several members of our class were not yet believers. One of them was Abe Froese of Tofield, who sat next to me. Later in the school year I had the joy of being present when he gave his life to Christ. What seemed a bit strange to us was that all the fellows sat in front of the classroom and the girls at the back. We were told this was to keep the boys from looking at the girls. The other way around evidently posed no similar threat.

Those students who came from farther away boarded at the school, but the school provided no living quarters. Parents were responsible for finding housing for their sons and daughters in the town of Coaldale, a half mile from the school. The Peter Penners, who lived about a mile from the school, had a large two-storey house and let out the entire second floor to Bible school students. Seven of us lived at the Penners that first year. A third-year student, Rudolf Hiebert, was one of the seven; the rest of us were first-year novices. We found it rather bothersome to have Rudolf around; it cramped our free-wheeling style. Most of us were away from home for the first time and we enjoyed our new freedoms to the full. How the Penners endured all the nonsense that went on upstairs almost every night, I am in no position to tell, and since Peter has been with the Lord for many years, I cannot ask him. It was a riot, to say the least.

I enjoyed Bible school. Bernard Sawatzky taught most of the Bible courses and a whole new world opened up to me as I listened to his expositions which were always intensely practical. In the class "Story Telling" ("speech" is the more sophisticated name), Mr. Sawatzky, first of all, demonstrated good story telling for us and then we all had to take our turn and tell the class a story. The teacher often supplied us with stories if we couldn't find one ourselves. After I had told my story and the class had discussed the presentation, Mr. Sawatzky made the remark, "Brother Ewert, you have good gifts." No one had ever told me that. Words of commendation were rather rare in our Mennonite communities at that time. The emphasis lay not so much on encouraging one another but on putting people down. How deeply his words affected me can be gathered from the fact that I should have remembered so casual a comment for the rest of my life. Since I had dropped out of high school after grade ten, and since I had never taken any real interest in my studies when I was in public school, I had no faith in my ability to study. Soon, however, I discovered that I could learn as quickly and as well as my classmates and that stirred interests in me that I had not discerned previously.

Bible school was not all study, of course. At noon we played ball (at least we beginners did; once you got to the third year it was assumed you were beyond such childish things). One day it occurred to us that we should challenge the baseball team of the Coaldale High School to a match. It was arranged after school. We had a hilarious time and completely buried the high school team. Mr. Quiring walked home that day and heard the shouting from the school baseball diamond. To his great disappointment he discovered that it was his Bible school students who were making common cause with "the world." The next day he had us in the faculty office reprimanding us for such very inappropriate behaviour.

During our winters on the farm we had normally spent Sunday afternoons playing ice-hockey, and so when we came to Bible school we continued this practice. One day Mr. Sawatzky made the comment in class that if we couldn't thank God for the blessing we had received from the hockey game, we ought not to play. I found that difficult to understand, but I had the highest respect for this man and so I laid my skates aside for good.

In spite of the many shenanigans we pulled off at Penners, and the fun we had during recesses and in the dining hall, I began to take my Christian life quite seriously. In fact, after my first year I decided that with God's grace I was going to make some radical changes in my deportment. I became very introspective and sin-conscious, to the point where the natural joys of life began to lose attraction for me. For Christmas someone gave me a diary as a gift and I began daily to record my failures and the few victories I had. I became withdrawn and spent less and less time with other people in spite of my gregarious nature. So ashamed did I feel about my progress in the Christian life that I began to sit in the last pews of the church so that as few people as possible would see me. The question of how to overcome sinful tendencies almost obsessed me at times. It took me a long time before I could believe that I was acceptable to God in Christ in spite of my weaknesses and sinful propensities.

It was the spring of 1940. First year Bible school was over and we were back on the fields. There was no question in my mind any longer that Bible school was the place for me the coming year, and this conviction made the summer work on the farm more meaningful and bearable. Moreover, I had now been introduced to books at Bible school and a whole new world was opening up to me.

Also, having committed my life anew to Christ and his kingdom, it became my firm conviction that I must be baptized in the name of Jesus and become a member of the Coaldale Mennonite Brethren Church. I held off until harvest season; then I told my parents of my decision. They were naturally very pleased. Dad let me use the car to visit the leader of our church, B.B. Janz, who lived about twelve miles away from us. He was very busy on his farm and I waited around for a long time till he had a few moments for me. He didn't say very much, but we prayed together and I went home.

At that time it was custom that baptismal candidates give their testimony of conversion before the entire congregation (all 600 of them) and the congregation then had the opportunity to ask whatever they wished of such candidates. I was frightened to death at the prospect of being interrogated in front of such an audience. We had no baptismal classes, no coaching, nothing! We were entirely on our own. As I reflected on my past life I could think of so many things I had done wrong and wondered whether I would pass the scrutiny of the congregation. My conscience was very sensitive at the time and so I made several difficult trips to people in the community, apologizing for little things of which most of them were not even aware. However, I had to do this in order to stand before the church with "a clean heart."

The interrogation went much better than I had anticipated and so that fall I was baptized with a number of other young people in the reservoir close to the Coaldale Mennonite Brethren Church. After the baptism we returned to the church where we were formally received into membership. B.B. Janz read some of the rules we as church members were expected to observe, but I had by then decided to order my life as best I knew how by the Word of God and did not need these rules. I now looked forward with anticipation to the second year of Bible school.

10

Spiritual Formation

In the fall of 1940 I returned for my second year of Bible school. Again, where I would live was a question. On the main street of Coaldale stood the Del Monte General Store, run by Martens and Sons. In conversation with them we discovered that they had an extra room at the back of the store, big enough for two students. They were kind enough to offer this facility to me and my friend, Abe Froese, from Tofield. The room had only a stove; we had to supply the rest. Water was available at the town pump. There was a back-door exit and so we did not have to walk through the entire store to come and go. The Martens must have had a lot of confidence in us, for we had access to all parts of the store day and night. To my knowledge we did not violate their trust.

Since many students took only one year of Bible school, our second year class was considerably smaller than it had been the year before. We sat three to a desk; Eduard Martens sat to my left and Abe Froese to my right. As in the first year, the fellows sat in front and the girls at the back. Two students who had taken their first year in La Glace, Alberta, joined our class in the second year. Lena Hamm and Elizabeth Konrad had come almost 800 miles from the northernmost church of our Canadian Conference at that time.

I felt an attraction for Lena Hamm almost from the day I first saw her, but we never went beyond a friendly greeting. Correspondence and dating were not allowed. Besides, I would not have had the courage at that time to ask Lena for a date, even if it had been permitted. All year long we sat in the same class and ate in the same dining hall. Often I watched her walking from school to the town of Coaldale where she and Elizabeth lived. At the close of the school year I said goodbye to her with a handshake. Both of us felt somehow the handshake was more than a mere formality. A message of mutual admiration and love had been conveyed, even though neither of us really knew how we felt toward each other. As it turned out, this spark of love eventually burst into flame and several years later we were to become husband and wife. However, since Lena lived hundreds of miles away we did not see each other during the next three years, nor did we correspond--we just waited, hoped and prayed.

What made the second year even more interesting than the first was the addition of Mr. J.A. Toews to the faculty. Toews had been a student at the Coaldale Bible School in the early thirties and then went on to study at the Prophetic Bible Institute in Calgary. Following that he had studied for three years at Tabor College, Kansas, and had earned a Bachelor of Theology degree. Naturally we looked the new teacher over rather carefully. Among the things that struck us was his curly hair and his laughter. In my youth laughter was not thought of as the most authentic way of expressing godliness, and perhaps that was why his friendly demeanour struck us. On one occasion, which I remember vividly, he asked a student in the Church History class for the name of the village (Dorf) which became the centre of Moravian activity, and he answered, "Zinzendorf." Toews turned to the blackboard away from the class and exploded with laughter.

We continued our studies in Bible, in Doctrine and Ethics, and in German Grammar. Mr. Quiring taught courses such as Child Psychology and Pedagogy, designed to equip us for Sunday school teaching. One subject that became most meaningful for me that year was Prayer. Mr. Sawatzky lectured on various aspects of prayer and we worked through O. Hallesby's classic on that subject. I have read books on prayer since then, but in my estimation Hallesby's is still one of the best in the field. Unfortunately the book is not widely known today.

The study of prayer had a profound effect on my life. Once the school year was over I decided to discipline myself in praying. For some time I used part of the lunch hour (when dad had his rest) for prayer. Also, I found a spot hidden among the trees on our farm where I could pray without being disturbed. In order to train myself in intercession I wrote out names of people or events or needs for every day of the week and mentioned these before the Lord in prayer. It was all a bit mechanical and stilted, but one has to begin somewhere.

When Bible school closed I was glad to get out into the fresh air again and prepare the land for seeding. Walking behind the harrows or sitting on the tractor all day, I had much time to reflect and to think. Bible school was opening up new perspectives on life of which I had not formerly been aware. Among other things, I began to feel a deep inner urge to serve the Lord in some capacity. An opportunity afforded itself that summer.

The Western Children's Mission had been accepted by the Coaldale young people as an avenue in which to express their mission interest. The church had elected a committee that gained permission from the trustees of public schools, lying around Coaldale in a hundred mile radius, to teach Daily Vacation Bible School for two weeks during the summer holidays. Two young men or women would spend two weeks in a school district. They invited the children of the community to attend classes in Bible and related subjects in the forenoons, from 9:00 to 12:00. Teaching aids were supplied, but otherwise the workers were left largely to themselves to improvise and to communicate the gospel to the children as best they could. At times the workers were allowed to live in the teacherage, if it was vacant, but more often than not they slept on the floor of the school house, cooked their own meals, taught the children and, if possible, visited the homes in the community to give a Christian witness.

After my second year of Bible school I volunteered to spend two two-week periods in this kind of ministry. My partner for the first two weeks was John Schmidt, who later became the speaker on the Gospel Light Hour from Winnipeg, and pastored churches for many years. We were asked to go to a country school near the town of Grassy Lake. We enrolled about a dozen children from the community. Most of them came from families that belonged to the United Church. Roman Catholic families at that time did not allow their children to come.

We did our best to teach the Bible lessons. We sang gospel songs with the children, memorized Scripture with them, and tried above all to make the way of salvation plain to the children. I was quite overjoyed when one of the girls expressed her willingness to have me pray with her that Christ might come into her life. The previous winter I had had the joy of leading a young man in the Coaldale community to Christ and had found that a source of great joy. In my eagerness to win people for Christ I prayed with my sister Margaret, as well as with my two younger brothers, Abe and Henry, as they turned in faith to Christ.

Since we had DVBS only five days a week for two weeks, John Schmidt and I felt we should make ourselves useful over the weekend. We had no vehicle other than our bicycles with which to get around, so we tied our instruments (John had an accordion and I had a guitar) to our bikes and made off for the town of Burdett on Saturday afternoon. Our plan was to hold an open air meeting on Main Street. However, the town seemed very dead that Saturday, and so we decided rather to cycle to the town of Bow Island. This town was alive on Saturday night and so we set up in front of a cafe and began to sing and to play. Both of us gave a word of testimony, played and sang some more and then handed out about a hundred tracts to those assembled on the sidewalk to hear us. By then it was dark and we cycled most of the night on gravel and dirt roads to get back to our school. When the neighbour, who wasn't particularly interested in our gospel, heard about our street meeting he couldn't help but commend us for our courage (he called it "guts").

The two weeks passed by and John Schmidt had to return home to Coaldale. In his place came Herbert Hamm, a former neighbour of ours with whom I had attended the Coaldale Bible School. A member of the mission committee came with his pickup truck and took us to a school about ten miles from the town of Bow Island.

The school had no teacherage and so we slept on the floor of the school house. One night it was so hot I decided to open the door and sleep on the front steps. When I was fast asleep a gust of wind blew the heavy steel-framed door shut and I received a deep gash in my sleepy head. We had no electricity and so we tried our best to attend to my wound in the darkness. Fortunately I was able to carry on with the work.

Again we invited the children of the farmers who lived in the community and conducted DVBS for another two weeks with about fifteen youngsters. It was a delight to learn to know a Christian family in the neighbourhood who not only sent their children but also invited us for a meal occasionally. On one occasion we felt we should cycle to the town of Bow Island to meet with the minister of the United Church who did not, as it appeared to us, have a great appreciation for what we were doing. Our "consultation" left much to be desired, to put it mildly. At the end of the two weeks, just as we had done in Grassy Lake, we invited the parents to come for a Friday night closing program. The children demonstrated some of the things they had learned and we used the occasion to give a gospel message in word and in song. After the evening program, Mr. Henry Nikkel, one of the directors of the mission, came to take us home to Coaldale.

I am not sure how effective our ministry was in these two schools, but it certainly did a lot for us. It took much courage to go from farm to farm and meet total strangers and ask them to entrust their children to us for two weeks. What I found even harder is to visit the homes and try to speak to the people about the salvation offered us in Jesus Christ. Admittedly we were short on knowledge, but no one could fault us for lack of zeal.

Upon my return from a month of DVBS work, August was upon us and I helped my parents bring in the harvest, eagerly looking forward to my third year of Bible school. Again the question of housing had to be faced. The principal of the Bible school, Mr. B.W. Sawatzky, had a small study, six by eight feet, which he thought he could spare. The salaries of the teachers were very low at that time and a bit of extra income through rent was much appreciated. The Sawatzkys were willing to have me stay at their house. I would, of course, take my meals at the school's dining hall. The room was so small that my Aladdin lamp would often go out on me for lack of oxygen, if I kept the door closed. The window, of course, had to remain sealed because of the cold. I tried not to interfere in the family life of the Sawatzkys and kept strictly to my room in the evenings. Occasionally Mr. Sawatzky would come into my room to talk to me about the things of God and to pray with me. Moreover, I had been elected student president and the principal occasionally wanted to discuss aspects of student life with me.

As in my second year, I once again became a member of a male quartet and found great satisfaction in singing the great songs of the faith. Occasionally a faculty member with a student group went on deputation to other churches in the province of Alberta, and it was my privilege not only to participate in the singing on these occasions, but also to give words of testimony, tell the children a story, or give an object lesson (they were popular at the time). In our desire to witness, several of us took the evening train to Lethbridge one Friday night and spent half the night handing out tracts and witnessing to people who were willing to listen. We got home in the morning, and I had the feeling that Mr. Sawatzky was not particularly impressed with this venture, but he was careful not to dampen our enthusiasm.

Again we had interesting subjects this third year. What was new was Homiletics. We made a great many sermon outlines that year, and although I took at least three more courses in Homiletics later in life, this elementary course proved to be invaluable. It taught us how to organize materials around a theme and to set forth several salient aspects of this theme clearly in sub-headings. Later, in graduate schools, where I had to write essays without end, I suspect my professors at times gave me good grades for the way I had organized my materials, rather than for the content of the essays.

The three years slipped by rather quickly and graduation was around the corner. I was asked to speak on behalf of the graduating class and I put a lot of thought and effort into the preparation of my valedictory address.

After school it was back to the farm and to work in the fields. I left Bible school with precious memories. The three years had been truly worthwhile. The teachers had tried to draw out latent gifts in the students and this had helped me to gain a new respect for myself. Also, God was continuing to work in my life, calling me to invest my time and energy in the kingdom of God. I had no inkling at the time what this would eventually entail. At the moment it was enough that I was willing to enter those doors open to me and not to despise the day of little things.

Once again there came the call for workers to serve in DVBS. This summer I teamed up with Cornelius Thiessen, and we were sent to a country school about ten miles west of Nobelford. Brother Thiessen was considerably older than I and had more experience in personal evangelism. In the classroom I could easily hold my own with the children, but I did not have the same grace as Cornelius did in approaching total strangers and giving a word of testimony to the saving death of Christ. Altogether it was a growing experience.

Again it was harvest season and the question that I had to answer was, "What next?" I had no inclination to spend the winter on the farm. I decided, therefore, to take a fourth year of Bible school in Winkler, Manitoba.

11

Winkler Bible Institute

The A.H. Unruh family left the Crimea in 1924 and arrived in Canada in January 1925. Unruh had wide experience as a teacher in Russia and in the years just prior to emigration had been on the faculty of the Tschongraw Bible School, which was established by the Mennonite Brethren in the Crimea after the Bolshevik Revolution. The school was under the leadership of Johann Wiens, who was a graduate of the Baptist seminary in Hamburg, Germany, and who had been a missionary to India. The curriculum of the Tschongraw school was modelled after that of the Baptist seminary in Hamburg.

The school had operated for only six years when the Soviet authorities closed it for good. The Unruhs then made their way to Canada and settled in Winkler, Manitoba. Here Unruh rented two rooms in the home of Mr. K. Warkentin and began a Bible teaching ministry. This led to the establishment of the Winkler Bible Institute, which is still in operation. In 1926 one of his former colleagues from Tschongraw, Gerhard Reimer, joined him in this new venture. By 1927 the former head of the Tschongraw school, Johann Wiens, had also come to Winkler and joined the faculty. To begin with all instruction was given in the German language, but soon English-speaking faculty members were added. Also, as time went on, a large school building was erected and students came to Winkler not only from Manitoba but from other provinces as well.

A number of young men and women from the Coaldale community went to Winkler after completing the Coaldale Bible School, since Coaldale had only three years. Moreover, the Coaldale Mennonite Brethren Church repeatedly invited Dr. Unruh for Bible conferences and he always impressed me with his thoroughness, his devotion and his sense of humour. Also, I had chanced to come into possession of a Winkler Yearbook which gave me a good insight into the life of the institution. All these factors contributed to my interest in this school.

I had no desire to venture out into the unknown by myself and so I persuaded one of my classmates from the Coaldale Bible School to join me. After I had helped my parents bring in the harvest, Eduard Martens and I boarded a Greyhound bus and made our way to Manitoba. After travelling a night and a day we arrived in Winnipeg. What had not been explained to us was that Greyhound did not serve southern Manitoba, and so we had to transfer to Grey Goose. After about two hours the bus suddenly drew to a halt in the middle of nowhere and we were informed that this was our destination. The driver went out and removed our luggage from the baggage compartment and the bus left. Later we discovered that we had been let off at Winkler Corner.

What should we do? We didn't know where Winkler lay. Besides, we couldn't carry all our things. We decided, then, to leave our baggage in the ditch beside the road and to walk in the direction of what appeared to be a town. After walking for a half mile we looked back and to our consternation saw a car parked beside the highway and the driver, so it seemed to us, was going through our stuff. We agreed quickly that Ed Martens would run back to retrieve what was left of our belongings and I would make my way to town.

A farmer came by with his car and offered me a ride to Winkler. I gladly accepted. I asked him if he knew the Bible school teachers. All he knew was that Mr. Wiens operated a garage in Winkler and he would be glad to take me there. As I walked into the garage I saw a small man in a heavy jacket sitting behind the counter. I introduced myself and discovered that this was Mr. Wiens. He didn't look very much like a teacher to me, but then my former teachers at the Coaldale Bible School also had to work at other jobs during the summers to make a living, and that helped to soften the initial shock. Mr. Wiens then offered to go to Winkler Corner with his car and bring the two of us with bag and baggage to the Hooge Home, where we were put up for the night.

To my pleasant surprise I discovered that Abe Froese, who had been my classmate in Coaldale for two years, asked me to be his room-mate. Ed Martens found a room in a private home, and Abe and I, together with several other students, found board and room at Miss Anna Banman's place, on the condition that we would take our turn cleaning her chicken barn every week (besides paying rent, of course).

Since I knew Dr. Unruh, I was hoping to take most of his classes, even if I did not finish my fourth year, but he very graciously talked me out of that. Fortunately he did offer a good course in New Testament studies in the fourth year and I enjoyed it immensely. Besides Unruh, the faculty that year included J.G. Wiens, H.H. Redekopp, G.D. Pries, A.A. Kroeker and A.H. Redekopp. With the exception of Mr. Pries, all these good men have passed on to be with their Lord.

I enjoyed my studies and my association with the many students from other parts of Canada. Among my classmates was Ben Froese, who went into medical work; Henry Derksen, who spent most of his life as missionary in Zaire; Henry Thielman, who entered the pastoral ministry; David Janzen, who became both college professor and pastor in the Conference of Mennonites; and Annie Dyck, who became missionary to Columbia.

By now World War II was raging in all its fury. On December 5 I turned twenty and promptly received notice from the Selective Service in Edmonton that I was to present myself for a medical examination in preparation for military service. I made an appointment with Dr. Wiebe of Winkler and was declared physically fit. Immediately I dashed off a letter to the authorities in Edmonton explaining to them that I was a conscientious objector to war and had no intentions of serving in the military. Without responding to my letter, my file was transferred to Winnipeg, since I was now residing in Manitoba. Rumour had it that after

Christmas a number of us would be sent to a camp for conscientious objectors in Clearlake, Manitoba. Meantime, however, Manitoba Mennonites had worked out an arrangement whereby those who would normally have to serve in such camps could go to Kapuskasing, Ontario, and work in the forest, cutting lumber. This was considered essential war industry, and as long as we stayed in these lumber camps, we were told, we would be free of the draft.

About twelve of us at the Winkler Bible Institute that year decided to go this route and so at the beginning of January we dropped out of school, purchased warmer clothing in Winnipeg, and left by train for Kapuskasing. We were joined by a great many Mennonite men from villages of southern Manitoba as well as from Winnipeg. After a long train ride we were put up in a lumber camp together with French Canadians. Besides working in the forest every day, felling spruce trees, cutting them into eight foot lengths, and piling them up in cords, we saw an opportunity for evangelism here. We organized meetings at which we proclaimed the gospel and sang gospel songs. It was a pleasant surprise to me many years later to meet a man in Manitoba who told me that he had been saved through a message I had preached in the lumber camp.

The work was very hard and we tramped in deep snow all day long with the temperature dropping to fifty below (Fahrenheit). After working for several weeks I began to wonder whether I had done the right thing in coming here, especially since I was an Albertan (all the others were Manitobans). Toward the end of January I wrote Dr. Unruh and asked him if I could still finish my fourth year if I returned immediately. He replied that if I worked hard it could be done. So I packed my bags and returned to Winkler. The people at the Selective Service at Kapuskasing agreed to let me go on condition that I report to the Winnipeg office as soon as I got to Manitoba. When I informed the Winnipeg authorities that I would be returning to my home province in spring, they gave me a letter to present to the Selective Service office in Lethbridge upon my return to Alberta.

My studies at Winkler went quite well, even though I had a lot of catching up to do, and I was glad I could complete the year and graduate with my class. What made the year even more interesting was that I had the opportunity of travelling with a singing group from church to church in Manitoba. It opened my eyes to the larger Canadian Brotherhood. We visited Morden, Manitou, Lena, Boissevain, Justice, Alexander, Elie, Newton, Wingham, Elm Creek and Winnipeg. Also, my circle of friends was greatly enlarged, for I learned to know students from Ontario to Alberta.

After graduation Ed Martens and I took the train home. It had been my first longer stretch away from home and I was glad to return to my family. Shortly after my arrival dad and I went to Lethbridge to report to the Selective Service. After introducing myself, I told the authorities that I had a letter from the Winnipeg office which I was to present to them. However, they ignored the letter and simply asked whether I had a job. Of course I had a job, for I was now back on the farm with my parents. "Well, then get out of here; we're here only to look for jobs for people." It was a pleasant surprise and a great relief to my parents.

Again the committee of the Western Children's Mission called for workers for the summer. I volunteered for two two-week terms of DVBS. Normally workers went out in pairs but this year there was an uneven number of volunteers and so I offered to go by myself. For two weeks I worked again at Nobelford, and then transferred to Claresholm for another two weeks. Neither of these schools had a teacherage; in fact, at Claresholm there wasn't even a cook stove, and so I slept on the floor and cooked my meals on a tripod in the back yard. I lived on very meagre fare, but it was a rich experience. Since I was alone, I had to prepare lessons to keep me going the entire forenoon. However, I still found some time to visit the farmers and in both schools we had a closing program at which I shared the gospel with the parents of the children.

My brother John, who had gone off to attend the Institute of Technology at Calgary after finishing his high school, had decided (under considerable pressure by the Selective Service) to join the air force. Since he had not been baptized and did not belong to any church he thought he had no right to claim conscientious objector status. After basic training he rose quickly in rank and became an instructor in radar at the RCAF's training centre in Trois Rivières, Quebec.

When he first wrote my parents that he had joined the air force they were completely broken up. Dad knew too much about life in the army from his own observations in the First World War, and feared not so much the physical, but the moral and spiritual dangers that life in the forces brings with it. They wept bitter tears when they read his letter, informing them of his decision.

One benefit of his training was that he became very meticulous about his dress and appearance--something he had considered rather unimportant till then. I had seen him last just before I left for Winkler. At the time it did not cross my mind that I would never see him again. In the middle of August 1943, we received the shocking news by telegram that the plane on which John had been instructing an observer had not returned to its base. All planes were out looking for the lost aircraft. The next few days at our house were intensely sad and sombre. We were in the midst of harvest and had to carry on our work, but our minds were elsewhere.

A second telegram arrived saying that the wreckage had been spotted in the Laurentians and that a rescue team, including medics, were cutting their way through the bush to get to the plane. From the air there were no indications of life. It appeared as if all five--the pilot, two instructors, and two students--had lost their lives. We did not give up hope, however; we prayed and prayed for his life. Dad said he wished he could be there cutting the path; indeed, he wished he could have died in his place.

The third telegram brought the shocking news that John, aged twenty-one, was dead, and that his casket accompanied by an officer was being sent by train from Montreal. We sank into deep sorrow and grief. Neighbours came to comfort us; cards and letters came from friends. Particularly meaningful was a letter from Dr. A.H. Unruh, who lost his son, Victor, in the war. Repeatedly at nights when we lay mourning and could not sleep, groups of brothers and sisters from the church would suddenly be at our window and sing songs of comfort for us.

We were at the railway station when the passenger arrived from Montreal with John's body. The officer came to our home; mother made him a meal and then I took him to the air base at Lethbridge. He tried to comfort us by stressing that he had died for his country, but I pointed out to him that there was salvation in no one else but in the name of Jesus. Since the casket was sealed, we placed it in the morgue at the Coaldale Hospital and prepared for the funeral.

First we gathered in the Readymade Church, where John had always attended as a boy. Mr. Isaac Janzen spoke on the text, "What I am doing you do not understand now, but afterward you will understand" (Jn. 13:7). It was a great comfort. Then we made our way to Coaldale. The air force had sent an officer with ten honourary pallbearers who were present at the service. Since he had been dead so long we could not take the body into the church building, but left it standing in front of the church. The Coaldale Mennonite Brethren Church was filled to capacity. B.W. Sawatzky spoke in German on Psalm 73:25, "Whom have I in heaven but thee? And there is nothing upon earth that I desire beside thee." I also gave a short message, after which J.A. Toews spoke in English on Amos 3:6, which in Luther's version reads, "Is there an accident in the city which the Lord does not do?"

After the service, burial took place in the cemetery behind the church. Following the burial we had a simple fellowship meal at the church. For some time I kept on praying for John; it had become too much a part of my prayer life. When the RCAF offered us a tombstone they asked us which words they might engrave on it. We chose the words of Paul: "Behold the kindness and the severity of God" (Rom. 11:21).

12

Prairie Bible Institute

It would probably strike a young person as exceedingly strange today for someone to attend Bible school for five years in succession, but the times and circumstances need to be taken into account. We were an immigrant family whose life revolved around the farm and the church. Higher education was not really part of our thinking. In fact we were constantly warned against it from the pulpit. Besides, I had not finished my high school and without grade twelve there was little one could do in the field of general education. The Mennonite Brethren Bible College had not yet been established in 1943. And so I decided to go to Prairie Bible Institute, in Three Hills, Alberta, for a fifth year of biblical studies.

I had never been to Three Hills, but the place was a household word for us, since we listened regularly to Prairie's Victory Broadcast on Sunday mornings. Prairie Bible Institute was a highly respected school in our Alberta churches. Its emphasis on godly living, discipline, and missions was greatly appreciated. The institute had its beginnings in 1922 and the image of the school was shaped largely by its founder and principal, L.E. Maxwell. Maxwell had a good reputation in Mennonite Brethren circles, except that he jumped around too much when he preached. Also, some of our people were critical of the fact that Prairie had women Bible teachers. When Miss Miller, the dean of women and an able expositor of the Word, preached a message on the radio one Sunday morning, my mother was visibly upset. To answer my mother I wrote to Maxwell to ask him why they had women teachers and preachers on their staff. In response he sent me a copy of the *Prairie Overcomer* in which both he and Miss Miller had addressed the issue. His explanation was that Paul did not forbid women to teach, only that they should not lead, and that policy, as he explained, was carefully observed at Prairie.

Through this bit of correspondence I was introduced not only to Maxwell, but also to the *Prairie Overcomer*--a monthly publication of the Institute which I received for more than forty years. In my earlier ministry this journal was a source of spiritual nourishment.

My parents were not overly excited about my decision to go to Prairie Bible Institute, but since a number of Coaldale students, older than I, had gone to Prairie, they did not try to prevent me from going. My parents had not yet come to see that there was a lot of authentic Christianity among non-Mennonite denominations, and since Prairie was an inter-denominational school, they feared I might lose my appreciation for our own church.

In the fall of 1943 I left Lethbridge by train and arrived via Calgary in the little hamlet of Three Hills (three "bumps" as Mr. Maxwell called them). Institute trucks were at the station to take the baggage of incoming students to the campus. After inquiring at the office I was told that my room was on the fourth floor of the men's residence, number 79, and that my room-mate was Jack Lindberg, from Seattle. I met Jack in the room and soon discovered that he was a man with a B.A. from Seattle Pacific College, and so I felt rather inferior to him from the outset. That changed, however, for soon it became obvious that although he had a much better general education than I had, he had only the most elementary knowledge of the Scriptures.

We lived very simply. Our room had an old-fashioned steel double-bed, closet space and two study tables. There was no running water. All we had was a washbasin, a container for water and a slop-pail. All the water for Prairie's thousand students at that time was hauled twenty miles by truck. In the morning we would fill a can of water at the boiler-house and, if we wanted it warm, we let steam from a boiler pipe into the can. There were no showers or bathtubs. All we could do was to give ourselves a wet rubdown standing on the floor.

I soon discovered that my Mennonite feelings for cleanliness were not particularly appreciated by my room-mate. He couldn't understand why we should wash the floors on Saturday; it seemed especially strange to him that we should have to wash under the bed. My wardrobe was very limited at the time, but Jack seemed to have a great supply of socks which he would wash in our wash basin and hang up to dry over both ends of the bed. I found it somewhat obnoxious to sleep with Jack's socks dangling over my head. Nevertheless, we managed to get along quite well.

After I arrived at Prairie and got settled in my room I went out to look over the campus and discovered that the Institute ran a big farming operation to support the school. Mr. Gowdie was just then supervising the cutting up of oat-bundles for feed when I came by and volunteered my help. It was the kind of work I was used to. Almost immediately Mr. Gowdie went to tell Mr. Maxwell that I was needed on the farm and that I would come in later to see him. Since I had already had four years of Bible training, Mr. Maxwell worked out a special two-year course for me (the minimum for graduation).

But now I was stuck in the barn for my gratis work for the rest of the year. All students contributed about two hours of free labour daily to keep the cost of schooling down. Between 4:00 and 6:00 PM, every day of the week except Sunday, I had to haul manure from the barn or ashes from the boiler room. Often there was more work than we could manage in the two hours and we barely made it in time for supper. Sometimes we ran as fast as we could directly from the barn into the dining hall for supper. On Saturdays I frequently accompanied Mr. Gowdie to the fields to get loads of straw. Also, because I knew how to handle horses, I was put on the "mystery crew" occasionally. Since we had no running water, large pails were used for toilets in the dormitories. These had to be emptied every day. This was done at night when everyone was asleep. In the case of the girls' dormitories we had to wait until midnight before we could complete our assignment. Because the whole undertaking was shrouded in mystery, we were said to belong to the "mystery crew." In my report on gratis work at the end of the year I received 96%, so I must have pleased Mr. Gowdie.

Men and women ate separately at all meals and each table had a table head who saw to it that proper decorum was observed. Mr. Maxwell always ate lunch with the students and sometimes supper. The meals were very simple, but we didn't suffer. Water had to be used economically and a half glass of water left over by a student at the table brought a word of admonition from the table head. There was, however, one day a month on which we did go hungry. One Sunday a month we spent the day in worship, prayer and reflection, and so we fasted until supper, when we made up for what we had missed during the day.

I enjoyed my classes by and large. Maxwell's Bible classes were always inspiring. Without realizing it at the time (and quite contrary to the perception of some of my colleagues), Maxwell weaned me from the dispensational interpretation of the Bible, made so popular by the Scofield Bible. Although the teachers I had had in Mennonite Brethren schools were only moderately influenced by the teachings of John Darby, the father of dispensationalism, I had absorbed a fair amount of Darbyism without knowing it. Maxwell helped me to understand the unity of the Bible and to see that salvation always was by grace through faith, both in Old Testament as well as in New Testament times. The laws of the Old Testament were not given as a way of salvation but to make Israel into the kind of people that God could use for his redemptive purposes in the world. That insight alone was worth spending a year at Prairie.

Since I was asked to conduct the Junior Choir, Mr. Malsebury, one of the music teachers, gave me some private lessons in Conducting. Leo Janz, of the well-known "Janz Team," was a student at Prairie that year and offered voice lessons; so I enrolled. He thought I had the makings of a good singing voice and brought me to the attention of Miss Anderson, head of the Music Department. As a result I was asked to join the radio choir, and occasionally to sing a solo on the Victory Broadcast, to which I had listened for so many years. Together with Ben Zerbe (who later became a missionary and a Mennonite Brethren pastor), Ralph Jacobson and Gus Kaiser, I enjoyed singing in a quartet on various occasions and in different places.

Just before I went to Prairie I had purchased a portable typewriter, thinking it might be useful in the writing of essays. After a few weeks at Prairie, it occurred to me that I should join the first-year typing class at the Prairie High School. In retrospect I must now say that typing was one of the most important things I learned that year. Throughout seminary and graduate studies, as well as later when I typed articles and book manuscripts for publication, not to mention sermon and lecture notes, I made use of the typing skills I developed at Prairie.

Since there was little water available on campus, it was always a grave concern to the administration that there be no matches anywhere in the rooms. Also, we had fire drills every so often. My assignment was to carry patients out of the hospital in case of fire. Two fellows would take a woolen blanket, roll up the sides, gently move the patient into the blanket and carry him or her as on a stretcher. On one occasion the alarm went off and we hurried over to the hospital to take up our duties. Without asking too many questions we raced up to the second floor, dashed into one of the wards and rolled a sick Bible school girl onto our stretcher and made off with her across campus. Although it was utterly hilarious, she must have been shaken up rather badly.

My room-mate, Jack, had a girlfriend in Seattle. He posted her picture and wrote to her regularly. This was not really in keeping with Prairie's regulations, but he thought nothing of it. Through his example I was encouraged to write my first letter to Lena Hamm, whom I had not seen for several years. However, before mailing the letter my conscience smote me and I threw it away. I didn't even know at the time that she was in Winkler that year for her fourth year of Bible school. She has never quite forgiven me for not mailing that letter.

When Christmas vacation arrived I was happy to take the train home to Lethbridge and to spend the holidays with my family. The RCAF had meantime sent home all of John's personal effects, including his New Testament. Mother had looked through everything, including his New Testament, to see whether perhaps there were any indications that he had read it, but found nothing. When I leafed through his New Testament I found that he had underlined with a pencil a phrase which recurs in John 6, "And I will raise him up in the last day" (vv. 39,40,44). It was a great comfort to my mother.

Christmas came and went and I was back at Prairie. With studies, choirs, and gratis work, the second term slipped by rather quickly. How it happened that I was chosen to be a member of the Banquet Committee I do not know, but several men and women of the Junior Class were asked to assume the responsibility of preparing the banquet for the spring graduates. Normally fellows and girls were not even allowed to walk together, but now all of a sudden a group of us met regularly for committee meetings. Soon I noticed that June Carlson was taking a special interest in me, and this made me uncomfortable. For a Mennonite boy to marry an English girl was viewed as a very serious breach of conduct, and so I played it cool, even though she was a likeable girl.

After the banquet we had a week-long missionary conference to which visitors came from all over Canada and the United States. I was sitting on the platform one day as a member of a music group when I saw Lena Hamm walking into the huge auditorium. I couldn't believe my eyes, and my heart skipped a beat. On her way home from Winkler she "had" to go via Calgary, rather than Edmonton, and decided to take in the missionary conference. (She confessed later that she had had another reason for stopping at Three Hills). She was in the company of other girls whom she had known in the Coaldale Bible School, and since dating was forbidden, we could at best walk from the auditorium to the dining hall as a group and exchange a few words. I was afraid she would leave before the conference was over and I would not have a chance to talk to her in private.

When the conference ended I packed my belongings and went to the railway station to leave for home. I was very disappointed that I had not had a chance to speak to Lena alone. But as the train left for Calgary I noticed all of a sudden that she was seated in the same train car, only farther to the front. There were so many other students on board that I did not have the nerve to go over and talk to her. However, as we detrained in Calgary, both of us, with several others, had to transfer from the CNR to the CPR station. We hailed a taxi and I managed to slip into the taxi with her. When we got to the CPR station I had just a minute to talk to her alone and I asked her if she would be interested in corresponding with me. The twinkle in her blue eyes and a positive response were all I needed at the moment. I rode home to Lethbridge on cloud nine.

It was 1944 and the war was still raging in all its fury. The Selective Service apparently had forgotten about me. However, when I arrived at home there was a letter ordering me to appear in the military barracks in Calgary within two weeks. We had to take quick action. Since I was now back on the farm we decided to make application for farm postponement. If such postponement were granted it could help us over the hump, for it appeared by then that Germany was fast losing the war and that the end to the struggle was not far away. We went to RCMP headquarters in Lethbridge to make our application. They were not very happy with our request but permitted us to file a petition for postponement.

Back on the farm we waited anxiously to hear from the Selective Service, but there was no word. One summer day an official came to visit us. I was home alone and he asked me to show him our farming operation, which I did. I suspected he had come to check whether the information we had given on our application was in harmony with the facts. He left without suggesting whether farm postponement would be granted or not. As long as I did not hear from them I was obviously free.

It was an exciting summer, for by now I was corresponding regularly with Lena in La Glace. Her letters were getting thicker and thicker and so important were they to me that I walked out into the fields at times where I could read them alone without disturbance. Often I read them over several times. The Danish theologian, Søren Kierkegaard, suggests that we should read the letters of the New Testament like love letters: one reads them over and over again. A fitting analogy! Occasionally Lena's letters had a picture or a pressed flower she had picked in the woods. Then the unexpected happened.

My highly respected teacher, B.W. Sawatzky, had been asked by the Alberta Home Mission Board to serve in the churches of northern Alberta in whatever way he saw fit. Very graciously he asked whether I would accompany him. It was a great honour for me. Today we stress the need for "discipling" others. That vocabulary was not known to us at the time, but there was in fact a lot of discipling. That was also the deliberate intention of Mr. Sawatzky when he asked me to go with him. For an entire month we worked in areas north of Edmonton, although we also visited Tofield, and served in the church there (located at that time in Lindbrook). At a place called Busby, northwest of Edmonton, lived a Mennonite family, the Mieraus. They were willing to take us in for a week. A vacant loghouse several miles from their farm was put into shape and we invited the children of the community for a week of DVBS. From here we moved to Barhead where we slept in the granary on the farm of another Mennonite family, the Nikkels. Again we cleaned a vacant building and had DVBS with the children of the district for a week. Also, we held preaching services in several places, often walking long distances, since we had no vehicle. I received no honorarium from the Mission Board, but just to be together with Mr. Sawatzky was reward enough.

One day he dropped a bombshell. Why not go up to La Glace for services? From Edmonton to La Glace by train in those days was a trip of some 400 miles. But why not? I knew how much the church in La Glace had appreciated the ministry of Sawatzky in the past and they would certainly welcome him. But what should I do? My friendship with Lena was still a secret. Not even my parents knew about it. A decision had to be made. I quickly wrote to Lena and asked her whether she would be willing to be publicly engaged if I came to La Glace. Her answer was a glad, Yes!

13

Lena Hamm

Things were moving faster than I had anticipated. When I left home to travel with Mr. Sawatzky for a few weeks I had not dreamt of making a trip to La Glace at this time nor of a public engagement to Lena. But here we were in Edmonton purchasing tickets for Sexsmith, Alberta, the closest railway station to La Glace. Before leaving I wrote my parents about what was in the offing. Also I quickly went to a jewelry store and bought an engagement ring, and then we were off.

It took the Alberta Northern almost a day and a night to reach Sexsmith. On the train we met Mr. and Mrs. Abram Funk, members of the La Glace Mennonite Brethren Church, who were on their way home from British Columbia. We told them about our anticipated ministry, but not about the planned engagement. As we neared our destination they noticed that I had put on a white shirt and that made them suspicious. Then as we pulled into the station they saw Lena with her father standing on the platform, and the secret was out.

I had never met Lena's parents before and I was a bit apprehensive, wondering whether I would be accepted into the family. Also, I was not aware of the custom of asking your future parents-in-law for the hand of their daughter. Mr. Hamm took Mr. Sawatzky and me, together with Lena, to their farm home in La Glace, where Mrs. Hamm had prepared chicken noodle soup for us and for her large family of ten children.

Martin and Anna Hamm had come to Canada in 1926 with three small children: Lena, Mary and John. They hailed from Sagradovka, a Mennonite colony in the Ukraine, where Mr. Hamm had been both a farmer and a teacher. Sagradovka had suffered terribly in the years following the Bolshevik Revolution, and it was only a miracle of God that the Hamms survived. The father of Martin Hamm was a Mennonite minister who had been cruelly put to death by the Machno bandits. The Martin Hamms had first settled in Linden, Alberta, but when it was rumoured that one could purchase land at reasonable prices in La Glace, they decided to establish their home in this area.

La Glace was the name of an Indian chief of the Beaver tribe, who had died in 1909 (the word, of course, is French). When the white settlers came into this area Chief La Glace proved himself to be an able mediator between Indians and whites. With the coming of European settlers, fur trading gave way to farming. Some early pioneers came to settle on homesteads; others purchased their land from the government. In 1916 the railroad from Edmonton to Grande Prairie was completed and more and more settlers moved north to the rich farmlands of the Peace River district.

Most of the early settlers were Norwegians. Many of them came via the United States. However, Dutch and English families also moved into the La Glace district. In the 1920s the Mennonites began to arrive and took up farming wherever land became available. When Martin Hamm, who had settled his family in Linden, Alberta, heard that a former friend from Russia, Aaron Janzen, had moved to La Glace, he also made his way north and purchased a quarter section of land for eight dollars an acre to be paid by crop shares.

The Hamms settled on a farm several miles from the little hamlet of La Glace, in 1927. The income in those early years was very meagre and the family was large. Life was not easy. Lena was the eldest. After her came six brothers and three sisters. Mr. Hamm was a minister in the La Glace Mennonite Brethren Church, and he wanted his children not only to embrace the Christian faith but also to receive a good education. His godly wife, Anna, shared this hope and vision. For the older children it was next to impossible to go on to higher education, but the younger ones had the opportunity. La Glace did not have a high school at the time.

Also, the work on the farm was so pressing, that the older children had to forfeit the opportunity of completing their high school. They were, however, able to attend Bible school for several years. Lena, in fact, had four years of Bible training. She had always wanted to train as a nurse, but this was simply not possible economically.

Lena had early come to know the Lord as her personal Saviour and was baptized in the La Glace Mennonite Brethren Church. She participated actively in Sunday school teaching, choir singing, DVBS, and other church activities. Under the teaching of Mr. Schierling in the La Glace Bible School she had become overly serious and forfeited many of the innocent joys of youth in order to exercise herself in godliness.

She had faithfully helped her parents for a number of years in the home and on the farm and had developed excellent culinary skills. Besides, she was a good seamstress. I had so much in common with her that it was not hard for us to get to know each other. Besides, our families were cut very much out of the same cloth, so that there were few cultural barriers to cross. It was a delightful experience to become a member of this large family. Mr. Hamm, in contrast to my father, was very talkative, and it was a new experience for me to sit with an elderly man and carry on a conversation on every imaginable topic.

It was Saturday noon when we arrived at the home of the Hamms. After lunch Lena showed me the room where I was to sleep and I took that opportunity to put the ring I had purchased in Edmonton on her finger. She was completely taken by surprise. We then knelt down beside the bed and prayed together, making our covenant before God and pledging our troth to one another. In the afternoon we went for a long walk in the countryside, we sat beside the creek where Lena had dreamt her childhood dreams, and we fantasized about the future that lay before us.

That evening after supper the entire family, including Mary who was married to Nick Siebert, gathered in the living room. Mr. Sawatzky had been asked to give a short message. We sang and prayed together and in this way made our engagement official. Next day was Sunday. Mr. Sawatzky and I were both to preach. I had prepared a message on Psalm 116. Because of the size of the family and the two guests we could not all go to church in one car. However, the church was only a mile away and so Lena and I chose the second trip. To prevent any gossip before the service began, Mr. Hamm suggested that Lena and I not sit together in the car. So we didn't. After the messages from the Word of God that morning, Mr. Hamm could hardly wait to announce to the congregation the engagement of their daughter Lena, to David Ewert.

Mr. Sawatzky returned home to his family shortly after the weekend but I stayed on for a few days longer. In the week following our engagement, Lena and I visited several neighbouring families. Also we went to Grande Prairie to apply for a marriage license. Moreover the Hamms had planned for some time to have a family portrait made and since I was to be a future son-in-law they asked me to be on the family picture, which was taken in a photo studio in Grande Prairie.

However, I could not stay too long. The Hamms were in the midst of the grain harvest and I knew my parents also needed my help at home. Mr. Hamm took Lena and me to the train station. Lena came into the train to give me a goodbye kiss--our first.

I worked in the harvest fields with great enthusiasm that fall. The farm postponement for which I had applied never came. Since the war was winding down, conscription was relaxed and I was free to do as I pleased. My plan had been to return to Prairie Bible Institute and to graduate and then to marry. But God seemed to have a different plan. Just before I went up to La Glace to be engaged I had received a letter from the chairman of the La Glace Bible school board, asking me to come up that fall to teach together with the veteran Bible teacher, Abram Schierling, and with Jacob Franz, who was to become a long-term missionary. It was very daring of me to accept the invitation, for I had little experience and my educational background was rather thin.

Mr. Franz, whose wife also came from La Glace, spent the summer in Coaldale. When he heard that I was to be his colleague the coming year, we discussed teaching subjects and other matters pertaining to the life of the school. One day I mentioned casually that my lady-friend lived in La Glace and wondered how the community would accept me as an unmarried Bible school teacher whose girl friend lived close to the school. "They won't," said Mr. Franz. "There are only two ways out: Either she leaves the community for the duration of the school year, or else you get married before the school year begins." That seemed like a rather radical solution, but I realized that my own community, Coaldale, would probably not have accepted any other solution either. "By the way," asked Mr. Franz, "who is this lady-love of yours?" When I told him it was Lena Hamm he said simply, but very meaningfully for me, "A golden girl."

Martin Luther was against long engagements: "Don't put off till tomorrow! By delay Hannibal lost Rome. By delay Esau forfeited his birthright .... Thus Scripture, experience and creation testify that the gifts of God must be taken on the wing." I could not ask Lena to leave La Glace simply because I was going to come there to teach. Very gingerly I asked her in one of my letters how she might feel about an October wedding? She was delighted with my suggestion and the date was set for October 12. Bible school was to begin shortly after.

On the church yard at La Glace stood the Bible school with its three classrooms and a teacher's office. Also there were living quarters for the students and a dining hall. Two teacherages were available: one, a two-storey building, the other, a one-room building which had been a granary. The Franzes lived in the larger building and provided Mr. Schierling with a room; Lena and I would live in the one-room facility.

About a week before the wedding I packed my few belongings and took the train from Lethbridge to Sexsmith--an 800-mile journey. I was met at the train station by Lena and her father and received graciously into the home of the Hamms, once again. The farmers were still threshing grain and life at the Hamms was very busy. Besides, wedding preparations were under way. But Lena and I spent long hours together.

Shortly before the wedding my parents arrived by train. They too stayed at the Hamms and the house was very crowded. I do not know where all the children slept during those days. Partly because I was nervous, I suppose, partly because of the change in water, I had a very upset stomach in the days prior to the wedding. However, there was no thought of delaying the wedding.

Lena had sewed her own wedding dress and she looked very adorable when she put it on on October 12, 1944. After taking the family and guests to the church, Peter Hamm returned to get me with my bride. It was a beautiful fall day and the church had been decorated appropriately for the occasion. Every last seat was taken and the aisle was so narrow that we could not even walk next to each other as we made our way to the front of the church. It was not custom at that time to have bridesmaids or bestmen, or that the father give away the bride. Two chairs, nicely decorated, stood just below the pulpit and here the two of us sat for the wedding service. Mr. Franz, who was to be my colleague that year, brought a message based on Joshua 1:8. Lena's father then spoke to us about serving one another with the gifts given to us, on the basis of 1 Peter 4:10. He also led us in making our marriage vows. Following a delicious meal for all the guests, Mr. John Hamm, Lena's cousin, had a third message for us and the congregation.

We received many lovely gifts from the friends who had come, and the evening was spent at home with the family and several relatives, opening the presents. There was no thought of a honeymoon. First, it was not a practice in our Mennonite communities at the time; second, we could not have afforded one; third, we had no car. So we simply stayed in the parental home for a few days and then moved into the little teacherage on the church yard. My parents waited until after the wedding to see what we might still need to set up housekeeping and then went to Grande Prairie with us to buy us their wedding gifts. Lena and I had already papered the walls of our little one-room house before the wedding and were very pleased to move into our first home.

The house had a range and a small wood burning stove to keep us warm in the winter, which can be frightfully cold in La Glace. There was no ceiling in the house and sometimes at night when the wind blew we felt the snow falling down upon us through the cracks. Every night during the winter I laid in a good supply of wood. If the fire went out at night our water in the pail froze (there was, of course, no running water).

Neither of us brought any money into our marriage and the school paid only a very modest salary. However, we had no complaints about our simple life. Today I hear young people contending that we as Christians should live a simple lifestyle, but I always find their understanding of simplicity rather lavish in comparison to the life we lived for twenty-one years before we got married and for many years after that. It was the only kind of lifestyle we knew about, and it was the only kind we could afford.

The first year of teaching was very difficult. The Old Testament Hebrews showed a lot of wisdom when they required that newly married men should be exempt from the army for a year. I too should have spent a year preparing for my classes, but that was not possible. I was simply thrown into the water and had to sink or swim. There were three classes and with only three teachers this meant about five classroom hours daily. Besides, I conducted the school choir. All I could do was to stay one step ahead of the students. By God's grace we survived the first year.

Friday nights were the highlight of the week, for then Lena and I always walked to her parents' home and had supper with the family and a delightful evening chatting with the parents. Also, it was very enjoyable to spend Christmas with the Hamm family.

Father-in-law had encouraged us to settle on a farm in the

community and take up permanent residence in La Glace. Just then several farms became available as some of our Mennonite people began moving away from the cold north to the Fraser Valley of British Columbia. By spring we would have to know what we wanted to do next summer. Bible school lasted for five months only and after that we had to look for some other means of livelihood.

My dad was able to make a downpayment on a farm just half a mile from our home in Coaldale and invited us to come to southern Alberta for the summer and farm this quarter section of irrigation land. We accepted dad's offer and so when school ended in spring we shipped our furniture by freight and took the passenger from Sexsmith to Lethbridge. After a few days at my parents' place we moved on to the newly acquired farm.

Dad let us use his machines to farm the land (in fact, the farm was in his name) and we did a lot of summer fallowing that year, hoping to put the land into good shape for the future. Also we renovated the house, tore down the old barn, and cleaned up the place as best we could. Whenever I could get away I went to help dad on his farm. In July, Lena volunteered to teach DVBS together with Helen Dueck and they were sent to a school district near Magrath, Alberta. It didn't take very long before I felt lonely without Lena. Fortunately I did not know at the time that I would be separated from her rather frequently for long stretches of time in the future.

That summer I received an invitation from Saskatoon to come and preach in what was later the Central Mennonite Brethren Church. Evidently it was the hope of some of the members of the City Mission Board that I would fit into city mission work. However, much as I enjoyed my stay with the H.S. Rempels, nothing came of this plan.

That summer my parents made a trip to British Columbia and came back with the resolve to leave Coaldale and to move to Chilliwack, B.C. That decision had profound implications for our future as well.

14

Farewell Coaldale!

After fifteen years on an irrigation farm my father was tired of walking in rubber boots all summer. He needed a change. It was decided, therefore, to sell the farm and to move to British Columbia. That also spelled the end of my dreams of being a farmer. Lena and I stayed until harvest had ended and then bade family and friends farewell. We made our way by train back to La Glace where I would once again teach in Bible school. Slowly the conviction that God was calling me to be a Bible teacher was growing within me.

Leaving Coaldale was not easy. The most formative years of my life had been spent in this community. It would always remain "home" to me. For my parents it was just as hard to cut their ties with the community in which their children had grown up and in which they had many close friends. Fortunately some of their neighbours chose also to settle in Chilliwack, British Columbia, where my parents purchased a dairy farm.

When Lena and I arrived in La Glace we were surprised to learn that her parents were also seriously considering a move to British Columbia. The many long and cold winters they had endured in northern Alberta made them long for a warmer climate. Also, the relative isolation of the La Glace community from the rest of the Canadian Mennonite community made them restless. Moreover, they wanted to give their younger children better educational opportunities than the older children had enjoyed. Other families in La Glace also decided to move to the west coast and that meant that the Bible school, which had operated for a good many years in this northern community, would probably have to close very soon.

Since the Jacob Franzes felt called to missionary service in

Paraguay, the Bible school was left with only two teachers for the 1945-46 school year--Mr. Schierling and I. However, we had three classes to instruct and this made the work even harder than in the first year. While Mr. Schierling and I taught two of the classes we also had to arrange for meaningful study periods for the third class. It was not an ideal situation, to say the least.

We had better living conditions this year. Since the Franzes left for Paraguay we moved into the larger teacherage. Martin, Lena's brother, roomed in our house and attended Bible school. Father-in-law with several of the boys had made a trip to the Fraser Valley just before Bible school began and they came back convinced that there was a better life waiting for them on the other side of the Rockies. They sold their land, had an auction sale at which they disposed of their cattle and farm implements, and moved to Chilliwack where they purchased a dairy farm, as my parents had done.

As I entered upon my second year of teaching the conviction grew within me that I needed to further my education if I was to continue in the teaching ministry. The question was, where could I do my grades 11 and 12 without having to spend two full years in high school? The Lord provided an answer in an unexpected way. One day I received a letter from Abe Voth, a Coaldale student who was doing his grade 12 in Hepburn, Saskatchewan. He wrote to tell me that Bethany Bible Institute, which had many students at that time who had not finished their high school, had arranged with the Department of Education to allow such students to work through as many subjects as they could between April (when Bible school closed) and June, when the Departmental exams in these subjects were to be written. Two teachers had been employed to help students with problems as they worked through their courses.

I had been out of high school for eight years and wondered how I would pick up Algebra and Geometry once again. The other subjects, I thought, should pose no problem. So I decided to review my mathematics from earlier years, while preparing my daily lessons for Bible school.

Spring came and I made my way to Hepburn. Lena stayed in La Glace for a while to be with her sister, Mary, who was expecting her first child and whose husband, Nick Siebert, was in the hospital with an illness.

I took the train to Edmonton and then to Saskatoon and Hepburn (at that time a passenger train still ran between Saskatoon and Hepburn). Hepburn in 1946 did not look nearly as inviting as it does today. Moreover, there were no houses for rent, but I was able to get a room in one of the houses owned by the Bible Institute. A neighbour lady took in boarders and so I ate at Miss Kroeker's, together with my friend, Abe Voth. Later when Lena arrived we simply continued to live in this room and to eat at Miss Kroeker's--an arrangement not at all to our liking, but there was nothing better available.

Classes began the second week of April and I had decided, if God gave me strength and wisdom, I would work through all eight required grade eleven subjects in the two months prior to the June exams. Besides, I decided to write Grade twelve German, for which I did not need to study.

Lena spent a lot of time sewing, embroidering and practising piano. It must have been rather boring for her, since she could not set up house. I spent most of my time with the books and when the June examinations were held I was able to complete my grade eleven.

While we were busy preparing for final exams, Mr. Jacob Epp, Principal of the Bethany Bible Institute, asked whether we would consider helping the school in the coming year by teaching several courses. It was a part-time arrangement which would allow me to complete my grade twelve in the local high school. We gladly accepted the invitation. The Bible school now permitted us to set up house in one of their buildings, supplied us with fuel, and paid us a salary of thirty dollars per month.

Since the University of Saskatchewan permitted students with grade eleven to enrol in university courses, we decided to move to Saskatoon after the June examinations and to enrol in the summer school of the University. An elderly couple, the Edigers, were willing to let us stay in their house for the six weeks of the session while they went on vacation. If we wished, they said, we could take in two boarders, which we did. One of our boarders was John Froese of Hepburn, and the other was John Goetz of Warman, both of them students at teacher's college.

I enrolled in Chemistry with Dr. Spinks, who later became the President of the University of Saskatchewan. It was hard work, but I found it interesting. We had classes in the morning and lab work in the afternoon. I was surprised at how well I did; I was even more surprised when a class-mate, who sat next to me and who had already earned a B.A., did so poorly. One day he asked me what I intended to do, and when I told him that I hoped to be a minister of the gospel, he said, "Dave, you're crazy!" When I received an "A" in the course I too began to wonder whether perhaps my calling lay elsewhere. If I could enjoy the sciences and do well in them, should I not rather think of medicine? This question was to haunt me for some time.

Back in Hepburn I began my grade 12 classes in the local high school at the beginning of September and when Bible school opened I taught my courses there. As I recall, I taught the Gospel of John, Homiletics and German. Also, it was our privilege to preach the gospel in a number of our churches in northern Saskatchewan--an invaluable experience. I had been in all the Alberta churches and had also visited most of the Manitoba churches during my year at the Winkler Bible Institute. Now I got to know the Saskatchewan churches. All this helped to broaden my understanding and appreciation for our wider Mennonite Brotherhood.

At the high school I enrolled in seven subjects (I had already written Grade 12 German) which were to complete my grade twelve. Our teacher, Mr. Neufeld, did not particularly like

Mathematics and when he discovered that only Alfred Schmidt (who later became a missionary to Zaire) and I needed Algebra to get into university, he decided not to teach it that year. Alfred and I decided then that we would simply get the grade twelve Algebra textbook and work our way through it on our own. We were convinced that if we could do all the exercises in the book we could pass the course. And that's what we did. We must have managed rather well for on one occasion a local school teacher ran into an Algebra problem in class and came to us to have it cleared up for him.

In the spring of that year, March 25, 1947, our first child, Eleanor Ruth, was born. Since we did not own a car and Hepburn had no hospital, Mr. Frank Froese, who worked for the Western Children's Mission at the time, was kind enough to take Lena to Saskatoon. After spending a week in the hospital, Mr. J.J. Toews, who taught at the Bible school that year, brought Lena and the baby home to Hepburn. Whatever would we have done in those years without friends? With the arrival of our first daughter a new chapter had begun in our family life.

As we came closer to the middle of June, I was busy boning up on all the subjects in which I would be writing final examinations. At the same time we began to pack our belongings for we had decided to leave Hepburn immediately after the exams and move to Vancouver, where I intended to enrol at the University of British Columbia. We chose Vancouver because both of our parents now lived in Chilliwack, about forty miles up the Fraser Valley from Vancouver. Again a friend offered to take us to Saskatoon together with our belongings. Here we boarded the CNR Transcontinental and with our three-month old daughter we headed for the west coast.

Lena and I had never been to British Columbia and we were completely overwhelmed by the scenery as the long passenger train snaked its way through the Fraser Canyon. The CNR ran through Chilliwack and both of our parents were at the station to welcome us and their new grandchild (my parents' first). We had not seen our parents for two years and it was a happy homecoming. Unfortunately I could stay only for a day or so because summer school at the University was about to begin and I had to be in Vancouver on July 2.

My brother-in-law, Martin, had been at teacher's college in Vancouver the year before and had reserved his basement room for me for the summer. It was on Fourth Street, not far from the waterfront. For some time I just couldn't get used to the beauty of the scenery with which we were daily surrounded, especially on Point Grey, with its gardens and forests, where the University was located. I allowed myself no recreational activities, other than walking, and gave myself completely to my studies. Since I had taken a university course in chemistry the previous summer I was told that I needed fourteen subjects to do a B.A. English 200 was required for almost every program regardless of major and so I enrolled in English with Professor Larson. The lectures began at eight every morning and that meant rising early for it took me more than an hour to get to the university.

Professor Larson lectured well and I read a lot of English literature that summer. In his first class session he warned us not to enrol in any other course besides English since the reading would be very heavy. I took him by his word and concentrated on English that summer. On several weekends I took the bus to Chilliwack to see Lena and our baby daughter who stayed at either my parents' or Lena's parents' place. Summer session ended the third week of August and I joined Lena on my parents' farm until classes began in the fall term.

Before I left Vancouver, however, I looked for a place where we as a family could live the coming year. Daily I scanned the papers to see what might look like a possibility. One day I saw a notice that two rooms with cooking facilities were available in a house on 49th Street. Immediately that evening I made my way to this address and was surprised to be greeted by a Mr. Henry Ewert (no relation). I asked him whether he would let us rent the two upstairs rooms for the price indicated in the newspaper and he agreed. When he asked me for my name and I told him, he was taken aback. "Are you a son of David Ewert who used to live in Coaldale?" I was. That made him uncomfortable. The reason was that my dad had signed a bank loan for him when he still lived in Coaldale. He had reneged on the repayment and my dad had to pay the bank a substantial sum of money because he had left the country and made no efforts to repay the loan. For years he had worked in the Vancouver shipyards and made big money, but the debt remained unpaid. My presence seemed to bring his conscience to life and he asked whether I would pay him half the rent and give my dad the other half as repayment for his debts. I explained to him that this was a matter between him and my dad and that I would rather pay my full rent. He agreed. My parents came to Vancouver on several occasions to visit us during that school year, but Mr. Ewert never once mentioned the money again. And so it remained until shortly before his death when he sent the money along with a friend and asked him to give it to my dad. Such things make dying hard.

We had had a breathing spell between sessions on the farm in Chilliwack and we enjoyed it thoroughly. The question that kept nagging me, however, was whether I should enrol in pre-medicine or go the liberal arts route. I thought and prayed much about it. Then it occurred to me that I should write to my spiritual mentor, B.W. Sawatzky, and ask him for advice. He encouraged me strongly to go the "arts" route because, as he emphasized, there was such a great need for Bible teachers. I took him seriously, but when I enrolled at the university at the beginning of September I decided to include Latin as one of my subjects, just in case I should decide at a later date to switch to medicine. (Latin was at that time still required for medicine.) My parents took us to Vancouver and we tried to make ourselves comfortable in our little two-room apartment on 49th Street.

15

University of British Columbia

Just before we left for Vancouver I received a call from the Chilliwack Bible School to join their teaching staff for the coming year. It was a temptation, if for no other reason than that it provided a means of livelihood. Our resources were very limited at that time and sometimes we wondered how we would make it through the year. Borrowing money was not a part of our thinking. However, we believed the Lord had called us to further our education with the hope that we might be more effective in future years.

After we had settled into our little apartment in Vancouver we were pleasantly surprised to find that we were within walking distance of the Mennonite Brethren Church, located on 43rd and King Edward. There was no other Mennonite Brethren church in Vancouver at the time and the congregation met in the basement. Funds for the superstructure were not yet available. Henry Klassen was the leading minister of the church, assisted by Jacob Thiessen and several others. I too was asked occasionally to bring a message from the Word of God. Klassen had worked for years in a sawmill, but had decided to take a year off to go to university. I recall taking first year Psychology together with him.

Besides Psychology I took Philosophy, Latin, and several German Literature courses that year. Latin demanded more work than the other subjects and whereas I took it, originally, in order to fulfil a pre-med requirement, it turned out to be helpful in other ways later. When I enrolled at McGill University, Latin was one of the languages required for a doctorate in New Testament and I was glad I had taken it. Psychology I found very helpful in learning to understand myself better. We had a brilliant lecturer in Philosophy, but I did not realize sufficiently at the time how important philosophy was for the study of theology.   I particularly enjoyed *Deutsche Kulturgeschichte*--a combination of history, language and literature, with many writing assignments, which Dr. Borden carefully corrected. One of my class-mates was Abe Schellenberg, who later in life became the editor of the *Mennonitische Rundschau.*

Although I had played ball and hockey as a boy, sports had not been part of my life since my first year of Bible school.   I was therefore quite upset when I discovered that Physical Education was compulsory for all first year university students. I could choose from a range of activities such as tennis, golf, soccer, swimming or badminton. Frankly I wasn't interested in any of them at the time and tried hard to get an excuse, but without success. It was not that I objected to playing, but it bothered me that I should be playing with unbelievers. Separation from the world had been so strongly emphasized when we were young, which we interpreted to mean that one should not associate with unbelievers. I should have chosen swimming, for although we had swum for years in our pond and in irrigation ditches when we were boys, we had never learned to swim properly.   However, swimming lessons meant "mixed bathing," and that was considered as totally unbecoming for saints. Finally I chose soccer and ran myself ragged, rain or shine, several times a week. Had I not had so many inhibitions I could have enjoyed it thoroughly and perhaps even had good opportunities to witness to my team-mates.

That I had at least given a "silent" witness became evident to me one day as I stood in the library. I was looking up something in the dictionary when a fellow from one of my classes edged up to me and told me that he wished he had the kind of faith I had. It took me by surprise for I didn't recall that we had ever discussed matters of faith.   However, he had observed me and had come to the conclusion I had something he did not have.

The normal academic load for a year at university was five full courses. However, I wanted to finish as quickly as possible and so I enrolled in six. About the middle of the year I received an invitation from the Winkler Bible Institute to join their faculty. Again it was a temptation, for I had enjoyed my year as student at Winkler and would have been glad to return there as teacher. But the Lord somehow did not give us the liberty to accept that invitation. I had full intentions of staying on at the university until I had earned my B.A. However, shortly after we had declined Winkler we had an invitation from the Coaldale Bible School to join their faculty. My beloved teacher, B.W. Sawatzky, was still principal at the time and the thought of having him as colleague was just too attractive. We accepted the call.

When university closed at the end of April, I had to look for a job since our money had nearly run out. I was able to get on with Commonwealth Construction and began working for them when our second daughter, Marianne Esther, was born. She arrived so speedily that we didn't have time to go to the hospital and the doctor came and delivered her in our bedroom and then called an ambulance to take mother and child to Grace Hospital. I quickly called our parents in Chilliwack who came and got Eleanor who was then a little more than a year old.

Before Marianne was born we had moved farther up the street to the second floor of a house owned by Henry Klassens, the leader of the church. Since two other adults lived on the second floor and we shared the bathroom with them we had to do a lot of adjusting. In fact Lena found it hard, after returning from the hospital, to cope with a one year old and a baby under such circumstances, and so she went to the Valley and spent some time with her parents. That spring, however, the Fraser Valley experienced very severe flooding and so she and the girls returned to Vancouver.

By then summer session had already begun and I was enrolled in Child Psychology and a senior German course (Lessing, Goethe and Schiller). The Child Psychology that summer was taught by a visiting professor from the University of Toronto, Dr. Blatz, educational advisor to the Dion Quintuplets. He lectured extremely well (without notes at that) and promised us all a "B" grade since, as he explained, anyone who had permission to enrol in such a "senior" course could obviously do B-work. If, however, we were not satisfied with a B, we could write on the final examination, "Please read carefully," and then we would get what we deserved. With fear and trembling I wrote these words on my paper and was fortunate to get an "A." Ten of the fifteen courses required for a B.A. were completed and I had five more left.

After summer session I worked in construction for a few more weeks and then we packed our belongings and shipped them by freight from Vancouver to Lethbridge, Alberta. After a visit with our parents in Chilliwack, they took us to Haney, B.C., where we boarded the CPR passenger for Calgary and Lethbridge. It did not occur to us in those days to take a sleeper, for we could not afford such luxuries, and it turned out to be a rather taxing journey with two restless little ones.

Upon our arrival in Lethbridge, Mr. Aaron Baerg and Mr. Peter Regehr, members of the Bible School board, met us at the station. They had rented a small house for us in Coaldale and took us there immediately. Next day we went back to Lethbridge to purchase some necessary household articles. Our furniture, such as it was, arrived from Vancouver in due time and we were able to set up house again.

The two brothers, Baerg and Regehr, had welcomed us very kindly, but on the way to Coaldale they shared something with us that had not been mentioned in earlier correspondence and that took us aback. The Board had decided (upon Mr. Sawatzky's request) that I should assume the leadership of the school. I had looked forward to being an associate of my former teacher, and just could not see myself as principal. However, the decision had been made and neither Mr. Sawatzky nor the Board were willing to take "No" for an answer. I finally yielded, with the understanding that Mr. Sawatzky would help me as much as possible. To his credit I can say that in the four years that we worked together he never made it difficult for me, even though he had been the leader for fifteen years. On the contrary, he was very helpful and made suggestions in gracious and tactful ways.

With more general education in my background I now felt a bit more secure in my classes. Even so I worked hard at the preparation of my lessons. We had four faculty members for three classes. The students had no spares and sat for six periods of instruction daily. All of us taught a variety of subjects. Among others, I taught Bible, Doctrine, Church History, Homiletics and German. Besides myself and Mr. Sawatzky, Aaron Warkentin and Alex Neuman were full-time faculty members that first year in Coaldale. With daily chapel periods at which the teachers took their turn and the many teaching hours per week we had our hands full. Added to that we participated in the preaching ministry of the local congregation and occasionally in churches somewhat farther away.

There was a marked increase in enrolment that first year and the church decided then that a new Bible school building was needed. In the spring of 1949 a large addition was made to the existing school. This gave us three large classrooms, an auditorium, a faculty room, a small library, and a full basement. Since our work as teachers (as well as our income) came to an end annually at the beginning of April, I helped in the building of this new facility. We worked nine hours a day and by the beginning of July the building stood ready.

In the course of our first year at the Coaldale Bible School it became clear that we could not stay in our rented house and would have to relocate for the following year. The church owned an acre of land in Nortendale (now incorporated into the town of Coaldale). On it stood one house in which the Aaron Warkentins lived. We were asked whether we would like to purchase half of that acre and build our own house upon it, and we were glad to accept the offer.

Since I had done some building before, and was engaged in construction at the Bible school for nine hours a day, we decided to build our own house in stages as we had money. I had only the early hours of the morning and the evenings after work to devote to this project and so it moved rather slowly to begin with. I dug the cellar with a spade, poured a foundation, put up the walls, built the chimney with cinder blocks, put the roof on, wired the house (I had a licensed electrician check it), hung the windows and the doors, built shelves and laid the floors. At the end of June, when the house was still in the rough, we moved in.

We were expecting our third child in June and the day after we moved in, June 29, our son, Ernest James, was born. Our neighbour, Mr. Sawatzky, had given me the keys to his Model A Ford which stood in his garage, in case we needed to go to the hospital during the night. His son, Waldo, later principal of the Mennonite Educational Institute in Clearbrook, woke up when I returned the car in the middle of the night and his father had to do a lot of explaining next morning, for he was certain that a thief in the night had stolen their car.

Lena was still in the Coaldale Hospital when the Canadian Conference convened in the Coaldale Mennonite Brethren Church. I could not attend, having two little girls to take care of. It was Saturday evening and I had them in the tub giving them their bath when Mr. J.A. Toews, Winnipeg, walked in on me. We had a good laugh and a friendly chat. Very likely he must have commented to some people in our congregation that it was a pity I could not attend the conference, for next day the Frank Duecks (parents of Abe Dueck, Professor at MBBC) came down and offered one of their daughters as babysitter so that I could attend the conference.

That spring the leading brothers of the Coaldale Mennonite Brethren Church asked whether I would be willing to be ordained to the gospel ministry. I had not had a spectacular call to the ministry but had grown into it step by step. Although I was only twenty-seven at the time, Lena and I were agreed in accepting the church's call to the ministry. It happened then that P.R. Toews, who had been at the Mennonite Brethren Bible College, and was returning to his native Coaldale with his family, was asked to join the faculty of the Bible school to replace of Alex Neuman. Since he had served the church from time to time in the preaching ministry it was decided that he too should be ordained.

The ordination was set for a Sunday in the month of October. Dr. A.H. Unruh, who had been my teacher in Winkler and, more recently, P.R. Toews's teacher in Winnipeg, was invited to be the guest speaker. Particularly meaningful for Lena and me was the fact that my parents came from British Columbia to participate in the event. Besides Dr. Unruh, our church leader, J.J. Siemens, and others spoke. Brothers Toews and I were asked to share with the congregation some of our experiences that had led us into the ministry. Hands of blessing were laid upon us and we were grateful to the church in which Brother Toews and I had grown up, that it was willing to affirm our gifts and calling and to identify with us in our efforts to preach and to teach the Word of God.

After it was all over and we were alone with my parents, they told us that when I was born there was little hope that I would survive the famine in the Ukraine. They had then humbly given me over to God with the promise that if God would spare my life they wanted to dedicate me to the service of Christ and his kingdom. It had been a well-kept secret and they must have had many doubts about my calling as they watched me struggle to adulthood. However, they felt that God had honoured that simple act of devotion on their part and they wanted me to know that. One almost hesitates to share such sacred memories.

16

Coaldale Bible School Teacher

Because of the move into an unfinished house and the birth of our son at the end of June, there was no thought of going to summer school in 1949. Instead I worked in construction much of the summer and in the fall I helped Jake Dueck, son-in-law of B.B. Janz, bring in his harvest. During the summer I discovered that the University of British Columbia had just begun to offer several courses by extension, and so I decided to enrol in Medieval History under the direction of Dr. Ormsby. The course demanded a considerable amount of reading and a number of essays on a variety of topics. It was a very valuable course and I was able to complete the assignments during the course of the year and write the final exam at the university next summer.

With three children, a fairly heavy teaching load, church work and studies, our second year at the Coaldale Bible School was rather crowded. Moreover, the Bible school had a marked increase in enrollment in the year 1949. About twenty young people who had come out of the Soviet Union with the collapse of the German armies had come to Coaldale, and the church offered them free tuition if they wanted to attend Bible school. Some of these young men and women had grown up without any religious instruction whatsoever; indeed, some of them were not even Christians. One of these was Frank Peters, who has spent most of his life as missionary in Brazil. It was a joyous occasion for us as faculty when he confessed Christ as his Lord and Saviour. Among these recent immigrants were some very able and promising students and it was a joy to see them adjust to the new culture and to grow in their Christian life.

As spring came round the question of where we might find a job for the summer became acute once again. Our salaries were rather low at the time and covered only half the year; for the remainder of the year we were on our own. We could of course not look for regular employment, for in the fall we had to be back at Bible school. Mr. Herman Wiebe, who had done construction work in Lethbridge for several years, was kind enough to get me a job on his crew. Since we did not have a car I travelled back and forth from Coaldale to Lethbridge in his car. His son, who worked with us as well, was tragically killed later in a highway accident, together with B.B. Janz's son, Peter.

At the end of June we were anxious to return to Vancouver where I wanted to continue my studies toward the B.A. Housing was at a premium and money was scarce, so we decided that Lena and our three little ones would stay with her parents in Chilliwack (alternating with my parents) for the seven weeks that I would be in summer school in Vancouver. We took the train through the Rockies once again, arriving at the CPR station in Mission, B.C. I stayed for only a few days and then left for Vancouver to write my final examination in Medieval History. Also, I had to look for a place to stay. An elderly lady offered me room and breakfast in her house on condition that I pay her a weekly rent and carry a pile of wood into her basement for the winter.

Having just completed a very good course in history, I enrolled for one of the finest courses I have ever taken, Ancient History, with Dr. Guthrie of the Classics Department. Half the course dealt with the history, literature, philosophy and architecture of ancient Greece, and the other half with the culture of ancient Rome. The course provided an excellent background for New Testament studies. I wrote my term essay on the Roman road system. Also I took Sociology with Dr. Topping. This class was less enjoyable because the professor, who had received training in theology, had become apostate and ridiculed those who identified with the church. He had taught DVBS in his younger years and one day he read us a letter from his brother who was a missionary in China. In order to find out what kind of students he had in class he asked all of us to write up one important experience in our life. I chose to write the story of my conversion and after that he had it in for me, even though I never argued with him.

The class of forty students was divided into groups for the purpose of debating sociological issues in the presence of the class. We were given the choice of doing research for the group or participating in the debate. I chose to do research. Almost at the end of the summer Dr. Topping came into class and wrote on the board the names of those who had done research. Since he had no way of knowing how much they had contributed to the debate, he wanted all of these to give a speech in class. He suggested to me that I speak on religion, but that I not make it too evangelistic lest the class laugh me to scorn. I explained to him that it was for that reason that I did not even want to speak on the subject. Alright then, he said, instead of a speech write an essay on the Mennonites--which I did. I was glad when the course came to an end.

We had come to B.C. on the train because we still could not afford a car. My parents now offered to take us and our three children back to Coaldale in their car. It was a tiring but enjoyable trip through Washington, Idaho and Montana, then through Glacier Park and finally to Coaldale.

A third year of teaching at the Coaldale Bible School slipped by quickly. I had been elected to the Home Missions Committee of the Alberta Conference and as the school year came to an end the committee agreed that we should go north to La Glace once more. The church at that time was without a pastor and was glad to receive some assistance. Also, we were to help the church in planning for DVBS in the area around Dawson Creek.

We had acquired an older car by now and at the beginning of April we packed the necessary belongings into our Chevy and made our way north. We took up residence in the old Bible school building. For three months we served the churches in La Glace and Crooked Creek, and tried to arrange for DVBS once the public schools would close.

At the end of June our term was up and we prepared to return to Coaldale from where we wanted to drive to Vancouver for my last summer session at the university. Peter Hamm, Lena's brother, had taught school on the Alaska Highway all year and he too wanted to go to Vancouver for summer session. We agreed then to take him with us. After the last day of classes he made his way south to La Glace. It was evening when he arrived, but we decided to leave for Edmonton and Coaldale immediately. By then it had begun to rain and darkness was setting in. Soon the dirt-roads turned into mud and we were slipping and slithering from one side of the road to the other. Splashing through water puddles on the road made our timer wet and we had to stop again and again and dry it out. When we got to Sturgeon Lake we drove through a deep puddle and again the motor stalled. It was raining so heavily that we did not dare get under the hood of the car for fear it would get wetter still. There we sat, three adults and three children, in the rain and the darkness.

Finally the motor started again and we were on our way. About four in the morning we came to a creek and saw that the bridge was washed out and a temporary structure had been erected to allow vehicles to pass. However, a big semi-trailer was on this make-shift bridge and his front end had slipped off and now blocked all traffic. A half dozen other trucks stood beside the road waiting to get across. The truckers were finally able to jack the front end of the truck up, but when the vehicle began to move his rear end slipped off the bridge. By moving over so far to one side there was now just enough room for a car to squeeze by. Several men steadied our car as we eased across the bridge. We had wanted to be in Edmonton by morning, but we hadn't travelled more than perhaps 150 miles.

Since I had been at the wheel all night, Peter Hamm agreed to take over. I sat down in the back seat with our girls and two-year-old son. He wanted to sit right by the window as children often do.

I didn't notice, however, that he had his hand on the door handle, and as we travelled along on the gravel road he pressed the handle, throwing open the door. As the door flew open he was thrown out. It all happened in a split second and as we looked back we saw him rolling on the highway. We stopped quickly and I ran out to pick him up. Blood streamed from his head and he turned white from shock.

What should we do? We were in the middle of nowhere. All we could do was to drive on until we came to a place where we could get some help. After travelling some distance we saw a sign beside the highway indicating that first aid was available at the next stop. We followed the directions and found a nurse who cleaned the little fellow up, put some antiseptic on the wounds and told us we would have to get to a doctor to have the wounds sutured. The closest hospital was at McLennon, about 200 miles away. There was no blacktop on the northern highways in those days and we didn't get to the hospital until late in the afternoon. It was evening when we drove into Edmonton. We had driven a night and a day.

By then we were tired and dirty but in no mood to stop. So we decided to drive through a second night. It rained almost all the way from Edmonton to Coaldale, but in the morning we arrived at our house in Coaldale. After washing up and eating breakfast we all went to bed.

It was the end of June and both Peter and I had to be in Vancouver for the beginning of summer school. We decided to leave the next day, but when I took our old Chevy to the garage to have it checked out, the mechanic told me we would never make it across the mountains unless we had a valve job done. This delayed us another day but finally we were on our way through the Crowsnest Pass, where it began to snow so heavily (end of June!) that our wipers would not take the wet snow. Also, we noticed that our car heated up again and again and we were constantly looking for water to fill up the radiator. The Trans-Canada Highway was not yet ready at the time and so we went through Idaho and

Washington and then up north to the Fraser Valley.

Again we imposed upon our parents. Lena and the three children stayed in Chilliwack and Peter Hamm and his brother Martin and I decided to batch in Vancouver. We rented two rooms on Lacarno Crescent overlooking the Bay and did our own cooking to save money. One rather interesting course I took that summer was General Linguistics, taught by Professor De Groot from the University of Amsterdam. It gave me perspectives on language which proved helpful to me later in the study of the biblical languages. The other course was the Psychology of Adjustment. The course was not what it had been cracked up to be, but I was glad I could complete the requirements for my B.A., and that fall I received my degree.

My one regret as I reflect on my university experience as an undergraduate is that I looked upon my studies as something that I had to get out of the way; a requirement I had to meet if I wanted to go on. My interests were in Bible and theology and I needed an arts degree to take advanced studies in these areas. I would have profited so much more if I had looked upon every subject as an opportunity to broaden my horizons and to stock my mind with valuable information. Even so it was a valuable experience, and I felt gratified when I learned that I would be graduating with First Class Honours.

Upon our return to Coaldale that fall, Mr. Sawatzky asked me to accompany him on a trip to the far north of the province. A number of Mennonites from Mexico had returned to Canada and had settled on crown land along the Peace River in the area of Fort Vermillion. Mr. Sawatzky had been there once before in an effort to bring the gospel to people who bore the Mennonite label, but knew next to nothing about the good news. On his first visit he had gone up the Peace River on a cattle boat. By now Fort Vermillion had a dirt landing strip for small planes. We took the train from Lethbridge to the northern town of Peace River, and from here we flew to Fort Vermillion. A police station, a store, a small hotel, and a large Indian residential school, run by Roman Catholic nuns, were all there was in this town.

After our arrival we found a farmer who was willing to let us use his horse and buggy for a few days so that we could look up the Mennonites living in small log houses along the Peace River on land reserved for trappers and hunters. We took along some canned goods in case we got nothing to eat, and so for several days we travelled from house to house to see whether perhaps it would be possible for us to conduct DVBS in this area. But there was no interest in that. Several families took us in for the night, although we also slept in granaries several nights.

It was Sunday morning and we decided to attend a church service of these Old Colony Mennonites. I had never witnessed anything of the sort. The hymns had up to sixteen stanzas and the congregation was helped through the many lines by *Vorsänger,* of which there were three. After the singing they all promptly fell asleep, only to be awakened by their desire for tobacco. One after the other left the church for a smoke and then returned to take his place on the platform. The prayers were spoken silently. The sermon was endless. The preacher read an eighteenth-century sermon from a sermon book. The topic was the Prodigal Son and we wondered for a while whether he had chosen that text because we were present. We had, of course, deliberately removed our ties, lest we be an offense, but we were obviously seen as intruders.

After the service we continued on our journey with horse and buggy and once we were out of sight of the church-goers both of us exploded with laughter. It was a most inappropriate response to a rather sad situation, but our emotions were so pent up, and we had to find release. We were quickly brought to our senses when we noticed that one of the buggy wheels was not functioning as it should. The steel rim had come off one of the back wheels and before we knew it one of the spokes broke, giving us a terrific jolt every time the wheel came round. We realized that we could not go on in this manner, but we were still many miles from Fort

Vermillion. With no one to help, we had to improvise. We found a sturdy log in the forest and stuck it under the axle and put the rear of the buggy on skids. It was a bit hard for the horse and so we walked behind the buggy most of the way back to Fort Vermillion. Fortunately the farmer was not overly upset when we returned the buggy with a broken wheel. We did pay him what he asked for.

Much more traumatic was the telegram that awaited Mr. Sawatzky when we returned to the Fort. The sad news was that his wife had been taken to Calgary for a cancer operation. We decided then to return home. The plane came to Fort Vermillion only once or twice a week and so we would have to wait several days if we wanted to fly out. We found a man who was willing to take us all the way to Peace River by car--a day's drive on very rough roads. Three nuns also wanted to go to Peace River and so with this holy company the driver barrelled over washboard roads all day, fixing one flat tire after another. Toward evening we entered Peace River where we took the next train home.

17

Wheaton College

Bible school was about to open its doors once again to a large student body in the fall of 1951. It was my fourth year as teacher and principal at this school and we didn't know that fall that this was to be our last year in Coaldale. Over the years the Lord had given us an interest in and concern for missions. After much praying and reflecting we decided to offer our services to our Board of Missions. I wrote to Mr. A.E. Janzen in Hillsboro, who was then the Executive Secretary, and before long he sent us the required forms to fill in. We had not set our minds on any particular field, but my interest was in the teaching/preaching ministry. We waited patiently to see what would come of all this.

Since I now had my B.A. I was also anxious to get back to theological studies if at all possible, and so I wrote to several seminaries to find out if I could do some work through extension courses. Central Baptist Seminary in Kansas offered a number of courses, and so I decided to enrol in Homiletics, Acts and Epistles, the Hexateuch, and Old Testament Theology. These studies proved to be very valuable.

In the course of the winter Mr. B.B. Janz came down for a visit one day and laid upon us the need for a church worker in Bage, Brazil. Janz had been our church leader for many years, but by now had given that responsibility to others. However, he was still a member of our General Conference Welfare Board. It sounded interesting and challenging as he described the Mennonite settlement of Bage for us. When he noticed a spark of interest he would not let us go (Janz was known for his tenacity) and asked me to visit him and we prayed about the matter once again.

At the spring meeting of the Board of Missions in Hillsboro it was decided that we should go to Copenhagen to work among the

Mennonite refugees from the Soviet Union who reportedly were stranded in Denmark. We now faced a dilemma. What should we do? First of all, I had to resign my position at the Bible school. With a conflict still raging in our minds, we decided to attend the missionary conference at Prairie Bible Institute in the spring of 1952. Mr. and Mrs. Jacob Franz, returned missionaries from Paraguay, went with us. It was a good conference, but there was no light for our next step. As we returned to Coaldale I went to the post office to pick up our mail and found two letters in our box, one from the Board of Missions informing us that we were to leave within a few months, and another from Mr. H.H. Janzen, President of the Mennonite Brethren Bible College, asking us whether we would consider joining the teaching faculty at the college.

In a split second I had the conviction that the college was the place for us. Had the Board of Missions offered to send us to some country where we could have taught in a Bible school, the story of our life might have been very different. But we could not imagine ourselves going to Copenhagen to look up Mennonite refugees (as important and legitimate as this might be). Moreover, I was then the chairman of the Alberta Home Missions Committee and we were trying to get a mission in Calgary established. It occurred to us then that if it was city mission work we were to do, we could do that in Calgary as well. We did not feel in the least critical of our Mission Board for their decision, but we did not have the conviction that our calling lay in the area they were suggesting.

The interesting thing about the whole process was that H.H. Janzen, who was a member of the Mission Board, had been present when the decision to send us to Europe was made. He then quickly went home to Winnipeg and wrote us a letter asking us to come to the college. Evidently he had also discussed the matter with B.B. Janz, for one day Janz was at our door again to let us know that if the college in Winnipeg desired our services, he would no longer insist that we go to Brazil. That settled the matter for us.

The Mennonite Brethren Bible College had been established in

1944 and had grown from a small beginning with Dr. A.H. Unruh as President to an institution that had a sizeable student body and a growing faculty.   There were very few in our Canadian Conference at that time who had advanced theological training, and most of those who did had already been appointed to the faculty of the college. I felt inadequately equipped to transfer directly from Bible school to college and the college agreed to delay my appointment for a year if I would spend the year in seminary studies.

It was only natural that we should apply for admission to Tabor College, where a three-year Bachelor of Divinity program was offered at the time. (This department was later moved to Fresno and became the Mennonite Brethren Biblical Seminary.) Tabor admitted us immediately upon receipt of my transcripts. I was given advanced standing and even the promise that they would provide work for me in order to reduce expenses. We had not asked for this and as it turned out later that statement made the American Consul in Calgary suspicious, thinking that we did not have enough funds to go to Tabor, and he refused to grant us a student visa.

I had written to the consulate asking for a list of documents required for us to study in the United States. By mistake they had sent me the requirements for an alien residence visa. We did not know this and went to the trouble of collecting innumerable documents in duplicate. When all was completed we mailed them to Calgary together with the letter of acceptance from Tabor. However, they were all returned to us with the explanation that the immigrant quota for people born in the Soviet Union was over-subscribed. I called by telephone to ask whether I could come in to see the consul personally, but he refused on the grounds that we did not have enough money to go to school in the U.S. When I asked him how much we needed he replied that there was no fixed sum, but he wouldn't tell me in any case for then I would go and borrow it. So the door to Tabor was closed.

It was through the reading of *Christianity Today* that I became aware of Wheaton College's graduate division, where one could earn an M.A. in Biblical Literature. I applied and was accepted. Since Wheaton's summer school ran for ten weeks it was possible to do the work of a semester during the summer months. We sold our little house to the church for the princely sum of $2,500, and prepared to move to Wheaton, Illinois. We were going to go on a visitor's visa, secretly hoping that once we would be in the United States we would be able to convert our visitor's visa to a student visa.

Before we left we traded our old Chevy in for a car that held a bit more promise. Also, we disposed of most of our furniture. With our personal belongings and our three preschoolers we began the four-day journey to Chicago and Wheaton. We had written to Wheaton to let them know of our coming to summer school, but Wheaton really had no housing for married students at that time.

It was a humid and hot day when we arrived in Wheaton-- something we weren't used to from the dry prairies. There was no place to stay, so we spent the first night in a motel about twenty miles outside of Wheaton. The next day we drove into Wheaton again but again had no success, and for another night we drove to a neighbouring town to find a motel. On the third day we met a Canadian family from Saskatchewan who had had a similar experience to ours when they first came to Wheaton, but now owned a house. These kind people took us in for a night. Also, they informed us that there was a young couple both of whom wanted to attend summer session, but did not know what to do with their baby during classes. This couple had two rooms upstairs in their house which they were willing to let us have on condition that Lena take care of the baby while they studied. It was a great relief to us to have a roof over our head--only that these upstairs rooms, without fan or air-conditioning, were almost unbearable in the summer heat.

We cooked on a hot plate and lived very simply and frugally that summer. Our children spoke only German when we came to

Wheaton and it was a difficult emotional experience for them to be thrown suddenly into an English-speaking world. They even went to DVBS in the Wheaton Bible Church that summer, and by the end of the summer spoke English.

My first course at Wheaton was Romans with Dr. Kenneth Kantzer (later the editor of *Christianity Today* and Dean of Trinity Evangelical Divinity School). Although I had taken Romans twice before I knew by now that God's Word is quite unfathomable and had no hesitation in taking the course in the two-week inter-session. We had four hours of lectures every day, had daily assignments to do, read through a major commentary, handed in a term paper, and wrote a final exam--a rather ambitious undertaking for a two-week session. Fortunately the library was air-conditioned so that one could at least study in comfort. The problem was that it was almost impossible to sleep at night because of the heat and the humidity.

After the inter-session came two four-week terms in which I was to take an accelerated Greek course. An entrance requirement for the M.A. program in Biblical literature was two years of Greek, which I did not have. The alternative was to take this accelerated course and follow it up with a third-year course. Dr. Gerald Hawthorne was our instructor. At first I managed quite well, but with three hours of class every day and a lot of homework it did eventually get quite heavy. In fact when we began working through the section on the Greek participle I floundered for a few days. But then the light broke through, and I was quite heartened when on one occasion when the professor could not be present, he asked me to lead the class.

All through the summer the question of what we would do at the end of August weighed heavily upon us. Turning back to Alberta was out of the question, for we had, as it were, burned all bridges behind us. If there had been more evangelical seminaries in Canada at the time we might have chosen one of these even before we came to Wheaton, but we did not know of any. As a last resort, I thought, we could return to Canada and pursue graduate studies at some university in a field other than Bible and theology. One day I paged through *Christianity Today* and my eyes fell on an advertisement announcing the academic program of Central Baptist Seminary in Toronto. I had never heard of this school and so I immediately wrote to the dean, inquiring about their offerings and about transfer credit. With five years of Bible school and several seminary courses, plus a summer at Wheaton, I should not have to start at the bottom, I thought.

An answer came back very soon offering us admission to the three-year Bachelor of Divinity program with two years of advanced standing. Theoretically I should be able to complete the B.D. in one year; practically this seemed next to impossible for the seminary required not only three years of Greek but also two years of Hebrew. Also, I was to write a thesis.

We decided then not to bother with a student visa for the U.S. any longer, but to move to Toronto and attend the Central Baptist Seminary. When summer session was over at Wheaton we packed our few belongings into our Ford and headed for Ontario--again into the unknown. Our only consolation was that my friend and former classmate from Bible school, Abe Froese (who had married Hertha Dyck, Vineland) lived in Ontario and they would certainly receive us into their home for a few days until I found housing.

It was a long day from Chicago to Detroit/Windsor and then on to Vineland. What we did not know was that the Froeses no longer lived there. When we arrived in Vineland the streets were dark and empty. We went to a telephone booth to find the Froese address in the phone book but without success. After several vain attempts to find out where the Froeses lived, we discovered that they had moved to St. Catherines. We got the address and made our way to St. Catherines. It was past midnight when we arrived and since they weren't sure about our coming, they were all fast asleep. Nevertheless, they were kind enough to take us in for the night.

The Froeses then offered to keep Lena and the children while I went to Toronto to look for housing. That turned out to be a bit of a nightmare. Every day when the *Toronto Star* appeared on the newsstands I went through the rental section and called from a telephone booth. But the moment people heard that we had three children, they hung up on me.

I spent five days in Toronto, eating very meagrely and sleeping in my car at night. To shave and to wash I went to the Union Railway Station. Finally at the end of the week I found a house in the Beverly Hills district. It was a new brick building and the owner, Mr. White, had found the mortgage payments too heavy and so he and his family had moved into the basement and wanted to let the upstairs out for rent. We could have the house for 125 dollars a month--at that time considered rather high, but it was the best we could do.

With great joy I returned to St. Catharines to get my family and to settle in. However, the Froeses asked us to stay for the weekend. Abe had already arranged that I should preach in the Vineland Mennonite Brethren Church that coming Sunday, and so we stayed. Monday morning, at the beginning of September, 1952, we moved to Toronto. Friends in Coaldale shipped a few items of furniture which we had left behind. We picked up several second hand items and soon Lena had our living quarters fixed up nicely and we were grateful to God for his gracious provision.

We had barely settled in when Ernest, our three-year old, threw my ink bottle into the toilet bowl without our knowledge and soon we had serious plumbing problems. We tried everything before letting the owner, Mr. White, know, but to no avail. He was very understanding and undid the bowl and turned it upside down and out came the ink bottle. Shortly thereafter Ernest fell against the steel railing on our front steps and cut a deep gash in his forehead. We were new in the area and did not know where we could find a doctor. Again Mr. White kindly helped us out and took me and Ernest to the doctor's office to have the wound sutured.

With the housing problem solved and the family settled once again, we braced ourselves for the coming school year.

Our family in northern Ontario, 1927. John and I sitting in the middle.

In grade 3, 1931; kneeling on the far right.

In grade 10, 1938; in front, 2nd from the right.

Our family in Coaldale; in the back next to my sister.

Sunday school picnic on our yard, early thirties.

Teaching DVBS at Bow Island, 1940.

Pretending to study.   With my room-mate, Abe Froese, in the Coaldale Bible School.

In lumber camp in northern Ontario, 1943; in front row, in the middle.

Graduates of the Coaldale Bible School, 1942; back row, far right.

Graduates of the Winkler Bible School, 1943. Back row, 2nd from right.

August 1943, at the funeral of my brother John. Our family.

The Hamm family in La Glace, Alberta. Lena in front, far right.

Our wedding in La Glace on
October 12, 1944.

Graduation from Central
Baptist Seminary, 1953.

Lena joins the Ewert family; at the back, far left.

Principal of the Coaldale Bible School; front row, 4th from right.

First year of teaching at MBBC, 1953-54; front row, 3rd from right (at annual ministers' course).

Instructor in the Bethany Bible Institute, 1946-47.

With our 5 children (Eleanor, Ernest, and Marianne at the back; Grace and Doreen between Lena and me).

18

Central Baptist Seminary

In the twenties when the battle between Fundamentalism and Liberalism tore the Baptist churches in Ontario apart, Dr. T.T. Shields, pastor of the Jarvis Street Baptist Church, had led a movement that broke with McMaster Divinity School and established a new seminary in Toronto. Shields' teaching and preaching could be characterized as highly polemical. If he wasn't blasting the Liberals, he was fighting Roman Catholicism. Dr. Martin Loyd-Jones of London, England, filled one of Toronto's pulpits one summer and exhorted Shields to stop fighting and rather to devote his energies to the proclamation of the gospel, but to no avail.

Several years before we came to Toronto, Dr. Gordon Brown, who was the academic dean of Shields' seminary, together with several of the faculty of the Toronto Baptist Seminary, left and established Central Baptist Seminary. When I came to this seminary in 1953 I was quickly brought up to date on these developments by the students. Since I did not understand the complexities of Baptist church controversies, all this meant very little to me. My main concern was that I have a profitable year of study.

Dean Brown had earned a Masters in Semitics at the University of Toronto and had then gone on to work on a Ph.D. under the famous Greek scholar, A.T. Robertson, in Louisville, Kentucky. He had already gathered most of the material for his dissertation when it was discovered that someone in another school had written on the same topic and Brown did not have the heart to start over again, and so did not receive his degree. However, he did have the training, and besides administering the seminary, he carried a full load of teaching. I had him for third-year Greek exegesis and second-year Hebrew. In Greek we worked our way through I

Corinthians very carefully and I recognized for the first time how crucial an understanding of I Corinthians was for the life of the church.

Mrs. Brown, who had earned a Masters in ancient languages at the University of Toronto, taught the first-year Hebrew course and second-year Greek. With the double dose of Greek I had received at Wheaton, I did not find the Greek classes too difficult, and so I spent more time on the Hebrew. We had a fairly good-sized class in Hebrew to begin with, but by Christmas all had fallen by the way except three. I was already looking around for a school that offered second-year Hebrew in summer session, since this would be the only subject I would lack for graduation, when the Dean called me in just before Christmas and asked me if I would care to join the second year Hebrew class after Christmas. This was startling good news and I decided to give it all I had. It was understood, of course, that I would continue with first year also till the end of the academic year. Since I had the Hebrew verb forms well fixed in my mind by Christmas, and some of the second year students had not reviewed them for a while, I discovered that with careful preparation I could keep up. The class was reading the Servant passages of Isaiah at the time and with God's help I completed both first and second-year Hebrew in one year. To my great delight, when prizes were awarded at graduation, I received the Hebrew prize.

Besides a heavy load in languages I took Systematic Theology, Church History (including Baptist History), Homiletics, and Missions. It was also expected that students participate in the seminary choir. For my thesis I chose the topic: "Sanctification in the Epistle of Romans." Shortly before the end of the school year I brought a bound copy of my thesis to the Dean who told me that this was the first time in the seminary's history that a student had his thesis completed and bound before graduation, but he was not at all displeased.

Since there was no Mennonite Brethren Church in Toronto at the time, we attended the People's Church, where Oswald Smith was the senior pastor. We enjoyed the Sunday morning services at which we heard not only Oswald Smith but also speakers from other lands. It was a year of widening horizons. The only time we felt rather uncomfortable was during the annual missions conference when great sums of money were collected and we poor students had to resist the pressure to give away the few dollars we had. The morning service was always broadcast by one of Toronto's stations and one Sunday when we couldn't go to church we listened to Dr. Smith on the radio and were completely taken aback when he preached on the topic: "Why I Do Not Pray the Lord's Prayer." The reason he gave was quite incomprehensible to me: because, he said, it begins with "Our Father," and since Liberals stressed the Fatherhood of God and the Brotherhood of man, we should not pray the Lord's Prayer. Unfortunately our Lord had not anticipated the Fundamentalists/Liberal controversy when he taught his disciples to pray!

One day as I sat in the seminary library I noticed a book on the shelf, written by Oswald Smith. I looked at it and found that it was on the subject of prophecy. It had been written before the Second World War and made predictions (in the light of prophecy!) about the future of Japan and other nations. Because I had the advantage of historical perspective (it was now 1952) I noticed very quickly that most of his predictions had failed to come true. It was a salutary warning not to speculate about political developments in the modern world on the basis of Old Testament prophecies. However, we enjoyed our year at the People's Church, although I do not recall that anyone in the congregation ever took any interest in us; we just came and went. When Oswald Smith's biography appeared in 1982, I read it with great interest. With all his weaknesses, he had a great heart for the mission of the church.

Eleanor was five years old when we came to Toronto and we enrolled her in a local kindergarten. One day she came home and recited the Lord's Prayer with great pride. She stopped short of the doxology and when I asked her to finish it she said she had. Her teacher was Roman Catholic and I did not realize at the time that in the Catholic Vulgate the Prayer ends with "and lead us not into temptation but deliver us from evil." I had already learned by then that my Greek text did not have the doxology either.

Our children had noticed the postman carry the mail from door to door and one day decided to imitate him. On my study desk lay a pile of cards which I used for memorizing Greek vocabulary. So they took my Greek vocabulary cards and distributed them from door to door in our neighbourhood. However enlightening they may have been for our neighbours, I was without my Greek cards from then on.

We lived on a shoe-string budget and were so delighted when at Christmas we received, quite unexpectedly, a hundred-dollar cheque from Mr. David Penner, Grassy Lake--the man for whom my dad had worked many years ago. John Esau, with whom I had grown up, had married an Ontario girl and lived in Ontario now. One day he went north and shot a bear. On the way home it occurred to him that he should stop in Toronto and supply a poor student family with bear meat. So there he was late one evening with a car trunk full of bear meat. What could we do but receive his gift graciously? Lena tried several ways of preparing it, but it never went down well. It was a general rule at our house that we did not fuss about what was on the table, and when Marianne, who was four at the time, asked at the supper table what kind of meat we were having, I told her that "meat was meat and that's that." "Yes," she replied, "and a bear is a bear." It was hard to say grace with a straight face that evening.

One evening after we had finished supper Eleanor came to sit on my lap. We chatted a bit and then suddenly she asked, "Daddy, how does one get saved?" What does one say to a five-year old in such a situation? I took her into my study and we talked about it for a moment and we prayed together and she received Christ into her heart. When Marianne heard that, she too wanted to be saved. This was all too much for us. After all she was only four years old.

We told her to wait till tomorrow and if she still wanted to be saved the next day we would try to help her. The next morning when we were still asleep she stood crying at our bedside, asking if she too could be saved. We prayed with her and to this day she claims that was the beginning of her life with Christ. I should add that we had not put any pressure upon our children. Indeed, I do not recall ever really discussing the question of conversion with them. We did, however, regularly teach them the Scriptures and pray with them. How strange are the ways of the Spirit!

Although I was very busy at seminary we did drive out to some of our Mennonite Brethren Churches in the Niagara Peninsula, as well as Kitchener and Leamington during the course of the year. In Leamington I spoke at a provincial Sunday school convention, in Kitchener at the Harvest Thanksgiving festival. On one occasion we were asked to come to Vineland for services and we stayed with some friends on the farm. However, something had gone wrong with the lemon pie and before the evening service at which I was to speak I began to throw up. Somehow I got through my sermon, but we left for Toronto immediately. Before we got home, Lena and the children were also throwing up. Next morning we got a call from our friends, the Peter Doerksens, informing us that their family was sick also and that it must be a case of food poisoning. Fortunately we all pulled out of it without harm.

Part of the Christmas holidays that year were spent in the Niagara Peninsula with the Abe Froeses and with the parents of Hugo and Harold Jantz--relatives of Lena. It was a pleasant change in the routine. For the Easter break Jim Sieberts invited us to their home in St. Catharines. Jim and I were friends from childhood, when the Siebert family lived with us on our farm in Coaldale. He was now an art teacher in the St. Catharines school division. It was a delight to have him as secretary of the college board later when I served as president of the college.

Having now lived in five Canadian provinces--the provinces in which our Mennonite Brethren churches were located at the time--I had a reasonably good grasp of church life in our Canadian Conference. Later when my duties at the college led me to serve in the various provinces, I was always happy to find friends wherever I went.

At the beginning of May, 1953, I graduated from seminary and wanted very badly to return to Wheaton College to continue with my M.A. studies. However, we had learned from experience the previous summer that Wheaton had no housing for a family such as ours and therefore we thought it best to drive across the country to B.C. Lena and the children would then stay with the parents and I would take the bus back to Wheaton for summer school.

Abe Froese came to Toronto with his pickup truck and took a few articles of furniture to their place. He shipped them to Winnipeg after we got settled there. We visited the Froeses once more to say our farewells and our thanks and then made our way west.

We took the route through upper Michigan, Wisconsin, Minnesota, the Dakotas, Montana, Idaho, Washington and from there north to Chilliwack, B.C. We had not travelled very far when the radiator began to boil. The fan belt had torn and so we spent a lot of time getting it fixed. Lena and the children stayed in the car, while I tried to get a new belt. Once we got into the central states the motor stopped on us repeatedly, often at the most inconvenient places. In the wide open spaces of Montana, where towns are often as much as fifty miles apart, our Ford refused to go any further. We were in the middle of the prairies; it was hot, and there wasn't a soul in sight. I left Lena and the children in the car and began to walk. Finally a traveller came along and took me to the next town. After sharing my dilemma with the garageman he volunteered to tow our car into his garage and try to solve the problem. He thought our fuel-pump was worn out and so replaced it at considerable cost. Now we were sure our problems were over, but not so. Finally a mechanic discovered a dirty gas filter and after cleaning it the problem was solved.

We were motoring through the beautiful mountains of Idaho on our way to Coeur d'Alene. As the sun began to set, a deer jumped out of the ditch right on to the hood of our car, and then slithered along the driver's side of the vehicle, giving our car a terrible bashing. We stopped. The deer was lying on the highway. Other motorists stopped also. We pulled the deer off the road. It appeared to be dead. However, one motorist explained that ninety percent of the times they were simply knocked out. Indeed, he suggested that we not report it to the game warden for that meant endless and useless red tape. We took his advice and travelled on, but with a badly battered car. The Lord's hand certainly had been over us, for if the deer had struck the windshield directly we may all have been killed.

Once we were in Chilliwack my dad was kind enough to buy the car from us and later sold it to Allen and Elizabeth Brandt (my sister). It was good to be home again with the parents. Our children were at the age where they were fascinated with the farm and both of our grandpas and grandmas enjoyed having them around. As we reflect on that summer now, we can't help but feel that we must have been a burden to our parents at times. However, we were grateful for the way they helped us out.

We had agreed that Lena and the children would stay in Chilliwack with the parents (either hers or mine) for the summer, while I returned to Wheaton. I tried to be of help on the farm before I left in the middle of June. When I took the Greyhound bus for Wheaton, I knew that I would not see my family for three months.

19

College Teacher

My first stop on the way to Chicago was Winnipeg. Here I met with President Janzen and several of the college faculty. They asked me to be prepared to teach Greek (both first and second year), Ancient History, Pastoral Epistles (in German), and a course in missions in the fall quarter. Subjects for the winter and spring quarter had not yet been allotted. It was all a bit frightening, but we had promised to come to MBBC and there was no turning back.

By the time I got to Chicago I was very tired, since there were no stopovers and I rarely sleep sitting up. When I arrived at Wheaton I was offered a room in Dr. Greene's house, where several other graduate students lived that summer. One of them, Earl Ellis, went on to become an internationally known New Testament scholar. I took my meals in the college cafeteria. Again I was to put in ten full weeks of study; first, two weeks of inter-session, and then two four-week sessions.

There were few options in the inter-session and I had decided to take a course in Old Testament Vocabulary with the Christian Jew, Dr. Neuberg. It was a kind of Old Testament theology built around key-concepts. When only eight students registered for the course the administration cancelled it, since ten was the minimum number for a course to be financially viable. This was such a great disappointment to several of us who had come long distances with the intention of taking this subject, that the graduate school reversed its decision and we got the course after all. It was in this course that I hit upon a thesis topic.

In the eight weeks that followed after inter-session I took Greek Exegesis of the Synoptics with Dr. Berkeley Mickelson. I also took a course in the Minor Prophets and in Thesis Research.

While engrossed in my studies I received a telephone call from

Lena, informing me that her mother had just passed away. This was a severe blow to our family. It came so suddenly and unexpectedly. She had worked hard all her life and had brought up ten children. My parents-in-law had just left the farm and moved into a new house they had built in Chilliwack, hoping to enjoy the evening of their life. But God's ways are not ours. Mother was a godly soul and we missed her very much. I was glad Lena could be with her in her dying hours. Unfortunately I could not attend the funeral.

My money was running out and I did not know where I would get the cash to buy a ticket for Winnipeg when summer session closed. I decided then to go to the employment office of the college and take on Saturday jobs such as cleaning houses and mowing lawns. One Saturday when I cleaned the washrooms of a rather palatial residence, the lady of the house engaged me in conversation. When she discovered that I was a minister of the gospel it was too much for her that I should be down on hands and knees cleaning floors. I thought nothing of it.

As summer session came to an end I heard of a student from North Carolina who wanted to drive all the way to Calgary, Alberta, and was looking for passengers. The Ken Davises (Ken was later to become the Dean of Trinity Western, Langley, B.C.) and Mr. Downey (who taught at the Canadian Bible College, Regina) and I travelled with this young man, first to Fort Francis, Ontario, where we left the Davises, then to Winnipeg, where I got off. Mr. Downey continued on to Regina.

Mr. H.H. Janzen had found a house for us on Stanier Street, close to the college. However it would not be vacant for another week and so I notified my family in B.C. to wait until we had permission to move in. I stayed in the college's Ebenezer Hall until my family arrived. It had been a long and lonely summer.

Lena with our three children took the train from Mission, B.C., and made the long journey to Winnipeg. Travelling by coach with three lively youngsters was not all that easy. I was at the CPR station when the train arrived in Winnipeg, but could not find them at first. Somehow we had passed each other and I wondered for a moment whether they had missed the train or whether there had been a mistake in communication. Finally I went back into the station and there to my great delight I saw them all. It must have been a sight to behold, for I had a child dangling from every limb for a while.

I took my family to Ebenezer Hall where we prepared a supper for ourselves (college had not yet begun). After supper we moved our belongings into the rented house and once again we were together and could establish our own home. Eleanor was now six and we enrolled her in the Lord Selkirk School. Marianne and Ernest were still below school age.

Soon the college students began to arrive. Some of them were my age and I felt very young and inexperienced beside people like H.H. Janzen and A.H. Unruh. In spite of my youthfulness, however, I was well received by my colleagues. Besides Janzen and Unruh, J.H. Quiring, I.W. Redekopp, Henry Regehr, J.A. Toews, and Mr. and Mrs. Horch, taught at the college at that time. Also, there were several part-time instructors.

The faculty met every week and I found the openness, the give and take, and the banter at these meetings rather enjoyable. My teaching load was heavy (sixteen hours a week) and I had little time for anything else than to prepare and to give lectures. However, I was afraid I would lose my knowledge of Hebrew and so I enrolled in an extension course in Hebrew offered by Oxford University.

We became members of the North End Mennonite Brethren Church (the Elmwood Church was just being built when we came to Winnipeg), and since we did not have a car we depended on friends to take us to church. The John Voths, Coaldale, were students at MBBC at the time and they usually made room for us in their car. By Christmas, 1953, the Elmwood Church was ready for occupancy and we were within walking distance.

Lena's mother had died in July and father-in-law felt desperately lonely. He had always wanted to travel, but family obligations and

economic necessity had kept him from it.   Now the opportunity
came to join a tour group to the Near East, led by Dr. F.C. Peters.
For him it was an unforgettable experience and gave him a thirst for
more travel.   After spending a good many weeks abroad he returned
to Canada just before Christmas, and since he had to pass through
Winnipeg anyway, he spent the Christmas holidays with us.   That led
to a new chapter in his life, for here in Winnipeg he was introduced
to Mrs. Wilms, who had been widowed two years previously, and the
following spring they were married.   Mrs. Wilms had four children:
Betty (Mrs. Jake Bergman), Herman (married to Mary Kroeker),
Helen (married to Albert Litz) and Bill (who was then a teenager).
For us this meant that we now had an extended family in Winnipeg.
After living in Chilliwack for a while they sold their home in B.C.
and moved to Winnipeg where they lived until both of them passed
away in 1982.

From time to time during the first year of college I was asked
to serve in the churches with messages from the Word of God and
this meant much extra work.   Particularly meaningful for me that
first year was a trip to Ontario at Eastertime, together with my
former teacher, Dr. A.H. Unruh.   We conducted a three-day Bible
conference in the Scott Street Mennonite Brethren Church.   Henry
Penners, whom I knew from Coaldale (Lydia and I were in the same
grade all through public school), put me up in their house and we
had a good time of fellowship.   Unruh and I travelled by train, since
flying was not all that common yet, and I was quite exhausted when
we arrived in Toronto.

Dr. Unruh was rather corpulent and found sleeping
compartments on the train inconvenient and therefore always
travelled coach in his later years.   It would have been very
inappropriate for me as a younger man to take a sleeper, and so we
sat in a coach for two nights and a day (he slept, I didn't).   One
question he asked repeatedly on that trip was, "Brother Ewert, what
does the Greek say?" He had not had the opportunity to study the
original language of the New Testament and always looked for

information that cast new light on the biblical text. I felt very honoured that I could travel and share a Bible conference with this highly respected man of God. After three days of meetings my friend, Abe Froese, took us to Toronto to the train station. However, we ran into a traffic jam at the Burlington Bridge, and when we arrived at Union Station the train had left. So we had to spend the night in Toronto and take the train the following day.

In the spring of my first year at college Mr. J.H. Quiring and I had the privilege of travelling to Coaldale together to attend the closing exercises of the Bible school and to lead in a Bible conference. He was Registrar at the college at the time, and since the college did not have an academic Dean in its earlier years, the Registrar did double duty. The greatest benefit to me that came out of our trip to Alberta was, as I recall, that he promised to relieve me of a new subject that I was to teach in the spring quarter. Mr. H.H. Janzen must have heard about this and asked whether I would relieve him of teaching Mennonite Brethren Missions. This request I had to decline for the simple reason that I did not know enough about the subject. As a result, my teaching load in the spring quarter was somewhat lighter than it had been in the fall and winter quarters.

With God's sustaining help we completed our first year at MBBC. It was Saturday night, June 13, the night before graduation, that I took Lena to Concordia Hospital and our daughter Grace Arlene was born. I hardly made it in time for the baccalaureate service that Sunday morning. We rejoiced in the birth of another healthy child. My original plan had been to spend the summer at Wheaton again in order to continue my studies on my Masters, but I could not leave Lena alone with a newborn babe and three other youngsters. Instead I worked on my Hebrew and prepared lectures for the coming year. Although I was to repeat several subjects which I taught the first year, there was a considerable turn-over of faculty that spring and that meant picking up new subjects.

Mr. I.W. Redekopp decided to leave college in 1954 and to

assume the leadership of the Elmwood Mennonite Brethren Church. For thirteen years he led this congregation, and our family has fond memories of his ministry. Although his sermons were not always as well organized as they might have been, he had a pastoral concern for all the members of the church. In some respects he was ahead of his times and some of us found it hard to accept the innovations he made. Although he was the pastor, Elmwood practised a multiple ministry and that meant that I, too, had to take my turn at preaching.

Mr. Quiring, after teaching at the college almost from the beginning, felt led to accept the leadership of the Winkler Mennonite Brethren Church. That left a vacancy in the Registrar's office. The faculty then asked me to fill that position. A normal teaching load at the time was fifteen hours a week. Mine was now reduced to fourteen, allowing one hour for this administrative duty. Quiring was also the editor of the college publication, *The Voice,* and with his leaving, that duty also fell to me--a duty which I carried out with joy for some ten years. There was an onerous aspect to this responsibility, however, and that was to see that faculty members got their manuscripts to me in time. Since some of my colleagues wrote with greater difficulty than others, it was not always pleasant to make changes and corrections in the material handed in. If one listens to the testimony of some of our older leaders, *The Voice* played an important role in shaping the theological thinking of the leaders of our Canadian Conference for a good many years.

Dr. A.H. Unruh, who finished his *Die Geschichte der Mennoniten Brüdergemeinde* during my first year at MBBC, decided to retire in the spring of 1954. He and Mrs. Unruh moved to Chilliwack where they lived with their youngest daughter, Lydia, until the Lord called them home.

As the years went by new faculty members were added and others left for different fields of service. All of them enriched our lives. Several of those who were on the faculty when we first came to MBBC have gone home to glory; others are still serving the Lord faithfully. For nineteen years in a stretch, our life was to be wrapped up with MBBC, sharing in its successes and its failures, its triumphs and its defeats. It was a good run.

20

Graduate Work

When I joined the faculty of MBBC in 1953 not one of the professors had an earned doctorate. A.H. Unruh had received an honourary doctorate from Bethel College; the others had bachelor's degrees in arts and divinity, except for Mr. Redekopp who had a Masters in Education. It was clear to all of us, however, that we would have to upgrade ourselves academically to keep pace with the growing interest in higher education among our young people. Since I had already completed half of my Masters program at Wheaton College, my first concern was to complete this program.

In 1955, after two years of teaching at MBBC, I left my family in Winnipeg for eight weeks in summer and attended two four-week sessions at Wheaton. I took Systematic Theology, Old Testament Introduction, and New Testament courses. One course in the Epistle to the Hebrews with Dr. Berkeley Mickelson stood out above the others. Mickelson had written his Ph.D. dissertation at the University of Chicago on the Epistle to the Hebrews and was thoroughly conversant with his subject matter. I worked my way through the Greek text of Hebrews (the vocabulary is very unPauline), wrote an exegetical paper on Hebrews 13, and handed in numerous word studies. When a class-mate asked me one day if I would let him see my returned exercises (the professor had advised him to do so), I was confident that Dr. Mickelson was pleased with my work. I was still labouring under feelings of inferiority as far as academic work was concerned and little things like this were important to me.

By now it was clear that my major would be Old Testament and it was time to get a thesis topic. In my first summer at Wheaton I had taken Old Testament Vocabulary and got interested particularly in the concept of *chesedh* (covenant loyalty). My proposal to write a thesis on this concept was accepted and Dr. Tenney, Dean of the Graduate School, appointed Dr. Manross to be my advisor. Nelson Glueck had already published his booklet, "*Das Wort Hesed im Alten Testament,*" and this gave me perspectives for my research.

During my third year at MBBC I not only taught a full slate of courses, carried out my duties as Registrar and as editor of *The Voice,* but I also wrote my Master's thesis. Hans and Elfrieda Kasdorf lived in Ebenezer Hall at the time and Frieda was willing to type the final draft of my thesis. (Dr. Kasdorf was to be my colleague later when I taught at seminary in Fresno, and we became good friends.) The following summer I took the finished copy with me to Wheaton and, after a fourth summer session, I completed my residence work and prepared myself for comprehensive examinations. The Lord helped me through these long hours of writing and when I got my report, saying that I had passed with "great distinction", I was overjoyed.

Graduation followed immediately upon summer school and I was happy to receive my M.A. in Biblical Literature. It would have been a much more meaningful occasion had Lena been there for the graduation, for she had played an important role in my studies. However, she was at home expecting our fifth child. A few days after my return from Wheaton, August 25, Doreen Elizabeth was born. Again we were grateful to God for a healthy child and, as we had done with the other children, we committed Doreen to the Lord and to his service.

In the few weeks between summer session and the beginning of college I felt very depressed, and I didn't know what was wrong with me. I see now that I had overtaxed my physical resources. But the opening of college brought new enthusiasm and strength. Having completed my Masters, I began to look around for schools where I could continue my studies in the biblical field. There was little available in Winnipeg at the time, and so I enrolled in several extension courses offered by Northern Baptist Seminary. The

Greek Exegesis of the Book of Revelation, together with the required readings, proved particularly helpful. My professor was Dr. Mantey, co-author of a Greek grammar which I used in classes for many years. However, if I wanted to earn another graduate degree I would have to look elsewhere.

The University of Manitoba had acquired the services of Dr. Wolverton, a graduate of Chicago's School for Oriental Studies, and in the academic year 1957-58 he offered a course in Hebrew and Septuagint Studies. With three others I joined this seminar which met for three hours every Saturday morning throughout the year. J.A. Toews had by then decided to do his Ph.D. in history at the University of Minnesota and since he needed another modern language, he decided to bone up on his Russian. Together we drove out to the University of Manitoba on Saturdays: he to study Russian and I to do Hebrew and Septuagint. A year later, when I enrolled at Luther Seminary in St. Paul, I received six quarter hours of advance standing for this course.

At first it looked as if the University of Manitoba might begin a Ph.D. program in Near Eastern Studies, but that did not materialize and I began to look around for a school where I could do graduate studies in summer session. I applied at Garrett Biblical Institute and stopped in at Evanston, Illinois, in late spring on my way to Fresno, where I was to give the graduation address at seminary. B.J. Braun was the president of the seminary at the time and he invited me to join their faculty, but we did not feel inclined to accept the invitation at the time. One day I saw an ad in a religious magazine in which the summer school offerings of the Lutheran School of Theology, Chicago, were listed, and so in the summer of 1958 I enrolled in a course on Parables, taught by Dr. Artur Vööbus, an Estonian scholar who had come to America after the Second World War. The other course was "Christianity, Buddhism and Hinduism," taught by Dr. James Scherer. Both courses were extremely valuable.

That summer I learned that Luther Seminary, St. Paul,

Minnesota, had begun offering courses that led to the Master of Theology degree in summer. St. Paul was only 500 miles from Winnipeg in contrast to the almost 1000 miles I had to travel to Chicago (always by train). When I returned home that summer I made application to Luther Seminary and was accepted into the M.Th. program, for which thirty-six quarter-hours in residence, plus a thesis, were required. Next summer, then, I took two valuable courses: "History of Christian Thought," with Dr. Tappert, and "New Testament Theology," with Dr. Rozentals, a former professor at the University of Riga, Latvia. I decided then to change my major from Old Testament to New Testament. That summer I learned that the seminary offered a goodly number of seminars during the regular session in three-hour blocks of time and so it occurred to me that I could possibly arrange my teaching schedule at MBBC in such a way that I would be free to go to Minneapolis/St.Paul weekly for Friday seminars.

When the seminary time-table was published I found that I could take three seminars, three hours each, on Fridays. At that time the Great Northern ran an overnight train between Winnipeg and Minneapolis, and so in the year 1959-60 I taught my classes at college Monday through Thursday, then I boarded the train in Winnipeg, travelled all night for twelve hours, and arrived in the Twin Cities at seven in the morning. This gave me just enough time to have a bite to eat and then I was off to nine hours of class. The return trip was just as long, and since I could not afford a sleeper, I sat in a coach two nights a week.

I was on my way home to Winnipeg one Friday night in September. The train was crowded and I sat beside a gentleman who had worked as ticket agent for the Great Northern for many years. When he discovered that I travelled to Minneapolis every week he asked me why I did not get a free pass on the railroad. I had never heard of such a thing, but he assured me that the founder of the Great Northern had left enough money in his will to cover the cost of ministers travelling the Great Northern. Upon my return home I mentioned it to Lena and she encouraged me to apply. But where? Go right to the top, I thought. So I wrote a letter to the president of the Great Northern and asked him whether they would consider me eligible for a free pass. We didn't have to wait long and a letter arrived informing us that our application would be considered if the moderator of our Conference would send a letter of verification and recommendation. Dr. F.C. Peters, my colleague at college, was the moderator of the Canadian Conference that year, and he quickly wrote a letter of confirmation, and within a few weeks I had my pass. This was a godsend for us, for our income was very low and with a family of five, very little could be spared for studies.

In the fall semester I took "The Church in the New Testament," with Dr. Preus, "Patristics," with Dr. Smits, (another Latvian scholar), and "Exegesis of the Apocalypse," with Dr. Rozentals. These seminars called for reading and papers and this had to be done at home besides my regular school work. In the winter semester I enrolled in "Old Testament Theology," with Dr. Frerichs, "Theology of Paul," with Dr. Rozentals, and a course in "Job," with Dr. Frost--all of them very valuable courses.

I needed one more summer session to meet my residence requirements. Since my free pass on the railroad was still good, I decided to go to summer school on it. On one of my trips to Minneapolis the conductor asked me to get off at the United States border and pay one-third the price of a regular ticket because, as he explained, it was now high season. I was happy to do so and from then on regularly purchased such tickets. But no conductor after that ever asked for them and so I went back to using my free pass. When I had finished summer school I estimated what I should have paid in tickets, had the conductors collected them, and mailed the cheque to the Great Northern. But they never responded.

This last summer I took a course in "Isaiah," with Dr. Halverson and a very interesting course in "Pascal," with the famous Norwegian scholar, Dr. Pere Lonning. Also, my proposal to do my dissertation on the "Christology of the Apocalypse" was accepted, and Dr. Rozentals, from whom I had by now taken several courses, became my advisor. I wrote the thesis during the 1960-61 school year and received my Master of Theology degree that spring.

The policy at MBBC at the time was that a professor who had taught for six years and who wanted to upgrade himself could have a half year off with pay or an entire year with half pay. To take an entire year off was out of the question for us, because we had five children, three of them in private school, and we could impossibly live on half our salary. My study leave was actually overdue, but in 1961 it was agreed that I might take the first semester off for further studies. Since there were no doctoral programs in Biblical Studies in Winnipeg or in the Twin Cities, I decided to return to Chicago, where I had earlier taken a summer session.

My family had to be on its own for three semesters (summer, fall and winter), while I devoted myself to studies in Chicago. Without a courageous and supportive wife I could not have undertaken this project. I took four courses in each of the semesters. In summer session I took "The Theology of *Sola Scriptura*," with Professor Watson of Garrett (a famous Luther scholar), "Worship in the Old Testament," with Professor Rylarsdam of the University of Chicago, "Contemporary Roman Catholicism," with Professor Lindbeck of Yale University, and "Gospels and World Evangelism," with one of the seminary faculty.

After summer school I spent a few weeks with my family, but at the beginning of September I was back in Chicago. I rented a small, unfinished attic room and ate in the Seminary cafeteria, except on weekends when the dining hall closed. Again I enrolled in four courses. J.A. Toews, who was then president of MBBC, asked me to return to college for registration, since I was still Registrar, and the college paid me a plane ticket, so that I would not miss too many classes in Chicago. I was to arrive in Winnipeg toward evening, but because of mechanical problems the plane arrived at 2:00 AM. Who should be at the airport to pick me up, but J.A. Toews? Next morning was registration and after just a day or two at home I flew back.

It was a very lonely year for me. On Sundays I usually took the subway to the Moody Memorial Church, where Dr. Alan Redpath was the pastor at the time. It was the only break in the weekly routine of studies.

When I returned to Winnipeg to teach, the second semester had already begun and I had to walk into the classroom immediately--something I was quite happy to do after almost nine months away from the family. Before leaving Chicago, however, I had a deep disappointment. I had now taken fourteen courses towards the doctorate and should have been allowed to sit for comprehensive examinations. Dr. Vööbus, however, paid little attention to the seminary catalogue, and asked that I spend the next few years in reading, and he gave me a book-list of about 125 volumes (many of them in nineteenth-century German). Other professors did not require this, but because he was such a famous man, the Dean did not want to put restrictions on him. For the next two years, therefore, besides teaching at college, I sat evening after evening wading through endless volumes on topics that were often far removed from areas of personal interest. It was a great test of patience.

21

Earning a Doctorate

I returned to Chicago the following summer to work in the library, since so many of the volumes I was to read were not available in Winnipeg. Also I took another course with Dr. Vööbus: "The Eucharistic Texts of the New Testament." In the summer of 1964 I went back once more for a summer session and took a course in the "Worship of Israel," and to sit for my comprehensive examinations (I had met the language requirements earlier).

Dr. Vööbus examined me for three days in the field of New Testament studies. Being a specialist in Syriac I might have expected his first question: "Write on the history of the Ancient Syriac versions." There was no time limit; I could write as long as I wished. After writing on New Testament areas for three days I had one day each for two sub-fields: Early Church and Patristics, and Old Testament. Besides writing for five days, I had an oral examination before the entire faculty.

Since it took the professors so long to read my exams it was not until Christmas that I heard the good news that I had passed. Dr. Vööbus, however, had a plan in mind of which I knew nothing, and once again gave me a reading list in the area of Rabbinics. Also, he insisted that I learn Syriac. Although several schools in the United States offered Syriac in their regular sessions, I had to find a school that offered it in summer, because I taught at MBBC during the year. Interestingly, Concordia Seminary, St. Louis, offered Syriac in the summer of 1965, and so I went down to study with Dr. Roehrs. I was glad I knew German for the Syriac Grammar we used was written in German. What made the summer more interesting and less lonely was the fact that Victor Adrian had decided to enroll in the doctoral program at Concordia and the two of us roomed together that summer. He even tried to teach me to play tennis in

105 (F) degree heat, but I'm afraid I did not offer him enough competition.

On my way home I decided to stop in Chicago and report to Dr. Vööbus that I had taken the basic course in Syriac and that I was anxious to begin my dissertation. He invited me to his home for dinner and after the meal took me into his living room where he laid out a grandiose plan he had had up his sleeve all along. He wanted me to do research in Syriac manuscripts. I was to compare them with the Greek and Latin Fathers and do the spade-work for the eventual publication of a new Syriac New Testament. My heart sank. This was a project that would take years to do and would involve travel to libraries all over the world. When I told Dr. Vööbus that at my age, with a growing family and with my very limited financial resources I did not see how I could possibly do this, he told me bluntly that he would not direct me in any other topic. This made me very sad, because we had always been on good terms and I thought he might be willing to direct me in a subject that was of greater interest to me. But no!

I went to talk to the Dean of the Graduate School and he told me that he had feared all along that I would run into a dead-end street. The fact was that in the fifteen years that Dr. Vööbus had been at the school, only one student had ever completed his doctorate under him. However, the Dean felt that not all was lost; they would simply give me a different advisor. To my dismay they gave me Dr. Granskou, a young Bultmannian, whom students tended to avoid. When I went to talk to him about it, he immediately informed me that he would have to retrain me, because he did not see eye to eye with his colleague, Dr. Vööbus. However, he was willing to be my advisor and suggested we pursue the concept of "The Son of Man in the Gospels." He called Dr. Stendhal of Harvard to see how he would view such a topic and was encouraged by him to go ahead with it.

I returned to Winnipeg, then, to begin another year of teaching and to gather all I could on this topic. By now I had resigned myself to the fact that it would take a long time to complete my doctorate. Besides reading on the "Son of Man" that year I decided to enroll in a course in Classical Greek offered by Queens University, Kingston, through their extension department. All my Greek courses till now had been in Hellenistic Greek and so it was good to get the classical background. The final exam was written at the University of Manitoba. The previous winter I had taken Latin in evening school in Winnipeg in an attempt to review what I had forgotten since I took Latin at the University of British Columbia.

In the summer of 1966 I left for Chicago almost immediately after college closed in order to spend as much time as possible researching my topic. One day Dr. Granskou called me in and asked me to read several passages from the Synoptics in my Greek New Testament. It was not a test of my ability to translate, but an attempt to bring me face to face with the Synoptic Problem and with the view of Bultmann that the Gospels are the creation of the early church and that most of the Son of Man sayings are not really the words of Jesus but words of early preachers put into the mouth of Jesus. I told him that I could not in good conscience accept that position. In that case, he told me, I could not write this dissertation. Only if I accepted his presuppositions would he direct me any further.

That meant that the many months I had read on the topic of "Son of Man" had brought me no closer to my goal. He suggested that we change topics and take something less critical. However, I was slowly coming to the conclusion that I was up against a radical liberalism which, for all its vaunted openness, was extremely dogmatic, narrow and defensive. I talked to the Dean about it and he sympathized with my dilemma, but encouraged me to pursue a different topic. At that moment I did not know what to say and made no promises.

After returning to my room I laid the whole matter before the Lord once more. I had by now taken eighteen courses, completed the language requirements, and passed my Comprehensives. And now this *cul de sac*. Five years of this was enough, I thought. I would leave. It was not easy for me to take the train home on that occasion. It was a dark night for my soul.

With a good part of the summer still left, I decided to enrol in a French course at the University of Winnipeg. In a year's time I would have the privilege of going on sabbatical and I was so disappointed with liberal divinity schools that I decided to spend my study year at a secular university, where one had the freedom to believe what one wished. In casting about for a Canadian university I found that only McGill University in Montreal offered a Ph.D. in New Testament at that time. (Today one can do similar programs at Toronto, McMaster, and other schools.) I applied for admission and was told that I would have to do a full year of residence, write comprehensive exams once more, have seven languages (four ancient and three modern), and write a dissertation. They would not carry over any of the work I had done for my doctorate in Chicago. It all sounded a bit overwhelming, but we decided to go to McGill for our study year.

I had taken four ancient languages (Latin, Greek, Hebrew and Syriac) and I knew English and German, but knew next to no French. After a summer session at the University of Winnipeg I enrolled in another French course in the evening school of St. Johns Collegiate the following winter. The summer of 1967 I spent at the University of Manitoba, taking more French language and literature.

Then it was time to move. Our eldest daughter, Eleanor, was by then in nurse's training, and Marianne and Ernest were going to be at MBBC. The two younger girls, Grace and Doreen, came with us to Montreal. We let out our house for rent, packed a U-Haul trailer and made our way to eastern Canada. The Anglican College had promised us a two-bedroom suite in Rexford Hall, the residence for divinity students.

We travelled around Lake Superior, stopped in Ottawa to view our nation's capital, and then it was off to Montreal. We arrived there during rush hour and with a heavy U-Haul behind our car it was not a very happy situation, especially since we did not know the city. Finally we found our apartment on University Street, just a stone's throw from McGill. It rained that night but in spite of that we unloaded our trailer and set up house on the second floor of Rexford Hall.

This was the year of Expo and before we had really settled in we had visitors from western Canada, whom we were happy to see. Shortly after arriving I had my first meeting with my advisor, Dr. George Johnston, a learned Scotsman who, after graduating from the University of Glasgow, had done his doctorate under C.H. Dodd at Cambridge. Dr. Johnston, first of all, offered me the job of teaching first-year Greek in the Divinity School. He promised to pay me a thousand dollars for the year. I agreed and this turned out to be a delightful experience.

Also, in my first conversation with Dr. Johnston, he suggested that I begin to think of a dissertation topic and that the concept of *pneuma* (Spirit) in Paul was one worth investigating. I responded very positively to such a topic, but since I had a whole year of class work to do and comprehensive exams and language tests to take, I put dissertation research on the back burner. The seminars which I took went quite well and again I had opportunities to learn many new things. In my spare time I prepared myself for examinations in four fields: New Testament, Old Testament, Church History and Theology.

When I sat for the comprehensives in spring I was asked to write for four hours on a saying of Bultmann to the effect that New Testament scholarship had now established that we could know very little about the historical Jesus. The ghost of Bultmann pursued me again, I thought. I decided to review the history of New Testament studies that had led to such a view, without getting involved in a debate over whether I agreed with Bultmann or not. After writing for several days I had to face the entire faculty in an oral. Once again God gave me the grace to survive comprehensive exams, and I was ready to begin my dissertation.

Since I had been elected moderator of the Canadian Conference in July, 1967, we came home to Winnipeg for the summer following our first year at McGill.   The Canadian Conference met in Clearbrook, B.C. in 1968 and so we made our way to the west coast for this event.   The rest of the summer was spent in reading and research.   I had had my sabbatical and was to be back at MBBC for the following year, but the administration granted us a leave of absence.   I did come back to Winnipeg to teach a two-week crash course in Pauline epistles.

A leave of absence meant that we would have no income in our second year, although Lena had been able to get a part-time job at Eatons in Montreal.   My advisor encouraged me to apply for a Canada Council grant, which I did.   I received four thousand dollars that year and that sufficed to see us through.   It was the first time a divinity student at McGill had received a Canada Council grant and Dr. Johnston was very pleased.

During the second year at McGill I followed a rigid schedule of research and writing.   Every morning when the library opened I sat down at the same place, worked till noon, then went home for lunch and a brief nap, and then it was back to the library.   The evenings I spent typing up what I had written by hand during the day.   Slowly my research began to take shape and form and by the end of the academic year I handed in five copies of my dissertation.   The thrust of the dissertation was to show that "Spirit" in Paul is an eschatological concept.

One more hurdle had to be overcome: the defense of my dissertation before the faculty and graduate students.   Three members of the Divinity Faculty, one professor from the English department and one from the Classics department formed my committee.   They had all read my work and had already reviewed the dissertation with me, but the final step was a public forum. After I had summarized my thesis, the professors began to ask probing questions.   Things were going quite well until one of the Divinity professors asked whether I believed in the *parousia* (the

Second Coming of Christ). I thought the question was unfair, for it was my thesis that was being examined and not my personal faith. In such situations, however, it is the part of wisdom to accept humbly whatever is thrown at one and so I answered with a simple "Yes." I waited for him to lower the boom on me, but neither he nor anyone else followed up the question.

After asking me to absent myself the committee deliberated for a while and then called me back to share with me the good news that I had passed all my exams and that I would be granted my Ph.D. at the June graduation. After all the trials I had had to endure in Chicago, this came as a great relief to me.

We had to stay in Montreal till the end of June so that Grace and Doreen could finish their school year. This also made it possible for my family to be present at my graduation, which was held that year in the Montreal Forum. The Earnest Dycks, who were stationed at St. Laurent at the time and whom we had befriended during our two years in Montreal, also came to the graduation.

As we looked back on our two years in Montreal we felt greatly enriched. First of all, they provided us with an opportunity to acquaint ourselves with eastern Canada. Although we were quite busy we made several trips into the Laurentians, to Quebec City, and to some other fascinating sites in Montreal. Almost weekly on Sunday afternoons we climbed Mt. Royal. Also, we were able to get in touch with our mission work in Quebec. When the Ste. Thérèse Church was dedicated I was asked to bring a word of greeting from the Canadian Conference and I dared to do this in my broken French. Also, we had the joy of meeting a goodly number of guests from western Canada who came to Montreal upon occasion. In our apartment block lived a number of student families with whom we were able to establish a good relationship. Among them was a family from England (for years we exchanged Christmas cards), one from India, one from Japan, and then a young Anglican couple from Quebec, our next door neighbours.

About two blocks from where we lived was the Montreal People's Church, where we attended on Sundays. Occasionally we also visited other churches, all the way from Pentecostal to high church Anglican, and in this way broadened our horizons. And then there were those special events when renowned scholars or church leaders gave lectures at McGill or in some church. I think of Dr. Eugene Nida, secretary of translations for the American Bible Society, of Stephen Neill, the great missiologist, of Dr. Samuel Sandmel, the famous Jewish scholar, of Dr. Samuel Terrien, of Union Theological Seminary, who lectured on Wisdom Literature, and many others.

Then there were those novel experiences which are hard to forget: to give a lecture in the School of Nursing on Mennonite theology, to discuss faith and baptism with a class of Roman Catholics from Loyola University, to speak repeatedly to a vibrant Chinese Christian Fellowship, and to have a Bible conference in the Mennonite Church in Ottawa. Then there were those many private conversations with students who were struggling to find firm ground to stand on in their theology. Also we had several opportunities to visit churches in Ontario and to proclaim the good news.

While in Montreal we received a call from our seminary in Fresno once again, asking us to join the faculty, but we did not have the freedom to accept. We felt we owed MBBC a debt and so we packed our U-Haul and made our way back to Winnipeg.

22

Ministries Here and There

The year 1969 was a year of graduations for our family. Having just graduated from McGill myself, we returned to Winnipeg for the graduation of our eldest daughter, Eleanor, from the St. Boniface School of Nursing. She gave the valedictory speech at the ceremony and we were proud of her. After living in nurse's residence for three years she decided to move back home. We had kept our house on 39 Sylvia Street, and after some renovations, we were happy to be back in our own home. Marianne, our second daughter, had spent the year in Waterloo and received her B.A. that spring from what is now Wilfred Laurier University. Ernest, after spending a year at MBBC had gone off to Vancouver and spent a year on the coast, working at odd jobs. He also returned home and enrolled at MBBC for a second year. Grace and Doreen were happy to return to the Mennonite Brethren Collegiate Institute after two years of absence.

Shortly after settling in, the Canadian Conference met in Winnipeg, and since I was still moderator, I had to lead the sessions. We had invited George Brunk and Dan Friesen to give several messages, but most of the time was devoted to business. (At that time we alternated between study and business conferences. The previous year we had had a study conference in Clearbrook, B.C.) Although the sessions went quite well, several issues surfaced unexpectedly which proved to be quite divisive. The Mennonite Central Committee reported that they had presented a brief to Ottawa urging the government to recognize Red China. This caused such a flurry that I hardly knew how to handle the situation, and we got ourselves into a delightful tangle.

After alternating business and study conferences for several years it became obvious that this was not the best arrangement and we decided to return to the earlier pattern of conducting conference business together with devotional exercises as part of the total experience. These annual Canadian Conferences contributed significantly to the unity and the strength of our churches which were spread over a wide geographical terrain.

Somewhat later in July, 1969, representatives from the various Mennonite theological schools met at Aspen, Colorado, for a consultation on theology. I had been asked to present one of the five papers that were read at that occasion. These papers were later edited and published by Dr. A.J. Klassen under the title, *Consultation on Anabaptist Mennonite Theology*. Four of our faculty members, Victor Adrian, H.H. Voth, H.R. Baerg and I travelled to Aspen by car. We had an enjoyable trip and the consultation was a good learning experience. Most of those in attendance came from the three Mennonite seminaries at Harrisonburg, Elkhart and Fresno. Faculty members from CMBC and MBBC represented Canada. An exciting sidelight of the conference was watching the first moonlanding on TV.

Eastern Mennonite College, Harrisonburg, was looking for an Academic Dean at the time and Myron Augsburger, then president of the college, approached me at Aspen to see whether I could be persuaded to accept this position. At that time I felt no inclination to accept, particularly since we had been gone from MBBC for two years and felt obligated to give the college a few more years of our life. Although I put the matter out of my mind at the time, this became the initial contact for our move to Harrisonburg in 1972.

That same summer, toward the end of August, the General Conference of Mennonite Brethren Churches met in Vancouver, and I was asked to give one of the messages. I spoke on "The Continuing Temptations of Jesus in the Church." Lena and I took the train all the way to Vancouver and back. It was a delightful trip.

I was happy to be back in the classroom at MBBC that fall. With formal studies out of the way I could devote myself completely to my teaching and administrative duties, as academic dean. MBBC had for years been an affiliate college of Waterloo Lutheran University in Waterloo, Ontario. In the year 1969-70 we were able to obtain a similar affiliation with the University of Winnipeg. This meant that students enrolled at MBBC could have their courses registered with the University and could apply them for their B.A. or B.Ed. degrees or transfer them to other universities.

In October, 1969, Lena and I, together with our family, our friends and our church, celebrated our twenty-fifth wedding anniversary. My parents came from Clearbrook to share with us in this joyous event. Lena's parents lived in Winnipeg and were close by. Since the church had always been so much a part of our family's life, we invited the Elmwood Mennonite Brethren Church to celebrate this occasion with us. Dr. John Regehr, my colleague at the college, brought a message from the Word of God, we shared some of our experiences with our guests, and at the tables in the lower auditorium our children presented a program. We received a number of fine gifts from friends, which we appreciated and treasured very much. Unfortunately most of these were lost when we lived in California, where we were burglarized several times.

During the Christmas vacation of that year I served once again at the annual three-day Bible conference, which had been conducted in Winnipeg since the late twenties. For ten years in succession it was my privilege to serve with messages at this conference. Besides A.H. Unruh and H.H. Janzen, who were speakers at this conference for many years, J.A. Toews, F.C. Peters and others served together with me in these three-day sessions. Mennonites from various traditions attended these meetings and the conference served as a unifying factor in the Mennonite community. The lectures of two such conferences, given by F.C. Peters, J.A. Toews and myself, were published under the title, *"Das Ringen um die reine Gemeinde,"* edited by H.F. Klassen, for many years editor of the *Mennonitische Rundschau.* Years later I returned from

California to speak at the fiftieth anniversary of this Bible conference and that year's expositions of Paul's letter to the Ephesians were then published under the title, "*Die Wunderwege Gottes mit der Gemeinde Jesu Christi.*" Eric Ratzlaff, who by then had become the editor of the *Rundschau,* edited this volume.

In May, 1970, Eleanor, our oldest daughter, was married to Raymond Martens who was in his final year of medicine at the University of Manitoba. It was a great event for our family. Lena sewed all the dresses and handled most of the preparations. Again we decided to celebrate the occasion in the context of our home church. John Regehr gave a message from the Word of God and I had the privilege of performing the marriage ceremony. After a fellowship meal in the lower auditorium the two families presented a program. It was a joyous occasion except that the weeks prior to the wedding had been made even busier because I was preparing to leave for India immediately after the wedding. Our Board of Missions/Services had for years participated in the work of Union Biblical Seminary, at Yeotmal, India (now at Pune) and several of our Indian pastors and teachers had received their training at this school. From time to time the Mennonite Brethren supplied the seminary with a visiting professor and I had been asked to serve in this capacity. By leaving at the beginning of May I would be able to serve our Indian churches for a month and then spend the first semester, which ran from June through September, at Yeotmal.

Since there was no direct flight to India from Winnipeg, Menno Travel suggested I choose three or four stops for which there would be no extra charge. I decided then to spend several days in Rome, in Athens and in Israel, before flying on to Bombay. After all the studies I had done in subjects touching upon the Mediterranean world it was a great delight to visit these ancient centres of civilization, especially the Holy Land.

We arrived in Bombay at night and I had to sit in the airport in the sweltering heat till morning, before I could get a plane to

Madras. That evening I walked the streets of Madras before going to my hotel and it was quite an eye-opener to see how people in that part of the world lived. Next day I flew to Madurai, South India, where Peter and Betty Hamm met me at the airport. After viewing the famous temple at Madurai we drove to Kodikonal, where most of our missionaries were gathered at the time of the summer heat. Since I knew most of them from earlier years (some of them as students at MBBC) it was a joy to visit Kodi.

Very shortly, however, together with the Peter Hamms, I made my way across country to Shamshabad in an old Willis Jeep. On our way we stopped at the famous medical centre at Vellore, where we had lunch with an American missionary doctor. I lost my lunch on the compound of the Vellore Medical Centre. Eating papaya and bobbing up and down in the jeep had upset my stomach. After a week or two in India, however, my body adjusted to the food and the water.

When we arrived in Shamshabad large crowds were gathering for the fiftieth anniversary of the founding of the Bible school of which Peter Hamm, my brother-in-law, was the principal at the time. We celebrated with a Bible conference at which I gave a series of expository messages. Also, there was much singing, readings, and endless servings of rice and curry. Another Bible conference was held with our missionaries almost immediately following this event at Jerchela, where I stayed in the home of the Dan Nikkels. I gave a series on the parables of Jesus.

From here we visited several of the other fields, among them Gadwal, where Dr. Peter Block and his family were serving, and Mabubnagar, where the Henry Poetkers lived. Later I returned for a week at Jerchela, where I served the hospital personnel (about forty in number) with messages every day. Dr. Jake Friesen and his family were kind enough to have me stay in their home.

After a month of travelling hither and yon in south India it was time for me to leave for Yeotmal. The missionaries dared me to travel third class, and that's exactly what I did. I travelled north all night, but did not sleep a wink, for there were six of us in one small compartment and I was afraid my brief-case with all my lecture notes might disappear, so I put it under my head and lay awake all night.

The train did not run all the way to Yeotmal, a village of 65,000, in the state of Maharastra, and so the last leg of the journey had to be done by bus. The faculty at Yeotmal received me very kindly and I was given a room in the principal's house. Kenneth Bauman was the principal of the seminary at the time and I had the joy of spending three-and-a-half months in their home. We became good friends and I was deeply saddened when Kenneth passed away in 1986. When I discovered that Professor Arthur Cundall, of London, England, who had also left his family behind for the semester, would be my colleague, I was comforted. We too became good friends and on a later occasion I had the privilege of visiting him and his family in their home in England.

The first time I walked into class at Yeotmal all the students rose to their feet and wouldn't sit down until I had asked them to. No one had warned me in advance of this kind of reverence. In fact the students were respectful in so many other ways that by the time I left India I was thoroughly spoiled.

It was a thrill to teach the students at Yeotmal. They were so eager to learn and I was cautioned by the principal not to make the assignments too heavy, for the students always did more than the teacher asked for and tended to overwork. In one subject, I recall, I had assigned a 20-page paper and received 70 pages from one of the students. The devotion of these Indian students who had come to know Christ and wanted to serve him with all their strength made a deep impression on me.

About the only change in the daily grind were the long walks Arthur Cundall and I took along the roads leading out of Yeotmal. Once in a while, Arthur, a good Englishman, insisted that I come over and have a game of darts with him. Occasionally we joined the students in a game of volleyball. The students had established a prayer chain and all night long on Saturday someone was in chapel praying. Sometimes I could hear them from where I lived, for they often prayed out loud.

G.W. Peters and J.J. Toews stopped in at Yeotmal for a few days on their way home from Indonesia and together we made a trip to Gandhi's old stomping grounds, which were only about twenty miles away from Yeotmal. Both of these men gave several lectures at the seminary before they left for home.

When the semester came to an end, the students gave me a great farewell, as only Indian students know how. Two students took me to the city of Nagpur with the seminary car and here I took an Air India flight to Calcutta. In Calcutta I encountered some difficulties with the Income Tax Department (even though I had not had an income in India), and the immigration authorities didn't want to let me leave India because I had no visa (after being assured twice by the Indian embassy in Ottawa that I did not need one). However, after a day and two nights in Calcutta, giving me just a bit of time to see this unusual city, I flew on to Bangkok.

Here I stayed in the Christian and Missionary Alliance guest house and enjoyed a day of sightseeing in the city and on the river. From Bangkok I flew to Hong Kong, where I spent a relaxed day sightseeing. When I wanted to board Air India to fly to Tokyo, I was told that I had to have a yellow fever shot before boarding the plane. I assured the people at the airport that I had taken care of this before I left Winnipeg and that my medical certificate indicated this. However, they contended that the doctor had forgotten to put in the date, and so I had to pay five dollars and get another yellow fever shot. In Tokyo I had a layover of two nights and a day to make connections with Canadian Pacific Airlines, and I used the opportunity for sightseeing. Also, I visited the Vernon Stobbies from Abbotsford, who had taught English in Tokyo for many years.

The flight across the Pacific was long and wearisome. I had been away from home for four-and-a-half months and had often been very lonely. I knew that Lena would be at the Vancouver airport to meet me, for my parents, in Clearbrook, were about to celebrate their Golden Wedding Anniversary and Lena had come from Winnipeg for this occasion. It was a great delight to see her again. We stayed at my parents' place for a few days and participated in the celebration of God's mercies in the many ups and downs of their fifty years of life together.

It was the middle of September and college had begun. Lena and I then took a flight to Winnipeg, and the next day I walked into class at MBBC.

23

Visiting Professor

A number of changes had taken place in the administration of the college over the years. After H.H. Janzen resigned in order to return to Europe, where he served the churches for many years, J.A. Toews became president and led the college for ten years. When he relinquished his post, J.H. Quiring accepted the presidency of the school. Just before we left for Montreal Victor Adrian had assumed the leadership of MBBC.

When I arrived home from India I was informed that a commission, appointed by the Canadian Conference, would be meeting in the next few days and that I was to prepare a brief on how I envisioned the future of the college. It was all a bit overwhelming. I had just come home from India after a long absence, was a week late for college, was trying to get in touch with my family once again, and now this unexpected happening. For the first time in many years at MBBC it appeared we had divided opinions on what kind of college MBBC was to be. I found this very unsettling.

Just before Christmas I received a call from the dean of the Canadian Theological College in Regina, Rex Boda, asking me to help them with their instructional program. They were about to establish a seminary division and needed faculty with doctorates. He suggested that I take a plane to Regina on Friday afternoons and offer two hours of lectures, stay over night, and offer two more hours on Saturday mornings and then fly back. The college in Regina offered to pay for the tickets on Air Canada. After Christmas, then, I commuted to Regina every week. The following year I was able to arrange things so that I needed to travel only every other week. I was glad to have a part in the training of ministers for the Christian and Missionary Alliance Church.

Also, in the course of the winter of 1970-71, I received an invitation from Dr. Jim Houston, Principal of Regent College, Vancouver, to teach in Regent's summer session. He asked me to teach two three-week courses in Greek exegesis and one three-week course in Synoptic Gospels. Before I could carry out that assignment, our Board of Missions and Services asked me to spend four weeks in Europe after the close of college in spring. I was to minister in our churches in Germany and Austria and for two weeks teach at the annual ministers' course at the European Bible Institute at the Bienenberg, Switzerland.

I left for Europe the day after college graduation, 1971. At the graduation I chatted with my old friend, Henry Redekopp, and he informed me that his wife had offered to pay Lena's ticket if she would go with me. At the moment that seemed out of the question for she did not even have a passport and we could not just leave our children and both go away for several weeks. However, I did have an extra application form for a passport and so Lena and I filled it out that night and agreed that whenever she got the passport she would come to meet me in Europe.

On the way to Europe I stopped in London to visit my former Yeotmal colleague, Arthur Cundall. Also, I spent some time sightseeing in London. Particularly significant for me was the London Museum with its manuscript collection. From London I flew to Frankfurt where I boarded an overnight train to Vienna. At the time the Mennonites had a small congregation that met at the Cottagegasse under the leadership of Helmut Funck. I stayed with the Funcks and gave Bible lectures both at the Cottagegasse and also in the home of the Abe Neufelds, whose apartment was crowded out Sunday by Sunday with visitors searching for God and his salvation.

After a week in Vienna I took the overnight Wienerwalzer to Basel, Switzerland, and then to Liestal, where together with Dr. Gruen, of the Baptist Seminary in Hamburg, I led in a two-week course for ministers and missionaries from Holland, Germany,

Switzerland and Austria. The first weekend at the Bienenberg a group of us decided to visit the Jura and look up some of the Mennonites in the French-speaking part of Switzerland.

Late one evening I was called to the telephone and Lena was on the line. She had just arrived in Basel and needed to be picked up. John Klassen, missionary in Lage at the time, was kind enough to take his VW and go with me to Basel to get her. After another week at the Bienenberg we travelled to Neuwied with a Viennese couple. Unfortunately we had an accident on the Autobahn and their new car was badly smashed up. However, none of us was hurt. At Neuwied Dr. Wieske and I served with messages at the European Mennonite Brethren Conference. From Neuwied, where we stayed with the Roland Marsches, we went to Neustadt-an-der-Weinstrasse, where the Mennonite Brethren Church had rented the facilities of the Methodist church for a four-day Bible conference.

We stayed at the Bayerischer Hof and enjoyed our fellowship with the Bachmaiers, the Gerhard Luthers and the Reuben Dirkses (Reuben was pastor at the time). The Luthers took us out one entire day to see Heidelberg and other historic sites in the area. After our assignment in Europe was completed we flew from Frankfurt to Amsterdam. Here we spent an enjoyable day, sightseeing and sailing along the canals of this ancient city. From Amsterdam our journey home took us to Brussels, where we boarded Sabena Airlines for our flight to Montreal, and then by Air Canada home to Winnipeg.

We hardly had time to get settled when we had to move on to Vancouver for our summer at Regent College. Grace had just finished grade 11 and Doreen grade 9 and they wanted to stay at my parents' place in Clearbrook and pick berries in the Fraser Valley. Doreen and her friend, Susan Klassen, finished school early and the two of them took the train to B.C. Grace came with us. Regent had rented Terry Winter's house for us (Dr. Winter and his family were away for the summer), which was located next to the Queen

Elizabeth Park. Often in the evenings we would climb the hill to see the flowers and feast our eyes on the beautiful city of Vancouver.

In the first three-week session at Regent I had a rather heavy teaching load--four hours every day. In the second term, when I taught only one subject, it was much easier. The association with students from all over the country and with visiting professors, such as Os Guiness and Bernard Ramm (who shared an office with me), as well as the resident faculty, was very enriching. All the visiting professors were expected to give one public lecture in the Vancouver area in the course of the summer and when I chose to give mine on "The Gifts of the Spirit," Dr. Houston was somewhat concerned, for he did not want to alienate people in the charismatic movement. To allay his fears I gave him my lecture to read in advance and he then apologized profusely for even having expressed concern.

The Fraserview Mennonite Brethren Church was without a pastor that summer and asked me to do a series of messages on Sunday mornings, which I was happy to do. We renewed our friendships with people in the church who were members of the church twenty-five years ago when I was a student at the University of British Columbia.

At the end of the summer we travelled home to Winnipeg together with Grace and Doreen. Grace came back somewhat unwillingly, for in the course of the summer she became involved with the Jesus People in Abbotsford and wanted to stay with them. That had, however, not been a good experience for her and she seemed to become progressively more indifferent to spiritual things--something that was a great burden to Lena and me.

Upon our return home we made preparations for the wedding of our son Ernest and his bride, Brenda Waighorn. The wedding took place at the end of August in the college chapel. John Regehr gave a message from God's Word and I performed the ceremony. Ernest had decided to take teacher training that year and we were glad to have them in Winnipeg for that year. After that we have always lived far away from them. Ernest taught school in Winkler for two years and then he and his family moved to Vancouver where he has taught school ever since.

In the meantime I had taken up correspondence with Myron Augsburger regarding a teaching position at Eastern Mennonite Seminary. They needed a New Testament professor and invited me to join their faculty. Dr. Augsburger, the president of Eastern Mennonite Seminary, and George Brunk, the Academic Dean, felt it was necessary for me to come to Harrisonburg so that we could get better acquainted before my appointment to the faculty was finalized. Since it was the practice at the Seminary to conduct a ministers' course annually in the month of January, they asked me to give several lectures on the Holy Spirit and to speak in the College's chapel hour. With some fear and trembling I took a flight to Harrisonburg where I was welcomed by George Brunk, who took me to his country home for the night. For the next few days I stayed closer to the college in the home of Dr. John Mumaw, President Emeritus of the college. In the midst of a busy schedule of meetings Dr. Brunk, who was an avid flyer, offered to show me Virginia from the air. We flew over the Blue Ridge Mountains all the way to Richmond and the Atlantic coast and back. The beauty of the Shenandoah valley was breathtaking. The lectures, given at the ministers' course, were later published by Herald Press under the title, *Encounter With the Holy Spirit,* edited by George Brunk.

We were about to begin our nineteenth year at MBBC and by then I had come to the conviction that it was time for a change. I had resigned as academic Dean and so in the fall of 1971 we made application to the United States consulate for a residence visa. At first it appeared as if this would be hard to obtain and we carried on endless correspondence. However, when the authorities discovered that I was an ordained minister, they advised me to begin all over again, for their was no quota for ministers. Myron Augsburger had to assure the American immigration authorities that they could not find anyone in the United States suitable to fill the position that I was to have. About the month of March we received notice that we could appear before the consul for our interview and from then on we had no more difficulties.

With that concern off our minds we had to tend to other things. We tried for some time to sell our house privately, but without success. Finally towards spring we engaged a real estate agent, and while I was in B.C., speaking at the graduation exercises of the Columbia Bible Institute, Lena called to say we had a buyer. House prices were depressed in 1972 and the man who bought our house re-sold it a few years later for three times the price.

At the end of the college year the Board of Higher Education had a special recognition banquet for Lena and me. We were given a plaque to remember our nineteen years of service to the college and a going-away present. It was hard to cut the ties that had bound us to MBBC for so long.

Before we moved out of our house at the end of June our daughter Marianne married Bob Worcester, an American student who had come to study at the University of Manitoba, and whom she had learned to know through her work at Pioneer Camps. Gordon Stewart, of Intervarsity, gave the message at the wedding and I performed the ceremony. Bob had just begun teaching Psychology at Vancouver City College, Langara Campus, and so after the wedding Bob and Marianne moved to Vancouver where they live to this day. With three weddings in two years our house seemed uncomfortably empty.

In the midst of the turmoil of obtaining visas, selling our house, speaking in British Columbia, the wedding of Bob and Marianne, moving Ernest and Brenda to Winkler, Grace graduating from high school and the birth of our first grandson, Jonathan Martens, I wrote a biography Of Dr. A.H. Unruh. The Board of Christian Literature of the General Conference had decided to publish a series of books on some of our denominational leaders of the past and asked me to do the one on Unruh. Fortunately we had the necessary materials for this project in our college library and the archives. I tried to follow a strict schedule of writing and by the time we were ready to move to Virginia I had the manuscript ready. It was published under the title *Stalwart for the Truth: The Life and Legacy of A.H. Unruh.*

We had to move out of our house at the end of June but did not plan to leave for Virginia until August. We sold a number of articles of furniture, gave some to Ernest and Brenda, and the rest we stored until August when we packed all of our belongings into a U-Haul truck. For the month of July we lived in one of the suites in Riverton Hall on the campus of MBBC.

Since we were not permitted to take a Canadian U-Haul into Virginia, I had to take a bus to Grand Forks, North Dakota, rent an American U-Haul and drive it to Winnipeg, load our belongings, and then drive it to the United States.

Raymond, our son-in-law who had married Eleanor two years earlier, had completed his medical studies at the University of Manitoba and they had applied for service abroad. MCC decided to loan them to the Eastern Board of Missions and Charities for service in Ethiopia. Before they left for Africa they were to spend a week or two in Akron, Pennsylvania, getting oriented. We gave them our car to drive to Virginia, and from there we would take them to Akron.

Before we left for the United States our extended family in Winnipeg together with some friends prepared a farewell supper for us in Kildonan Park. We probably never said so many farewells as in the summer of 1972. First we said goodbye to Ernest and Brenda when they moved to Winkler. Then we said farewell to Bob and Marianne who left for Vancouver after their wedding. Also we had to separate from Lena's parents and other family members in Winnipeg. Once Raymond and Eleanor were in Akron we parted with them. They left for a three-year term of service.

Our four-day trip to Virginia was uneventful but tiring. Lena and I with our youngest daughter, Doreen, rode in the cab of the truck. Grace wanted to stay in Winnipeg to the end of the summer and then come to Harrisonburg on the bus. We had made arrangements earlier to rent a small house from Dr. G.I. Lehman, my colleague at the seminary. He had built a new house on the lot next to his old house and for three years we rented his old house from him. One of our first tasks was to buy furniture, for we had not brought very much with us from Canada. We needed Virginia insurance for our car, but we could not get insurance without a Social Security number. After finally receiving Social Security cards we were told that before we could buy insurance we had to get Virginia license for our car. The Harrisonburg license bureau, however, would not sell us a license if we could not produce the bill of sale for our car (which we had not kept). Then we got word from Washington that Lena's fingerprints, made at the US consulate in Winnipeg, were not clear enough and would have to be redone. We were just not used to this kind of bureaucracy.

We had barely unloaded our U-Haul truck when a Mennonite pastor called to ask if he could come down and discuss with me the "headcovering" mentioned in 1 Corinthians 11. It was a sensitive issue among Mennonites in that part of the country and I had absolutely no desire to get involved in a hermeneutical controversy. I offered him my lecture notes on 1 Corinthians 11 and he seemed to be satisfied. Once seminary had begun, and I began to exegete 1 Corinthians, the students insisted that I have a debate with the College Dean (who held that women should always wear a headcovering at worship). The Dean invited all of us over to his house and set forth his case. I then gave my interpretation of 1 Corinthians 11, but before we could get into an argument someone turned on the television and Richard Nixon was telling the nation about his innocence in the Watergate debacle. The conversation quickly turned from headcovering to world politics and there were no winners or losers in the debate we were to have.

I was happy to be in the classroom at the beginning of September. Lena found that with fewer household duties, now that three of our children were gone, she had some extra time and so she worked part-time in the Senior Citizens Centre on the edge of the college campus. Grace enrolled at Eastern Mennonite College and Doreen at Eastern Mennonite High School. We joined the Parkview Mennonite Church as associate members, since we did not want to give up our membership in the Mennonite Brethren Church. The local congregation, however, treated us as full-fledged members and in our second year I was even asked to serve on the church council, to lead in Bible studies and occasionally to preach. We were so pleased when Doreen, shortly after we settled in Harrisonburg, renewed her commitment to Christ.

After our first year in Harrisonburg we made a trip back to Canada. I was still a member of the Board of Spiritual and Social Concerns, and so we wanted to attend the Canadian Conference which met at Three Hills in 1973. Also I had an invitation to speak at the Conference of Mennonites, meeting in Edmonton that summer. Grace had returned to Winnipeg right after her first year at Eastern Mennonite College and spent the summer in northern Manitoba doing an extension course in Indian Studies. Doreen came with us to Winnipeg and stayed with her friend Susan Klassen, hoping to be baptized in the Elmwood Mennonite Brethren Church. Lena and I drove to Hepburn, where we visited her sister Anna and her husband, George Geddert. From here we travelled to Alberta. I spoke first in Edmonton and then came to Three Hills. After the conference we drove up to La Glace to visit Lena's sister, Mary, then followed the highway from Dawson Creek to Williams Lake, where Lena's brother, Martin, was superintendent of schools. After a brief visit there we drove through the Fraser Canyon and on to Clearbrook where my parents now lived. When we returned to Winnipeg we found a very disappointed daughter. Doreen had gone to the pastor of Elmwood to ask for baptism but he had said it could not be done because she had to take a course which took eight weeks to give. Sometimes rules seem more important than people. Fortunately she did not become disenchanted and after moving to Fresno she was baptized in the Butler Mennonite Brethren Church.

We made our way to Harrisonburg, Virginia, to begin our second year of teaching at Eastern Mennonite Seminary.

24

Eastern Mennonite Seminary

The Shenandoah Valley is picture-book country. From our living room window we could always see the Blue Ridge Mountains. To the east of us lay the Allegheny ranges. Mennonites had settled here even before the Civil War and one of the churches in the valley celebrated its 150th year of existence when we were there.

Eastern Mennonite Seminary, where I taught for three years, is located on the campus of Eastern Mennonite College. Dr. Myron Augsburger was president of both college and seminary at the time. It was a privilege for me to work together with Myron and with the well-known evangelist, George Brunk, and others on the faculty. As the only Mennonite Brethren on the faculty I wondered at first how I would be accepted, but my fears were soon dispelled. We were received so kindly that Lena and I often thought the Virginia Mennonites had a special gift of making people feel welcome and appreciated.

During my first year at Eastern Mennonite I shared an office with Dr. Herman Reitz, with whom I got along very well. During that year the seminary expanded its facilities and after that I had an office to myself. Although I was asked to serve on the Administrative Committee of the seminary, my administrative duties were relatively few and so I could give myself to study, teaching and preaching.

Among the courses I was asked to teach were Greek Exegesis, Pauline Epistles, Hermeneutics, New Testament Introduction, the Book of Acts, and the Book of Revelation. The study of the Revelation worried me a bit, for I had heard that Dr. George Brunk was a staunch dispensationalist and might not take kindly to my classical pre-millennarian interpretation of the last book of the Bible. However, I was greatly comforted when Dean Brunk said to me one day, "David, I do not know what your views on Revelation are, but let your light shine!" He didn't realize at the time that he had taken a great load off my heart. Brunk's greater concern was that all faculty members have a high view of the inspiration of the Scriptures. The year before I joined the faculty, a professor with rather liberal views had been released, and I was asked to take over his subjects.

Before we moved to Virginia I had tried to inform myself to some extent on the views of the old Mennonite Church, for we were somewhat fearful that we would not fit into a community which had a rather different history from ours. Since I had read that the wearing of jewelry was a sensitive issue in the Mennonite Church, I always removed my wedding ring when I preached in the churches. However, we soon noticed that the majority of the people in the congregation in which we made our home wore more expensive jewelry than we could afford, and so we forgot about that subject.

Not only were we well received at the seminary, but also by the churches. On one occasion I was invited to lecture for a week, together with Dr. Don Jacobs, at the Keystone Bible Institute in Lancaster, Pennsylvania. I spoke on the parables on Jesus during the day and in the evenings I gave an interpretation of the book of Revelation. The lectures on the Revelation were televised and it was not exactly a comfortable situation to be under television lights and cameras for such long periods of time. On another occasion when the Mennonite Churches of Pennsylvania and Ohio had a conference, Don Jacobs and I were again privileged to work together in a lecture series. Many years later it was my joy to spend a week with Don Jacobs at the Bienenberg, Switzerland, where we led in a ministers' course.

During our first year at Eastern Mennonite our granddaughter, Jacquie, was born to Ernest and Brenda, who lived in Winkler, Manitoba at the time. We decided then that Lena should go to Manitoba and be with the children for a while. This was also the time in which the General Conference of Mennonite Brethren Churches was to convene in Reedley, California, and since I was on the Board of Reference and Counsel, I flew to the west coast and participated in the Board meetings and the conference. It was my privilege to write the resolution on the "charismatic" issue which our churches faced about that time. Also, upon my suggestion, the Board decided to revise our Conference practice with regard to non-immersed members who had been received into local churches, but who were not allowed at that time to transfer freely from one church to another. I was asked to write the resolution which was later accepted by the Conference that those who had been baptized on confession of faith by some other mode than immersion should not only be received into the Mennonite Brethren Church but should also have the privilege of transferring their membership freely from one church to the other. Fifteen years later I was again a member of the Board of Reference and Counsel and was asked to widen the 1972 resolution to the effect that ministers who had been baptized on confession of faith but who were baptized by another mode than immersion need not be re-baptized to serve as pastors in the Mennonite Brethren Church.

I flew home before the conference came to an end because of my teaching duties in Harrisonburg. In Los Angeles I boarded the midnight flight to Washington with the hope that I would be able to get a few hours of sleep before going back to class. Dr. Eshelman, our neighbour, had given me some sleeping pills that I could use for such overnight flights, and had the stewardess not roused me from my stupor when we landed at Dullas Airport, I would have flown on to New Jersey. I had parked my car on the airport's parking lot and after a three-hour drive by car I arrived in Harrisonburg ten minutes before my lecture.

The first Christmas we spent in Virginia we had the joy of having Ernest and Brenda with their two girls with us for the holidays. Ernest was completely taken in by the historic sites of Virginia and spent a good many days exploring the country. History was one of his favourite subjects. In the spring of our first year Bob and Marianne motored all the way from Vancouver to the east coast and paid us a visit. Together we made a short trip to Washington, D.C., and other places of interest. It was a joy to have two of our married children visit us during our first year in Harrisonburg. Ray and Eleanor wrote regularly from Ethiopia, but we did not see them for the three years they spend in that land.

Our Board of Missions and Services asked me to go to Europe once more and at the end of the seminary year I left for several weeks of ministry in our churches in Germany and Austria and to teach at the annual ministers' course at the Bienenberg. This time round I had the privilege of working together with Dr. Marlin Miller, later president of the Associated Mennonite Seminaries in Elkhart.

Upon my return we made a trip back to Canada during the month of July, and during the month of August I wrote a series of lessons on the Minor Prophets which were published by our Board of Christian Education for our church schools. Then it was time for the academic year to begin.

Eastern's year was divided into three semesters, with the Winter Semester divided into three sessions of three weeks each. This enabled pastors from the districts around Harrisonburg to continue their education. Since I had taught a rather full load all along, it was arranged so that I would have one of the three-week periods off. Our Board of Missions and Services had asked me to go to South America and to serve in ministers' retreats. I left immediately after Christmas, 1973, and spent two weeks in Paraguay. John Wall, who was then the pastor of the German-speaking Mennonite Church in Asuncion, picked me up at the airport and I spent a few delightful days with the Walls and in a ministry in Asuncion.

From Asuncion I flew to Fernheim, in the Chaco. It was frightfully hot at the beginning of January and I found the work in the churches very exhausting. In Fernheim I stayed in the home of the Erich Giesbrechts. Erich had been our student years ago at the

Mennonite Brethren Bible College in Winnipeg. He was now the pastor of the Mennonite Brethren Church in Fernheim. There in Fernheim I was also able to witness the marvellous work of God among the Lengua and Chulupi Indians. One of my friends, Jacob Franz, and his family had spent some twenty years in the Chaco, working among the Chulupi Indians, and it was quite overwhelming to see the fruits of his labours and of others who had worked with him.

From Fernheim we travelled to the Neuland Colony, where I stayed in the home of the leader of the Mennonite Brethren Church. Neuland was a colony carved out of the Chaco bush by Mennonite refugees from the Soviet Union following the Second World War. When I was there the colony was celebrating its 25th anniversary.

After several days of ministry here we drove back to Fernheim where I was to take the plane back to Asuncion and then to Curitiba, Brazil. Since the landing strip at Fernheim had no asphalt, the plane was delayed for some time because it had rained a bit. The result was that I missed my connection from Asuncion to Sao Paulo. I got to Sao Paulo on a Saturday evening. Next morning I was to speak in Curitiba, but I wasn't sure I would get there. In any case I had to spend the night in Sao Paulo. The taxi driver was to take me to a hotel close to the airport, but he took me all over the city so that in the end the taxi bill was higher than the cost of the room for the night. Next morning I was prepared to shell out another twenty American dollars to get back to the airport, but to my surprise I was there in a few minutes. Then I realized that the taxi driver the previous night had really taken me "for a ride."

We left Sao Paulo later than scheduled and when the plane finally landed, we were not in Curitiba but back in Sao Paulo. Curitiba was fogged in. The church at Joinville did without me that morning. I arrived in the afternoon and was welcomed into the home of the John Boldts, where I was to stay for three weeks. Ministers from Paraguay, Uruguay and Brazil had gathered for a three-week course of studies. All the lectures were in German and we followed three different streams: how our Bible came to us, hermeneutics, and an exegesis of 1 Corinthians. During the day we met in the Bible Institute and in the evenings in one of the churches. These were very heavy weeks for me and when I wasn't lecturing I was preparing. The first weekend I travelled to Witmarsum for a morning service. The second Saturday the ministers got together to drive to the coast and to swim in the warm Atlantic. As a boy I had been in many a lake, but this was my first experience of swimming in the ocean and I found it exhilarating. After five weeks of ministry I had to make my way back to Washington and Harrisonburg to the seminary classroom.

During that second year in Harrisonburg I was invited to lead in a Bible conference in the Fairview Mennonite Brethren Church in St. Catharines, Ontario, where Harvey Gossen was then the pastor. Harvey had been our student at MBBC and had a fine record of service in the church. We were all saddened when he passed away at a relatively early age.

Also, the executive of the United States Mennonite Brethren Conference asked me to visit the black churches in North Carolina and serve them with Bible messages. This was a new experience for me, but it proved to be quite enriching. I preached in Boone, Bushtown and Lenoir, and was kindly received by our churches there.

During that year it occurred to me that I should really put pressure on my aging father to write his memoirs. All of our relatives had stayed in Russia and, should my parents pass on, a great amount of interesting information about our past would be lost. To get my dad started on this project I wrote out about a hundred questions and asked him to answer them for me. As it turned out he soon forgot about my questions and wrote for weeks, filling up one notebook after another. He wrote in German Gothic script. When he was done he sent the material to me. After ordering it, I wrote it out in English and had about a hundred copies made under the title Pilgrims and Strangers. Although it was written for the immediate family, it has been read with considerable interest by others as well.

The Canadian Conference was to meet in Vancouver in the summer of 1974, and I had been asked to present a paper on "The Place of the Woman in the Church." This was becoming a sensitive issue and the Canadian Conference had never dealt with the subject formally before. Respondents to my paper were Henry H. Voth and Esther Wiens of the college faculty in Winnipeg. The paper was generally received well, although some felt I had given the sisters in our churches too much space. One of the women at the conference liked it so much she threatened to give me a kiss. Ironically, several years later when I wrote the resolution on this question for the General Conference that met in St. Catharines in 1981, in which I had expressed essentially what I had said in my earlier paper, I was charged by some with being restrictive.

In the meantime the Canadian Conference had gone on record as favouring a joint seminary program at Fresno, California. This meant not only that Canada would accept financial obligations, but that the faculty would also reflect the Canadian participation in this venture. We were asked, then, whether we would not join the faculty once the seminary had become a joint school. We found it hard to break with Eastern Mennonite Seminary, for our experience in Harrisonburg had been rather enjoyable. At the same time our loyalties to the Mennonite Brethren Church had remained strong, and so after weighing the matter for some time, we decided to move to Fresno after another year of teaching at Eastern.

Since I would be going to Vancouver in July for the study conference, I decided to come home via Fresno and to look for a house in Fresno. Aaron Warkentin helped me in locating a house in Butler Park and we let a seminary student live in it until the summer of 1975, when we moved to Fresno.

That fall Lena and I made a few short trips to places of historic interest, such as Williamsburg, Jamestown, Montecello and others.

Since we would be moving to the west coast in a year we decided also to make a trip to the Maritimes while we were still in the east. Together with Doreen we drove north to Ontario to visit Peter and Betty Hamm, in Hamilton. Peter, Lena's brother, was working on his doctorate at McMaster University at the time. Also, we visited our friends, Abe and Hertha Froese, in St. Catharines. They had just lost one of their sons through a tragic accident. The Froeses had been so helpful to us when we came to Toronto to study in 1952.

From the Niagara Peninsula we motored to Toronto and then to Montreal to visit some of the sites we knew so well from the days when I studied at McGill University. We crossed the St. Lawrence and motored east to the maritimes--provinces which we had never yet visited. We drove through New Brunswick, Prince Edward Island, Nova Scotia, and then back to the New England states on our way to Boston, New York, and home to Harrisonburg.

After my third year at Eastern Mennonite Seminary I made another trip to Europe to serve several of our churches and teach once again at the Bienenberg. This time I was teamed up with Dr. John Howard Yoder. I have always found my visits to the Bienenberg enjoyable.

The most exciting event in the spring of 1975 was the return of our children, Ray and Eleanor, from Ethiopia. Lena, Doreen and I drove to Dulles International Airport to meet them. When we entered the airport whom should we see first but our three-year old grandson, Jonathan, whom we had not seen since he was a baby. It was a joyous meeting and we were glad they could stay with us for a few days.

Since Lena and I were going to be driving a U-Haul across the continent from Virginia to California and didn't really want to take our old car with us to California (where one needs air conditioning) , we gave it to Ray and Eleanor to drive to Winnipeg where Ray had decided to enter a two-year residency in Pediatrics. Doreen had a job in Harrisonburg and wasn't really all that interested in moving again. She agreed to come to Fresno by bus at the end of August after we got settled there.

Several friends, among them Herb Swartz, who used to teach at MBBC and whom I had introduced to the faculty at Eastern Mennonite College, helped us load our U-Haul and so about the middle of June we made our way across the vast country of the United States.

25

Fresno, California

We arrived in Fresno on a hot afternoon. Since we had a house waiting for us we moved in immediately. Several seminary students helped us unload our truck. Henry H. Dick, president of the seminary, took us to Reedley the next day where we bought a good second-hand car with air conditioning.

After a few days some friends invited us to come to the Wednesday night meeting of the Butler Mennonite Brethren Church. We were told, however, that in Fresno one must be careful to keep everything under lock and key. We thought we had taken the needed precautions, but when we returned from church our back door stood open. Without giving it much thought we went to bed, commenting only on our carelessness. Next morning, however, I noticed that the board fence around our back yard was broken down at one place, and as I went to inspect it, I saw my new camera lying in the sand. Then it dawned on us that we had been burglarized. Someone had gone through the bathroom window and had opened the back door and the thieves had in fact made off with a lot of things. Among them were my electric typewriter, my tape recorder, which was a gift from the students of MBBC, and a host of other things. We had no theft-insurance and so we suffered considerable loss.

One evening I told Lena to keep her eyes on the garage for a few minutes while I drove to the library of Pacific College to pick up Doreen. (It was too dangerous for her to walk alone in the dark in our district.) I wasn't gone five minutes when thieves entered the garage and stole Doreen's ten-speed bike.

We had been in Fresno only for about a week when we left for Canada. The General Conference of Mennonite Brethren Churches was to convene in Winnipeg in July and since I was on the Board of Reference and Counsel we felt we should attend. We drove the 1,100 miles to Vancouver in two days and stayed for a few days with our children in Vancouver and our parents in Clearbrook.

The drive through the Canadian Rockies and the Prairies brought back many memories of the years when we lived in the western provinces. In Winnipeg we stayed with our children, Ray and Eleanor, who had just settled in an apartment at the Health Sciences Centre. Just as we walked into the door of their apartment the telephone rang. It was a long distance call from Fresno. The seminary student who had agreed to live in our house in Fresno called to say that he had gone out to preach on Sunday and when he returned the kitchen window had been removed and that we had been burglarized again. It gave us a sinking feeling, but it was something we would have to learn to live with. Several years later, after we had moved close to the seminary, we were burglarized once again.

The Conference in Winnipeg that summer formalized the agreement of the Canadian and the American Mennonite Brethren Churches to operate a joint seminary in Fresno, and I was able to participate in the formulation of the articles of agreement. Also the Board of Reference and Counsel had for some years worked on a revision of our Confession of Faith. It had been my privilege to have a part in the final stages of the revision and I was asked to read this revised Confession to the conference. The confession was well received. Some concern was expressed that we had no statement on the Millennium in our Confession, but since there had never been a statement on that subject in our earlier confessions, there was little interest in introducing it.

Lena's parents, who lived in Winnipeg, had arranged for a reunion of the Hamm family in the Okanagan Valley that summer, and so on our return to Fresno we stopped in Osooyos to meet Lena's brothers and sisters who lived in different parts of Canada.

From here we made our way via Vancouver to Fresno. Doreen came to Fresno by bus. She didn't enjoy her first few weeks in

Fresno at all, but once Pacific College opened and she made new friends she adjusted to the new situation and spent three enjoyable years at the college. We were delighted when she decided to follow the Lord in baptism. Christmas, 1978, she was married to one of our seminary students, Sam Myovich, a native of Fresno. This became an occasion for all our children to come to Fresno and we were glad to have the entire family together once more. By now Grace also had decided to come to Fresno and with transfer credit from Eastern Mennonite College she was able to complete her B.A. with an English major in one year. After graduating from Pacific College she decided to stay in Fresno and work. Several years later she took teacher training at the local university and began her teaching career in Los Angeles.

Doreen graduated a year later. She was valedictorian and we were proud of her accomplishments. After teaching for a year at the International Language Institute in Fresno, Doreen received a scholarship to go to Notre Dame University for her Masters in English. Sam decided to take his second year of seminary at the Associated Mennonite Biblical Seminaries and so they moved to Elkhart, Indiana. A year later they returned to Fresno, where Sam completed his M.Div. at our seminary.

After our first year at our seminary, the president, Henry Dick, and his family moved to Reedley, where Henry assumed the leadership of the Mennonite Brethren Church. They offered to sell their house to us and we never regretted buying it, for now we lived across the street from the seminary. This made it convenient for us to host many a visitor who came to the seminary for speaking engagements.

I found my classes at seminary quite enjoyable, although when I first came there I was asked to pick up courses which lay somewhat outside the field of my interest. However, as Dr. D. Edmond Hiebert slowly retired from teaching I took over some of his subjects. Since most of the students in our classes felt called either to the pastoral or teaching ministry, one always had the feeling that the information one passed on in class would be useful to them in the future and that made the work even more meaningful.

We made the Butler Mennonite Brethren Church our home church and from time to time I served the congregation in preaching and in the pastoral leadership committee. Lena worked three hours daily in the church's preschool.

To keep from getting stale I tried to do a lot of reading and also to enroll in summer sessions. One summer we drove up to the Vancouver School of Theology where I took in the lectures of Dr. Bowker, of Cambridge, and Dr. Minear, of Yale. It was also a good opportunity for us to visit our children, our parents and our brothers and sisters who lived in the Vancouver area. Another summer I took a course offered by Dr. Bruce Metzger, of Princeton, at New College, Berkeley. I returned to New College once again when Michael Green gave a weekend seminar on the Holy Spirit. In another summer I studied the Early Church under the famous Roman Catholic scholar, Dr. Raymond Brown. The course was offered at St. Mary's College, Moraga, California.

When we came to Fresno it was still a custom to exchange professors with other Mennonite seminaries during the inter-session in January. I was asked to teach a course in the Book of Acts at the Associated Mennonite Biblical Seminaries, Elkhart, during our first year in Fresno. It has always been an enriching experience for me to serve in schools that stand in somewhat different traditions from our own.

During our years in Fresno I was also frequently involved in study conferences of one sort or another. On one occasion I gave a paper on the Genesis record at a meeting of the Evangelical Theological Society, which met in Los Angeles. At another occasion I spoke to the Mennonite Mental Health Society, meeting in Anaheim, on the biblical view of homosexuality. At a study conference in Clearbrook I spoke once again on "The Place of the Woman in the Church." At another study conference which met in

Fresno I gave a paper on the meaning of "The Last Days."

Some time earlier I had written a series of articles in the Mennonite Brethren Herald on eschatology. The one on "Israel" created considerable controversy in the constituency. That became the occasion for writing a book on the subject of eschatology which was published in 1980 by Herald Press under the title, *And Then Comes the End.* The book was well received and was reprinted after the first 5000 copies were sold out. In 1987 a translation into Spanish was published by Herald Press.

The reception of the volume on eschatology gave me the courage to prepare other manuscripts for publication. That same year the seminary asked me to edit a book in which each faculty member contributed a chapter in the area of his discipline. The book was published by the Christian Press under the title, *Called to Teach.* Although we did not use the word, it was meant to be a *Festschrift* for Dr. D. Edmond Hiebert, Professor of New Testament. Also, David Wiens, speaker on the Russian Gospel Light Hour, which was produced in Winnipeg, asked me to write a booklet on the Holy Spirit. He had it translated into Russian and *Licht dem Osten,* Stuttgart, published it.

A number of years ago our churches had to come to terms with the charismatic movement and I was asked to prepare a paper on the "Baptism with the Spirit" for the study conference in Denver, Colorado. That was even before I had decided to do my doctoral dissertation on a related subject. Also, I wrote a series of articles in the Mennonite Brethren Herald on the Holy Spirit. All this (I can see it now in retrospect) was in preparation for the publication of a volume published by Herald Press in 1983, *The Holy Spirit in the New Testament.*

So far I had done most of my writing while teaching full time, but in the 1979-80 seminary year I was given two quarters off for study and research. I spent the fall quarter in preparing a volume on the history of the Bible. By Christmas the manuscript was ready

and when I attended the meetings of the Society of Biblical
Literature in San Francisco, Stanley Gundry, academic
book editor for Zondervan Publishing House, asked whether I
would care to submit the manuscript to Zondervan. I sent it in and
it was accepted for publication in 1983 under the title *From Ancient
Tablets to Modern Translations.* It went through several printings
and by 1992 had sold about 16,000 copies. That same year I was in
the process of writing a series of articles on 1 Corinthians for the
Mennonite Brethren Herald. When the series came to an end the
editor of the Board of Christian Literature asked whether the
Kindred Press had permission to print these chapters. The book
was published in 1987, under the title *The Church in a Pagan
Society.*

At the end of our first year of teaching in Fresno, I was asked
to go to Paraguay to teach in what was called the *Theologischer
Arbeiterkursus.* I left in June, the day after seminary graduation, and
flew to Miami, where I boarded a Varig airliner and flew to Sao
Paulo and then on to Asuncion. John Wall, who was then
missionary in Paraguay, once again picked me up at the airport and
took me to the home where I would be staying. Mr. and Mrs.
Wieler, a young couple from the Chaco, were to be my hosts for six
weeks. Willi Jantz, from Curitiba, Brazil, had also come to sit in on
the classes and he shared a bedroom with me. I lectured for three
hours every day and since I had to translate all my materials into
German, I worked hard. What made it even more difficult was the
cold. I left California in the heat of summer, and in Asuncion it was
now winter. The houses there were not heated and so I put on
almost all the clothes I had and sat at my desk preparing lectures.
Eventually I was provided with a
small propane stove which I placed next to my chair. I found it
rather strange when I was asked to speak at a harvest festival in
July.

The students in the classes were mature people and eager to

learn and it was a delight to teach them. In between I was asked to spend a long weekend in Fernheim and give a series of lectures on eschatology. Since I did not follow the rather more complicated system of John Darby, known as Dispensationalism, some people found my presentations overly simple. Evidently they expected me to deal with some exotic aspects of eschatology rather than to trace the major biblical themes.   After six weeks of teaching and preaching I left Asuncion very exhausted. Again it had been a time in which friendships were made and several couples came all the way to the airport to see me off.   I flew Braniff via Bolivia, Equador, Panama and Miami, and then across the country to Los Angeles and finally Fresno. Shortly after arriving home the fall quarter was about to begin.

I enjoyed ministering in churches during the years I taught at seminary. Some of the American Mennonite Brethren churches in which I served during those years when we lived in Fresno were Arleta, Bakersfield, Clovis, Dinuba, Lodi, Reedley, Kingsburg, Fig Garden, Visalia, Bethany, and El Camino. In Freemont, San Jose, Dalles (Oregon), Federal Way (Washington), Amarillo (Texas), and Fairview (Oklahoma), I had weekend Bible conferences.

A number of the Bible conferences in which I participated during our seven years in Fresno were in Canada, where I always felt more at home than in the American churches. In 1976 I was asked to participate in the annual Bible conference in Winnipeg when they celebrated the fiftieth anniversary of this conference. On another occasion I was invited to give a series of lectures on Christian ethics at a provincial conference that met in Saskatoon. Perhaps I was invited to speak on this topic because I had published a booklet in 1967 entitled *An Approach to Problems of Christian Ethics,* through the initiative taken by Harold Jantz, editor of the Mennonite Brethren Herald. On several occasions I was invited to minister in the Alberta churches: Vauxhall, Linden, Gem and Coaldale (the church of my youth). On one occasion I spoke at the Christian workers conference at Camp Evergreen and from there went to Red Deer, Alberta, to speak at the provincial convention of the Baptists.

After our second year at seminary we were invited to a retreat of the Mennonite Brethren ministers of the Central District of the USA, at a camp near the Peace Gardens, in North Dakota. Ken Reddig picked Lena and me up at the airport in Minot and we had a delightful time with the pastors from the various churches. Following the conference our son-in-law, Ray Martens, came to the camp to take us to Winnipeg, where we spent a few days with our children and grandchildren before we flew back to Fresno.

In 1980 Ray and Eleanor, who had earlier spent three years in Ethiopia, left for another term of service, this time to Tanzania. Before they left they paid us a visit in Fresno. By then we had lived in California for five years, but had not yet been to Disneyland, and so this became the occasion. It was fun taking our two grandsons on rides and to participate in their excitement. We were scared to death when suddenly our four-year old grandson, Matthew, was gone. We ran hither and yon but couldn't find the little man. Fortunately he had not lost his head but had gone to one of the servers at an outdoor restaurant, where we had eaten lunch, and told her his name and that he was lost. What a relief to find him among the many thousands that visit Disneyland every day!

26

Abroad

The leaders of the Tulpengasse Church in Vienna, Austria, had invited us to lead their ministers in a month-long study of a variety of Biblical subjects. The lectures were, of course, to be given in German and this meant endless hours of translating my English materials into German.

The seminary had granted me leave for the spring quarter, and so at the end of March, 1980, Lena and I took a KLM flight out of Los Angeles to Amsterdam, and from there to Vienna. Willi Giefing picked us up at the airport and took us to an apartment on the seventh floor of a building not too far from the famous Schoenbrun palace, which we visited on several occasions. In order to allow also those who had to work during the day to get in on the classes, it was agreed that we would have two hours of lectures from 4:00 to 6:00 PM, have a coffee break, and then follow that by another two hours of lectures. The attendance grew and it was a very worthwhile experience. On Sunday I was asked to preach at the Tulpengasse. We broke up the month into two two-week sessions. At the end of the first two weeks Lena and I boarded the Wienerwalzer which took us to Basel, Switzerland.

Here I was to give daily lectures at the Bible Institute, Bienenberg, until the school closed in May. Upon the request of the administration I lectured daily on the Book of Revelation. Also, I had been invited by Dr. Külling, Rector of the Freie Evangelische Theologische Akademie, Basel, to lecture on NT Theology and the Apocalypse. We lived at the Bienenberg and I arranged to have someone take me to the FETA for my lectures. The classes here were large. In the course on the Apocalypse I had over a hundred students. The FETA offers a five year seminary program of theological studies based on the completion of *Gymnasium*. The language of instruction is German. With classes at the Bienenberg and at Basel at the same time, my weeks were very full. Lena made herself useful by helping the ladies in the laundry and other departments of the Bienenberg.

On those days when I had classes both in the morning and the afternoon at the FETA, Dr. Külling always had me eat lunch with him and his wife and with any other visiting professors who happened to be lecturing that day. I never felt entirely at ease with the Rector because of his rather belligerent attitude to those with whom he disagreed. It struck me as exceedingly strange that we could never eat a meal in his dining room without listening to a lecture on the inerrancy of the Scriptures. Although I had no problem with confessing the Scripture's inerrancy, I had never found it very edifying to hear it defended so vociferously.

For some reason or other I had always had the impression that students in Europe were more respectful of their teachers than their North American counterparts. In this regard, however, I was disappointed. When something was said in the lecture that struck the students as new, some of them protested in a manner that I thought was quite outrageous. At the end of the term Dr. Külling asked me how it had gone, and when I told him that I was somewhat taken aback by the reaction of some of the students, he insisted that I give him the names. That was the last thing I wanted to do, for I already knew that a number of students, after five years of study, had not been allowed to write their final exams because of some disagreements. In fact five of them had come to Fresno to finish their seminary training there. Some of my Mennonite friends in Switzerland doubted that I would stay to the end of the term at the FETA, because other professors before me had not fared very well. In retrospect, however, I can say that it was a good experience.

The Tabor Seminary in Marburg, Germany, annually sponsors Easter Bible conferences, and I had been invited to be one of the speakers for the Easter weekend that year. Lena and I took the

train from Basel to Marburg. The train was so crowded that I had
to stand or sit in the hallway almost all the way to Marburg. The
director of the seminary, Mr. Hopp, received us very kindly and
since we had an hour before the evening meal he took us around
the city and pointed out the historic sites to us, among them the
famous castle where the Reformers had their debate over the Lord's
Supper, known as the Marburg Colloquy. For the next three days
we had meetings. About a thousand people, many of them young
people, had come from all over Germany, and it was an unusually
enriching event for us. Although the seminary stands in the
Lutheran tradition, it is pietistic in its orientation and it was
interesting to see how much we as Mennonite Brethren have in
common with Lutheran Pietists. We returned to Basel after Easter
to continue our teaching ministry at both the FETA and the
Bienenberg.

On one weekend Samuel Gerber, the rector of the Bienenberg,
and his wife took Lena and me for a day-long outing to Zürich,
where we looked up the old Anabaptist haunts. On another
weekend we had the pleasure of travelling to Geneva with Paul and
Heidi Hofer. Paul and Heidi spent two years at MBBC and Paul
has been for many years the leading minister of the Schänzle
Mennonite Church.

While at the Bienenberg the school arranged for a weekend
Bible conference for leaders from the Mennonite churches of
Switzerland, France and Germany. A delegation had come also
from the Mennonite Brethren Church in Frankental,
Germany--recent immigrants from the Soviet Union. Evidently they
had appreciated some of the emphases at this conference and asked
whether we would come to Frankental for a weekend of services.
Our schedule was very tight, but I felt I could not decline this
invitation to minister to these recent immigrants. They sent a car
all the way to Basel to pick Lena and me up and to take us to
Frankental, Germany, where we stayed in the home of Mr. Woelk,
a boyhood friend of J.B. Toews, Fresno.

The church met on Saturday and Sunday for lectures on the New Testament concept of the church. On Sunday morning I was taken aback a bit when the leading minister asked me to speak for a full hour, adding that he would follow that up with another sermon (ordinarily, he explained, they had three sermons). The entire Sunday morning service reminded me of the church services in Coaldale when I was a child. Fifty years in Canada had changed the nature of our worship services considerably; the worship services of those who had remained behind, however, had remained unchanged.

Following the weekend in Frankental the Bienenberg held its annual ministers' seminar for a week, and I was asked to lecture on the topic of Hermeneutics. My associate this year was Wilfred Becker from Hannover, whose subject was Counselling and Pastoral Care. Well over a hundred pastors and other Christian workers registered that year and we had a rather exciting time.

At the end of this course Lena and I took the train back to Vienna for another two weeks of instruction at the Tulpengasse church. Besides lecturing daily I served also in their midweek services. We kept one weekend open so that we could make a trip to Prague, Czechoslovakia. Special visas were required for this trip, but that did not create a problem for us. We were to be part of a tour group, but when we got on the bus that was to take us to Prague, we noticed that we were on a regular bus. However, we tried to make the best of our visit and, aside from the intolerable waste of time at the border, the trip went well and we could add another chapter to our experience.

After our services in the Tulpengasse church came to an end, Willi Giefing took us to Steyr, Austria for a day-long conference on the biblical concept of the church. The conference was under the leadership of Franz Ratmeier who later came to Fresno to study. On the evening of the same day we boarded an overnight train in Linz and made our way to Hannover and from there to Lage, where we stayed with the John Klassens and served in a short Bible conference in the Mennonite Brethren Church. We also ministered in the church in Bechterdissen and Bielefeld.

From here we took the train to Neuwied, where we had a service and spent the night with the J.J. Toewses. Next day we made our way to Neustadt-an-der-Weinstrasse, where again we had an evening service. The following day we returned to Vienna, where Dr. Fritz Lippert, a Christian judge and his wife, kindly received us as guests into their home for the night. The following day he took us to the airport where we boarded Jordanian Airlines for a three-week trip to the Near East.

I had been to Israel on a former occasion, but I had not been to Jordan and Syria, and so it was with great anticipation that we landed in Amman, Jordan. We took a hotel in the downtown area, not realizing that we were close to a minaret and so we were roused from our sleep every few hours by the call to prayer. Next day we hired a taxi and drove twenty-six miles north of Amman to the ancient city of Gerasa (Jerash) with its massive archaeological ruins. On our way back our Arab driver asked us who we were and when he discovered we were Mennonites he got very excited. He had learned English from the Mennonite Stolzfus sisters in Hebron. Also, he was so grateful to the Mennonites for having given them their irrigation system. If Allah willed, he said, we should have tea in their house that evening. Perhaps his wife hadn't willed, for in the evening he came to our hotel together with his brother, who had just graduated from Eastern Mennonite College, and so we had a lot to talk about.

Having befriended this Arab taxi driver he was eager to take us to Petra the next day. This famous capital of the Nabateans with its ruins of temples and houses is always a great tourist attraction. We arrived early, hired horses and guides, and rode into this rocky fortress through a narrow gorge which opens into a plain, surrounded by massive cliffs of red and variegated sandstone. I tried changing films in my camera while on horseback, but evidently I didn't get it right and found out later that none of the pictures I had taken had turned out.

The ancient city of Damascus was another attraction for us and so we decided to go by public transport. Crossing the border into Syria was a nightmare. We must have gone through at least ten checkpoints. After we were done with the red tape, we could soon see Mt. Hermon in the distance. Our hotel in Damascus left much to be desired, but we spent most of our time on the streets, anyway. We explored this fascinating city with its markets, its mosques and of course the "Street called Straight," of which Luke speaks in Acts. While in Damascus Lena developed stomach disorders which plagued her for the rest of our trip. After returning to Amman we got ready to leave for Israel.

To go to Israel from Jordan one has to get permission from the Ministry of the Interior. The manager of the taxi company which we had patronized offered to take us there and also to take us to the Israeli border. We had to go from one office to the next before we finally got our documents (the alternative was to fly to Cyprus and to enter Israel from there, but that was costly). Crossing the border into Israel took us four hours. Every piece of baggage had to be unpacked and checked. As we crossed the Allenby Bridge, we met an Australian archaeologist who advised us to go to the Jaffa Gate in Jerusalem. Here we could find information on tours of special interest to biblical scholars. We followed his instructions and also found very modest but adequate accommodations in a Franciscan guest house.

We began with a walking tour guided by an Armenian Christian scholar. He gave us more information than we could absorb in one day. Our next venture was to visit Massada, an old Herodian stronghold, taken by the Romans after a herculean effort in 73 CE. On the way there we passed by Qumran, where the famous Dead Sea Scrolls were found. On the return trip we stopped at Engedi--an oasis where David sought refuge from Saul. It was desperately hot in June and we stopped in Jericho for a cold drink. The manager of the café asked us who we were and when he heard that we were Mennonites he insisted that I tell Herb Swartz to write him a letter. (He thought Herb and Margaret Swartz, who used to be MCC directors in that area, were some of the finest people he had ever met.)

On Sunday in Jerusalem we attended an Anglican church service in the old part of the city and were impressed with its evangelical tone and emphasis. In the afternoon we did a tour of Bethlehem and its environs. By now we had contacted the director of MCC in Jerusalem, Mark Siemens, and we were happy to visit him and his family in their home. Mark took us on a tour next day to see some of the MCC projects in the Hebron region and, of course, the ancient city of Hebron itself.

One of the most meaningful trips was the one we made to Galilee, together with a Presbyterian missionary couple from Africa and our Arab Christian guide. We drove through the central plains, visited Kana, Nazareth, Tiberias, Capernaum, and other places. We circled around Lake Galilee on the Golan Heights and then crossed over to the western side where Lake Galilee empties into the Jordan. Once again we drove through Jericho on our way back to Jerusalem. Since I had seen the southern coast on a former visit we decided to do a tour of the northern coast as far as Haifa. On this occasion we had a Jewish guide whose information was mostly of a political nature (very different from our Christian Arab guides). A highlight of the tour to the coast was the visit of Caesarea Maritima--so important in the history of New Testament times.

By now we had covered most of the land and were ready to fly on to Greece. We had a round ticket back to Vienna and were to fly out of Amman via Beirut to Athens. However, we had no desire to go back to Amman, and so I tried to have our tickets changed so that we could fly out of Tel Aviv. An Israeli travel bureau informed us that this would cost us an extra $1,300. I couldn't believe what the man said, and so we decided to return to Amman. Fortunately we had kept the document which stated that we could return to Jordan, and the Israelis had not stamped our passports (only a loose leaf inserted into the passport) and so we had no trouble crossing the border.

We returned to the hotel in Amman where we had stayed earlier, and the following morning we flew to Athens on Swiss Airlines. From Athens we made several extensive tours of Corinth and the Mycenean Peninsula. Also we visited ancient Delphi and other important sites on the way there. One day was reserved for the Parthenon and Mars Hill. On the way we stopped at the Museum of Classical Antiquities. Since I had been in Athens before, we concentrated somewhat more on sites outside of Athens rather than those in the city.

From Athens we returned to Vienna where we had left most of our baggage. Dr. Fritz Lippert, who was on vacation in Germany at the time, had told us that we should spend the night in their apartment when we returned from the Near East. A medical student stayed in their apartment for the summer and she took us in for the night. Next morning we took a bus to the airport and soon we were on our way to Amsterdam, Los Angeles and finally Fresno. After three months away from home we were bone weary but rich in experiences.

27

Return to Canada

Having had my sabbatical, we settled in for what we expected would be another six-year stretch of seminary teaching. Before the fall semester began I flew to St. Catharines, Ontario, to attend the General Conference of Mennonite Brethren Churches. It was my twelfth consecutive year on the Board of Reference and Counsel and we had a number of resolutions to present to the Conference. I had been asked to write the resolutions on "Ordination," "Homosexuality," "The Gifts of Tongues," and "The Place of the Woman in the Church." These resolutions were accepted by the Conference except the one item in the resolution on ordination was referred back for further study (the Conference was not agreed that we should require re-baptism of candidates for the ministry who had been baptized upon their faith by some other mode.).

During the Conference I stayed with our old friends, Abe and Hertha Froese. Abe took me to Buffalo, New York, after the Conference, and from there I flew home to Fresno with an old friend, Dr. G.W. Peters. Shortly after returning home the 1981-82 seminary year began.

That fall our children, Sam and Doreen, whom God had given a baby boy in August, decided to go to Warsaw, Poland, to teach English under the auspices of MCC. They got their visas, but just before Christmas, Poland declared martial law and all visas were cancelled. However, they made new applications and by the end of January they were ready to leave for Akron, Pennsylvania, and then to Europe. It was initially to be a three-year term and we were somewhat saddened at their leaving, especially since little Samuel was then the only grandchild we had close by.

We decided to go to Vancouver for Christmas that year. My parents were on in years and Lena and I had not been at my home for Christmas for some 35 years, because we always lived far away. Also with two married children and several grandchildren in Vancouver we had every reason to go. Moreover, Sam and Doreen had decided to leave from Seattle for their MCC assignment, and so they too came to Vancouver.

We had an enjoyable time with our children, our parents, and our brothers and sisters in the Vancouver area that Christmas. On one occasion we arranged for a family gathering in the social hall of the Kennedy Heights Mennonite Brethren Church.

On New Year's day we left Vancouver to return to Fresno. It was raining hard and soon the rain turned to snow. As we travelled through Oregon the roads got heavier and heavier until we came to a road block. The police allowed no one to proceed unless they put on chains. It was pitch dark by now and I had never yet put chains on our car, although we carried a set in our trunk. So with flashlight in hand I lay in the snow under the car experimenting with putting on chains. On occasions like this my upbringing on the farm stood me in good stead. I had often been in circumstances as a lad where I had to be inventive and imaginative. We were finally permitted to proceed. Fortunately we had reserved a motel in Ashcroft in advance, otherwise we would have been without lodging, for no motorist dared to go south beyond Ashcroft in that kind of weather.

Next morning we had travelled but a short distance when a link in one of our chains broke and shortly thereafter a second link snapped. Fortunately there were mechanics parked along the highway at different places offering "chain" service for a price. We had our chains repaired and drove on into the Mt. Shasta region. Here in the High Sierras we encountered not only icy roads but a fierce blizzard that reduced visibility almost to zero. We slithered along following the red tail-lights of the car in front of us. It was awfully dangerous and when we saw cars lying in the ditches and gullies below we whispered prayers for protection.

Lena seemed to be in good humour and insisted we stop to take a picture. We just barely got back on to the highway. By noon we were able to remove the chains--a messy job, to say the least--and when we drove into Redding, we were greatly relieved to be on dry ground once again. Had we travelled north instead of south we would have had to spend the night on the highway, for the road north was blocked with thousands of cars returning home from the Rose Bowl parade in Los Angeles.

It was the first Sunday of 1982. Seminary classes were to begin next day. Lena and I were sitting in our family room and listening to the evening news, when the telephone rang. On the line was Dr. Abe Konrad, chairman of the Board of Higher Education of the Canadian Conference. He wanted to know whether I would consider talking with the Board about assuming the leadership of the Mennonite Brethren Bible College in Winnipeg. Dr. Henry Krahn, who had been president for eight years, had resigned. The call came like a bolt out of the blue, even though I had often had MBBC on my mind. We were glad that several of our seminary faculty, such as Drs. Howard Loewen and Allen Guenther, had formerly taught at MBBC. In fact the majority of the seminary faculty at the time had been either students or teachers at MBBC. So what could I say? Certainly I was willing to talk.

When I shared the call with Lena, she did not seem overly excited. She had enjoyed her years in Fresno. Besides, if we returned to Canada, it would mean leaving our one unmarried daughter, Grace, behind. Dr. Konrad had agreed to call back in a week to find out the direction of our thinking. When he called, I said that I would be willing to come to Winnipeg for an interview with faculty, students and members of the Board. Since the Council of Boards of the Canadian Conference met at the end of January, I was invited to come to Winnipeg for that occasion.

Before I flew to Winnipeg I thought I should let President Elmer Martens and Dean John Toews know about the purpose of my trip. They were quite uneasy about this development and assured me that they wanted me to stay on the seminary faculty.

The consultations in Winnipeg, however, led us to the conviction that we should return to Canada and take up the challenge of leading MBBC. Faculty and Board were unanimous in their request to have us come and so I called Lena from Winnipeg to let her know how things were shaping up. We agreed then to accept the call to MBBC. It was announced on Saturday at the Council of Boards meetings.

Before returning to Fresno, I visited Lena's parents, the Martin Hamms, in their apartment in Winnipeg. We had an enjoyable time, looking at slides (something father-in-law loved) and rejoicing at the prospect of returning to Winnipeg and being close to them in their old age. On Sunday I preached in the Elmwood Church where we had previously been members for twenty years, and then I returned to Fresno. The news of our decision to leave seminary did not sit well with my colleagues at first, but they were all gracious enough to accept it.

A week after I had returned to Fresno we got a long-distance telephone call from Betty Hamm, our sister-in-law, telling us that Lena's father had passed away. He had enjoyed good health for eighty-two years, and without suffering long he had died of a heart attack. The Institute for Church Ministries was in progress at Fresno at the time and I had lectures to give. Also, I carried a full class load, and so we agreed that Lena would go to the funeral without me. We were sorry our father would not be there when we moved back to Winnipeg.

At the end of April the Executive of the college was to meet and they asked Lena and me to come to Winnipeg once again. I was to speak to the students in chapel, attend a banquet with students and faculty, and participate in a program at which the outgoing President, Dr. Henry Krahn, and the Dean, Dr. James Pankratz, were to be recognized. The Krahns were going away for a year of study and the Pankratzes had accepted a three-year leave of absence to serve with MCC in Bangladesh. Also I had been asked to speak in the Sunday morning service of the Fort Garry

Mennonite Brethren Church.

We had the good fortune of finding a buyer for our house in Fresno almost immediately when it became known that we were going to leave. It was agreed, of course, that we would be allowed to stay in our house till the end of June. The visit to Winnipeg at the end of April gave us an opportunity to look around for a house and although we were rushed, we were able to purchase a house.

I taught a full load of courses that spring quarter at the seminary but often our thoughts were taken up with moving. My dad called from Clearbrook and told me not to drive a U-Haul truck across the country again, as I had done on former occasions. He was willing to pay the extra cost of a moving van. However, we had already discovered that a moving van cost more than twice as much as a U-Haul truck and so we decided once again to do our own loading and moving.

We loaded our U-Haul in the middle of June, 1982, hooked our car behind the truck, and started a five-day journey across the States and then north to Manitoba. We had an otherwise uneventful and rather tedious trip. The roar of the engine made conversation almost impossible. In Nebraska we had the misfortune that someone got into our car while we were parked by a rest-stop on the highway and stole the suitcases which contained Lena's clothes. We didn't notice this until we checked into our hotel in Omaha.

Since the house we had purchased in Winnipeg was vacant (the former owner had been transferred to Minneapolis), we were able to move in almost immediately upon arrival. Several college faculty members gave us a hand and before long we were comfortably situated in our home once again. All my life I had walked to school, but now we were too far from college and I had to get used to driving a car to college every day.

A week after our arrival in Winnipeg we were on our way to Three Hills, Alberta, for the annual meetings of the Canadian Conference. It was also my first opportunity to attend the College Board meetings, to lead in a few workshops in which I spelled out my vision for the college, and to give a short message at the Conference on the importance of Christian higher education.

The week after we returned from Three Hills our children, Ray and Eleanor, and their three children (we had not seen the youngest, who was born in Tanzania) returned to Winnipeg from Africa. It was a high point in our lives to welcome them. Ray had decided to join the Froese brothers in their clinic in North Kildonan and in a few days he was at work.

In the remaining weeks of July I tried to prepare for college opening. I had promised earlier to visit some of our churches in Europe once again and to teach at the ministers' course at the Bienenberg, Switzerland, in August. Since I was going to Europe anyway, I decided to go a week early to visit our children in Warsaw, Poland. At the beginning of August, then, I flew to Amsterdam and from there took Polish Airlines to Warsaw. Our children were at the airport when I arrived late in the evening, but it seemed as if I would never get through customs. Finally, however, we met.

Sam and Doreen with little Samuel lived in downtown Warsaw, on the 14th floor of an apartment building that left much to be desired. The view of the city on the Vistula, however, was breathtaking. During my stay in Warsaw we made several interesting trips to a variety of historic sites in Warsaw. Poland was still under martial law and soldiers patrolled the streets everywhere.

While in Warsaw I became acquainted with some of the Baptist leaders. In fact our son-in-law had arranged for me to speak a few words to the Baptist congregation in Warsaw on Wednesday night. Later several of the church leaders came to the apartment, and since they knew English, we were able to gain some valuable information on the Baptist church in Poland.

To my delight I discovered that Sam and Doreen would be going to Holland for the annual MCC retreat at the end of the week and so we arranged to travel together as far as Berlin. We took the train and that gave us a chance to see the Polish and East

German countryside. The security checks at the borders reminded us that we were not in the free West. We had several hours to wait in Berlin. My train for Salzburg, Austria, left at 9:00 in the evening; Sam and Doreen were to leave for Holland at midnight. It was hard to say farewell--even harder after seeing how and where they lived in Warsaw.

I travelled all night from Berlin to Munich and got very little sleep, sitting up in a smoke-filled coach. By noon I arrived in Salzburg where the Gerhard Jantzes received me kindly. Gerhard had arranged for meetings in both Salzburg and Lietzen. In Lietzen Gerhard and I slept on the floor in the attic of the house in which the church met.

After completing my assignment in Austria, I took the train to Basel. Lisel Widmer, secretary at the Bienenberg, was at the station to meet me. This was my fifth visit to the Bienenberg. On this occasion it was my privilege to lead in a ministers' seminar together with my good friend, Don Jacobs. Although Don had to speak by interpreter, he broke the ice quickly by explaining that to work with a translator was a bit like kissing one's wife through a window pane. The audience roared and he had their attention. I lectured on the doctrine of the Holy Spirit.

Again I was able to serve the Mennonite congregation near Basel, as I had done on former occasions. Daily I went for walks in the beautiful forest that surrounds the Bienenberg. My thoughts often wandered off to Winnipeg where new assignments awaited me. College was to open at the beginning of September and here I was in Switzerland.

After my last lecture I flew from Basel to London where I had to spend the night in order to make proper connections. Next morning I left Heathrow for Toronto and Winnipeg. All I remember from that long flight across the Atlantic was the showing of the film "Chariots of Fire," which I found quite moving.

28

College Administration

Upon my return from Europe at the end of August the faculty met for several days to plan the opening of the college year. The enrolment that year looked very promising. The Board, together with the faculty, had planned an inauguration service for us. Dr. Elmer Martens, Fresno, gave the address, our students and faculty provided the music, and I gave a short response in which I tried to spell out what I thought MBBC was all about. We received a great many letters from church leaders all over the country, wishing us well and promising their support. It was all quite overwhelming. I knew, of course, that it was the honeymoon period.

What I did not know when I returned to MBBC was that the college was involved in a self-study, designed to clarify its objectives and operational policies. With both the former president and dean gone, it was not all that easy to pick up this huge project in mid-stream. A time-table had been established by our Board and there were deadlines to meet. The faculty met every week to work through the goals, the administrative structures and a host of other matters.

It was my concern that the college work in close harmony with our churches. Also, I wanted MBBC to send clear signals to its constituency that we were there to prepare young people for life and service in the church, and so we tried to sharpen up our emphasis on missions and evangelism. Moreover, I hoped that MBBC would be a place where students could experience spiritual formation in a spirit of Christian love and discipline. Besides, I wanted our churches to know that our faculty was deeply committed to the Word of God and to our church's Confession of Faith.

After several revisions and after a visit to our campus of a team of external examiners, we presented our new Vision Statement to a group of twenty-five Conference leaders. From here we sent this statement to all the MB churches in Canada. Finally, in 1984, it was accepted by the Canadian Conference.

It was our Board's concern that the college be tied more closely to our supporting constituency, and I tried to do this by accepting as many preaching engagements as time and energy allowed. I visited numerous churches, attended provincial conferences, gave lectures here and there, spoke at harvest festivals, and tried by God's grace to be an ambassador of good will for the college. Our churches responded favourably to this approach and we received a lot of affirmation.

Another way in which we tried to strengthen the ties between college and church was by holding an annual Institute for Church Ministries on our campus. Upon our initiative, our Canadian Conference Board of Faith and Life declared itself willing to make this a joint-venture. Both college and constituency profited greatly from this Institute. Over the years we had some outstanding resource people who helped us grapple with subjects such as "The New Testament Concept of the Church," "The Mission of the Church," "Church Growth," "Marriage and Sexuality," "Hermeneutics and Proclamation," "The Holy Spirit in the Life and Work of the Church," and others.

When I left seminary in Fresno to become president of MBBC, I was chided for leaving the classroom to become a fund-raiser. However, I wanted to remain in the classroom, if at all possible. Fortunately our Campus Administrator, Harry Olfert, had the gift of collecting money for the college and carried much of the burden of balancing the budget year after year. So I was able to teach at least half-time and speak in college chapels regularly. In my opinion preaching is not being modelled sufficiently well in our colleges or at our seminary. The result is that students do not aspire to excel in proclamation. But that's what our churches are looking for.

I had no grandiose plans of building up the college campus when I accepted the leadership of MBBC. But with a good enrolment and good support from our churches we launched a building program. Our first step was to build a new dining hall, student centre, and Conference offices--all under one roof. Then we went on to rebuild two of our student residences, turning them into attractive structures with brick facing. Finally, in my sixth year in administration, a college gymnasium was built. Much of the credit again goes to our Campus Administrator.

These new facilities made it possible for the executives of the Board of Missions, Evangelism, Christian Education, Publications and Finance to be on our campus--people with whom college faculty and students could rub shoulders. Also, our facilities were soon greatly in demand by Christian organizations for conferences, banquets, retreats and so forth.

Administration, teaching and preaching did not leave me too much time for writing, but I was able to contribute a few items. Upon request I wrote a chapter for a *Festschrift* published in honour of my mentor at McGill University, Dr. George Johnston. Also I was invited to contribute a chapter to a projected *Festschrift* for Dr. Berkeley Mickelson, who had been one of my NT professors at Wheaton College. Upon the request of Dr. Bruce Metzger, Princeton, I contributed a lengthy article to the revised *Harper's Bible Dictionary* on ancient texts and versions. Also I wrote a commentary on the Thessalonian Epistles for The Evangelical Bible Commentary, published by Baker Book House.

During the summer months I participated in a variety of retreats and summer schools. In 1984 I taught a course at the Southwest Baptist Seminary in Vancouver, together with Dr. Roger Nicole of Gordon-Conwell Seminary. I was somewhat taken aback by the narrow dogmatism of several of the students, who somehow felt that when they heard something new it must be heresy. On another occasion I was invited to lecture at the summer session of the Baptist Seminary in Toronto. Students here had great difficulty with the warnings of Scripture, since the doctrine of eternal security was so central in the theology of the school.

On several occasions it was our privilege to lecture at the meetings of the Christian Medical Society. One summer we spent an entire week at Camp Oshkidee, in northern Saskatchewan, where the Society had its annual retreat. Then there were retreats at Camp Arnes, north of Winnipeg, at which we participated from time to time. On one occasion we motored to northern Manitoba to speak at the Christian workers' retreat at Camp Simonhouse.

One summer our mission board held its missionary training sessions on our college campus at which I lectured on the biblical basis of missions. On another occasion the Mennonite teachers, preparing to go to China, met for a retreat sponsored by MCC. Here I gave a series of talks on God's call to service. I also gave a few lectures at the meetings of Inter-Mennonite Council on Missions held in Minneapolis. The discussions between sessions at these various gatherings were often as profitable as the regular sessions and greatly enriched my own thinking.

Then there were the many Bible conferences in churches usually held Friday through Sunday. I recall with pleasure the conferences in St. Catharines, Kitchener, and Virgil in Ontario; Forest Grove, Regina, and Nutana in Saskatchewan; Coaldale, Calgary, and Gem in Alberta; Clearbrook, Willingdon, and Prince George in B.C. Frequently it was my privilege to have such conferences in non-Mennonite Brethren churches, particularly in Manitoba, where the EMC, EMMC, and GC churches often requested weekend Bible studies. It's a pity that the practice of having an annual Bible conference in the local church is slowly disappearing.

Then, too, there were the annual provincial conferences, ministers' and deacons' conferences, and the like, at which I had the opportunity to speak on biblical or related topics. Occasionally I flew to the United States for lecture series. Hillsboro requested a series on eschatology, the (Old) Mennonite Conference of Colorado requested a series on the Holy Spirit, and so it went.

On several occasions I travelled with our college choir, visiting churches in various provinces. Choir programs usually called for a message from the Word of God. In the summer of 1985 I flew to Germany for a Bible conference with the Aussiedler in Gummersbach, and then for a week of lectures at a ministers' retreat at Willingen. From here I flew to Basel for a week of lectures on Hermeneutics at the ministers' course held at the Bienenberg.

For eighteen years I served on the Board of Reference and Counsel of the General Conference of MB Churches. We planned study conferences on a variety of issues, formulated resolutions, and tended to numerous issues concerning our churches. I always found the bi-annual sessions of the board exhilarating, as we grappled with doctrinal and ethical issues. What was disappointing was that delegates at the conventions often accepted recommendations which individual churches (particularly larger churches) ignored, making some of our work an exercise in futility. Also, as the years went by it seemed to get harder and harder to get all of our churches to agree on some of the articles in our Confession of Faith. Seemingly the only way it was possible to maintain a semblance of unity was to go the way of compromise. This was due, in part, to the fact that many of our pastors received their basic theological training in non-Mennonite schools and did not fully understand our concept of the church.

Much of my work in churches and conferences was done over and above my administrative and teaching duties, but it helped me personally to stay close to the life of the church. The college was, after all, only a servant of the church, and it was my conviction that we could train our young people for service in the church only if the professors participated in the life of the church--which, of course, most of them did with great dedication.

And, talking about professors, MBBC was blessed from its beginning with some outstanding teachers, and it was our concern that this tradition be upheld. The strength of a school lies in its faculty. In a Christian college the faculty must be strong, not only

academically but also strong in the faith. Students
need to be guided in their Christian life and so it is important that
Christian teachers model for their students the way of discipleship.

Since, however, the college was also an academic institution
we wanted to have teachers on our staff who were well-trained in
their own disciplines. Academically, I believe, we were able to
maintain a high standard. Ten of our 15 faculty members had
earned doctorates in their field of teaching, and were well-versed in
the subjects they taught. Spiritual standards are harder to measure
and, in any case, must be worked at constantly. One of the
awkward aspects of leadership in Christian schools is that one
cannot avoid confrontations, which sometimes lead to growth, but
can also lead to the dismissal of faculty members--something always
rather painful.

It was the hope of our Board of Higher Education that a unified
system of Christian education be developed within our Canadian
Conference. Initially the plan was to have a tiered-structure, with
Christian high schools at one end of the spectrum and the seminary
(operated jointly with the U.S. Conference) on the other. The
many Bible institutes that were established in the past had been
reduced to three (not including the school in Quebec). These
schools, however, wanted to upgrade their programmes and become
colleges in their own right. Eventually Columbia Bible College,
Clearbrook (operated jointly by the Mennonite Brethren and
General Conference churches of B.C.), became the college of the
west coast, and MBBC (now Concord College) was supported by
churches in the other Canadian provinces.

As often happens when something new is undertaken, the old
is vilified. And so we who worked at MBBC, before it became
Concord College, had to endure a lot of name-calling. Constructive
criticism can be very helpful, but the abusive kind, in which
unwarranted and false accusations are made, don't help to build the
church.

One aspect of MBBC's programme that was often under attack

was our affiliation with the university. Many did not understand this arrangement and had forgotten that this association was worked out with the full endorsement of the Canadian Conference many years ago.

To begin with we were affiliated with Waterloo College (now Wilfred Laurier University). In 1969 we associated with the University of Winnipeg. The university placed no restrictions on our curriculum and in no way determined the spiritual emphasis at the college. Also, the president and dean of our college were invited to sit regularly on the University Senate.

For our students it meant that they could now cross-register most of their college subjects with the university and in this way earn their B.A., while studying under Christian professors at MBBC. Unfortunately some people interpreted this arrangement to mean that we were interested primarily in the academic advancement of the students, rather than in their spiritual formation and their training for church ministries and missions. God in his grace, however, called a great many of our graduates into church-related services. Many went on to seminary where, from my own observation, their training at MBBC stood them in good stead.

It was understood at MBBC that faculty members retired at age sixty-five, although they could be engaged as lecturers on an annual basis after that. I reached that age in December 1987, and so after a total of twenty-five years at MBBC, our work at the college came to an end in the spring of 1988.

That summer the Canadian Mennonite Brethren Conference was about to celebrate a century of life and witness. Winkler, Manitoba, where the first Mennonite Brethren church had been founded a hundred years ago, was chosen as the appropriate venue. This celebration would bring numerous guests to Manitoba and so the Board of Higher Education, without our knowledge, had planned a retirement festival for us, just prior to the conference.

I thought it rather strange that the Jubilee Auditorium should have been reserved for the occasion, since I couldn't believe that more than a sprinkling of friends would make the effort to attend such an occasion. However, we were totally overwhelmed when we saw a filled auditorium. Harry Heidebrecht, chairman of the Board of Higher Education, led the evening's programme. Former colleagues and friends spoke generous words of appreciation, laced with a bit of humour, and college students offered several beautiful numbers in song, under the direction of William Baerg. Our eldest daughter, Eleanor, gave an "inside" view of our family life, and I shared something of my spiritual pilgrimage with the audience.

Abe Dueck, Academic Dean, surprised us with a *Festschrift,* to which a dozen colleagues in the teaching ministry had contributed a chapter each. A scholarship was established in my name for students entering biblical studies. We received several lovely mementoes, and at the end of the programme all the guests were invited to a meal in the college dining hall. It was all done with such grace and generosity that our words of thanks and gratitude seemed utterly inadequate.

What made the evening even more special for us as a family was the fact that our four daughters had come from considerable distances for this event. (Our son and his family came later in the summer.)

There was no question in our minds that we wanted to continue to participate in the life of the church and to serve the Lord in the way that he enabled us. The college had asked us to stay on as lecturer, but from my observation, past principals don't always adjust too well in such a role, and so we chose not to stay at the college. Pastoral service was also an attractive option. Then, too, there were writing projects to be undertaken. However, the opportunity to serve abroad once more, seemed to have the greatest appeal at the time. Our children were all away from home and we were still in good health, and so we decided to begin our retirement years by going abroad. We now received our pension, which was quite adequate for us to live on, and so we decided that in the years to come we would serve churches and schools gratis.

Since we had children and grandchildren living in Vancouver and all of my family and most of Lena's family lived in the Fraser Valley, we decided to sell our house and furniture and settle in B.C. after our return from overseas.

Thirty-five years ago, after teaching in Bible schools for seven years, we were prepared to go abroad under our mission board. Then came the call to join the faculty of MBBC, which changed the course of our family's life. However, in spite of all the mistakes we must have made in those many years, we had no regrets. The work was challenging and rewarding right to the end. Moreover, I had had the privilege, during those years at MBBC, to serve in India, South America and, on a number of occasions, in Europe. Now we were bound for Africa.

29

Africa

Our teaching assignment during our first year after retirement was to be at the Nairobi Evangelical Graduate School of Theology, in Kenya. However, before we left, I flew to Toronto where I had promised earlier to teach in the inter-session of the Ontario Theological Seminary. Also, I completed a few writing projects, among which were eight articles for a *Dictionary of Christianity in America,* published by InterVarsity Press in 1990.

We left Winnipeg on a cold day in January and flew to London. Here we boarded Egypt Air for Cairo, where we had arranged for a three-day stopover to overcome jet-lag and adjust to a nine-hour difference in time. This gave us an opportunity to see Cairo with its many millions. Our hotel was actually located in Giza on one of the branches of the Nile, a city of five million.

Our travel agent in Winnipeg, John Schroeder, had arranged for a guide to show us the places of interest and so after a night of rest at the St.George's Hotel, we were off to see the Colossus of Rameses II, the Sphinx, the pyramids of Giza, the necropolis of Saqqara, the Papyrus Institute, the citadel built by Saladin who fought the Crusaders in the 12th century, and the mausoleum of Mohammed Ali, nineteenth-century viceroy of Egypt. Three days were hardly enough to visit even the most important sites of this ancient land.

It was Friday afternoon, and we were preparing to leave on Sudan Airlines for Khartoum and from there to Nairobi. Suddenly an Egyptian travel agent came to our hotel to inform us that Sudan Airlines had cancelled its flights. (In Africa people joke that Sudan Air flies only "if Allah wills.") Our agent, however, had arranged that we fly Egypt Air to Khartoum and from there Kenya Air was to take us to Nairobi. We thanked him for his help, but had no idea that we were getting ourselves into deep trouble.

We went to the airport in good time, but Egypt Air did not leave until two in the morning, and that meant we would miss our connection in Khartoum. We arrived in Khartoum early in the morning. Kenya Air had left by then and there would be no flights to Nairobi for the next few days. (The Sudan was actually a war zone, with Muslim Arabs in the north fighting Africans [mostly Christian] in the south.)

Immigration officials took our tickets and passports and shut us up in a waiting room. We hadn't slept a wink all night and were quite exhausted. Finally a representative of Egypt Air came to inform us that we had to fly back to Cairo, because there were no connections to Nairobi. That was a devastating blow, especially when they refused to return our passports and tickets and only said that they were in security.

About nine o'clock Saturday morning, when we were to arrive in Nairobi, we were back in Cairo. To our dismay we discovered, after waiting till two in the afternoon, that there would be no flights to Nairobi until Sunday night. Also, we were told to remain in the local airport till that time (all doors were locked and soldiers with automatic rifles guarded them). On the third floor was a primitive hotel where we could stay. They still had our documents. We felt a bit like Israel in Egyptian bondage. I tried phoning Nairobi to let the seminary know about our delay, but without success.

By Sunday afternoon I was getting seriously concerned about our documents and our baggage. What would we do in Nairobi if our bags with our clothes and necessary teaching materials were lost? Finally I went to the desk to press for information. From a pile of passports an official pulled out ours and took me to the other end of the airport where mounds of baggage lay stored up in long rows. But ours wasn't there. Perhaps it was outside, suggested the official. Sure enough, there lay our four bags with Khartoum stickers still on them. We removed these and put Nairobi tags on them. I felt much better after this, for now we knew that our passports and tickets were in the hands of Egypt Air.

Again we waited far into the night for our flight to Nairobi to depart, but finally we were airborne and arrived safely at our destination at 6:30 Monday morning.

Since we had never been at the Nairobi seminary before, we had no idea where to go. The school had sent a car to the airport three times hoping we would be on a flight from Egypt, but without success. So we asked a taxi driver to take us to the seminary, but he had no meter and charged us an exorbitant sum upon arrival on campus.

We were given a gracious welcome at the school and moved into an apartment which had the essentials for daily living. (We had no hot water, bathtub, spring-filled mattresses, sofas, or other such comforts which we take for granted in Canada.) To my great disappointment I discovered that my new typewriter had not survived the arduous journey and so for our entire stay in Africa I had to write everything by hand.

We lived in the midst of student families who came from different countries of Africa--Kenya, Tanzania, Uganda, Burundi, Ethiopia, Zaire, Liberia, Ghana, Madagascar. Most of the students were married and had children, and so we were constantly surrounded by children.

The teaching faculty included several visiting professors from America, England and Australia. We were the only ones from Canada and the only Mennonites. The school is inter-denominational. The principal and his wife were from Sierre Leone. There were also several Kenyans who had studied in America on the teaching staff. The language of instruction was English. A retired engineer and his wife from Germany, Hohneckers, were spending their retirement years constructing student and staff housing and (eventually) rebuilding all the seminary facilities.

The day after our arrival classes began and we were welcomed by the principal in the morning chapel period. Since Africans put great stock in family we were introduced as a couple that had five children and twelve grandchildren. Not much more was needed to be accepted in this African community. The classes went well. The students were college graduates and were preparing themselves for a variety of church ministries. They were eager to learn and dedicated to the work of God's kingdom. Teaching was a delight.

Since we had no car and the school was ten kilometres out of Nairobi, we were very much restricted to the campus. Fortunately several of our colleagues had vehicles and frequently offered to take us along. Nairobi has a comfortable climate year round because of its altitude, even though the equator passes through Kenya. The scenery is breathtaking. Beautiful flowers, tropical fruits and the purple-blue Ngong Hills in the background create a picture-book country. If only the malaria-carrying mosquito could be eradicated! Daily we went for walks along dusty roads of red earth--quite messy when it rains.

Our colleagues made us feel welcome and took us with them to various churches on Sundays, to mission establishments in different parts of the country, to the Rift Valley, to the game park and to other interesting places. One Sunday we travelled by train with two other couples to Lake Naivasha in the Rift Valley. During the break between semesters an Australian couple travelled with us by train to Mombasa, on the Indian Ocean, where we spent a few days sightseeing and holidaying.

MCC had asked us to go to Zambia for a week between semesters to give Bible expositions for church workers from the Brethren in Christ mission field and had booked us on Air Zambia. We had a lovely flight from Nairobi to Lusaka. In the distance we could see the snows of towering Mt. Kilimenjaro--a mountain our son-in-law, Raymond Martens, had climbed when he and his family served in medical missions in Tanzania. We were welcomed at the airport in Lusaka and taken to the MCC Guest House for the night. Next day we travelled all day by van to the Sikalonga Bible Institute where about 80 people had gathered for a four-day Bible conference. (The lectures were translated into Tonga.)

The spiritual fervour of these African church leaders, who live and work in great poverty, was quite overwhelming. We enjoyed the hospitality of two missionary women from America and that of Zambian Christians. Participating with me in the conference was Bishop Kipe from Pennsylvania. On our way back to Lusaka three soldiers asked for a ride, so we had them with us all the way. We regretted that we had not been able to see Victoria Falls, which were not too far away, but time did not permit. As we stopped on a street in Lusaka to let the soldiers off, a taxi bashed into the rear of our van. Its grill was smashed and the driver was furious. However, the soldiers told him to "lay off," for it was entirely his fault, and so we drove on. Once again we enjoyed a night in Lusaka--this time in Marion Buckwalter's apartment. Among other things we indulged in the "luxury" of a warm bath. The next morning a kind Zambian woman took us to the airport and we were on our way.

Back in Nairobi, the next semester was about to begin. I gave lectures in the Mennonite Church in Nairobi for the elders, and preached in the morning service (with translation into Swahili). Several times we met with MCC and Mennonite mission workers at the Mennonite Guest House in Nairobi. We were always impressed with the sacrificial service that these servants of God render in distant lands. Among them were the Willie Reimers from Winnipeg. Willie worked in relief efforts in war-torn Sudan.

Suddenly on May 29 I was called to the school telephone. MCC had just received a telex with the sad news that my father had died. He was 94 years of age and we had said our farewell to him when we last saw him in the Tabor Home in Clearbrook. It was our understanding that should the Lord call him home during our stay in East Africa we would not be able to attend the funeral. We sent a telegram to mother. The principal, Dr. Taylor-Pearce, also telexed mother condolences on behalf of the seminary. The community shared in our loss-- something Africans are better at than we. One student family after another came to pray with us. One family brought us four eggs as a gift. Our prayer group came to our apartment to mourn with us. Don and Emma Yoder, Mennonite missionaries in Nairobi, came to pray with us. Letters and cards of sympathy came from a number of friends and loved ones in Canada. To lose one's father is a wrenching experience. However, we were thankful for his godly life, his generosity in giving, and the Christian example he set for us. He is now with his Lord awaiting the great resurrection day.

I had been invited to lead a four-day Bible conference in the Mennonite Church in Mogadishu, Somalia. On June 14 I took Somalia Airlines for this city on the Indian Ocean. Although I had an entry permit, getting through customs was a nightmare. Finally, however, I emerged from the seething masses of people and was welcomed by Kevin Yoder, who took me to their house.

Mission work in this Muslim country is exceedingly difficult. Church buildings are not allowed; meeting in homes is dangerous. We had our meetings in the Roman Catholic Cathedral, which is looked upon as a kind of sacred enclosure even by Muslims. Abdullah, a member of the church, took me for a long walk and bus ride through the city. Yoders hadn't been out of the city for a long time and took me with them for a drive in the country--a rather barren and dreary part of this world. Because Friday is the Muslim holy day, the church had its main services on this day as well. On other days we met for two hours each evening.

When the time came for my departure it appeared I was not a confirmed passenger. It seemed I would be stuck in this unattractive place for a few extra day, for there were only two flights a week to Nairobi, and the planes are always crowded in these countries. As an answer to prayer it was discovered that a mistake had been made and I was on the list. Checking in took a good half day. The airport was hot and humid and very crowded and I was glad to return to the cooler air of Nairobi.

At the end of July our stay in Kenya was coming to an end.

The last days were filled with visits with students and colleagues. The year ended with elaborate graduation exercises. (Africans love to celebrate with colour and flare.) Our German friends, the Hohneckers, offered to take us to the airport, and after endless red tape we finally boarded British Airways for a direct all-night flight to London.

Heathrow was jammed with passengers and it took us all of three hours to check in for our flight to Toronto. Our daughter-in-law, Brenda, and two of her children, who were in Europe at the time, had come to the airport in London to meet us and so we had lunch together and a short visit and we were off for Canada.

After an all-day flight we landed in Toronto and were glad to be back on Canadian soil where there is more "breathing space." (The small country of Kenya has a population equal to this vast country of ours.) We were so worn out from travel that we chose to spend the night in Toronto before flying home to Winnipeg. Next day we were welcomed by Ray and Eleanor, our children in Winnipeg, and three of our grandchildren. We stayed with them for about two weeks. It was wonderful to meet so many friends who had prayed for us. On Sunday we were able to share a few things with the Elmwood congregation and proclaim the Word of God. With that, our first year following retirement came to an end. The next assignment was about to begin.

30

Europe

Before leaving for Europe we made a trip to the west coast. On the way we stopped for a weekend in Kelowna, where Lena's brothers and sisters (the Hamms) met for a family reunion. From here we left for the Fraser Valley to celebrate my mother's 89th birthday. She was still grieving from the loss of her husband, our father. In Vancouver we visited our two children and our grandchildren. Some sixteen years ago they left Winnipeg to teach in Vancouver and we had been far away from them during these years.

Also, we made a downpayment on a condominium that was to be built in the coming year, in Abbotsford, so that we would have a place to stay upon our return from Europe. Although we had signed a contract for a fixed price, we were unpleasantly surprised when in the course of the year, after prices had risen dramatically, the people in charge threatened to sell the unit to someone else at a good profit. However, since we had met all of our commitments this did not happen. So much for business ethics!

After returning to Winnipeg we had only a few days to get ready to leave for Switzerland. I had promised to teach for a year at the European Mennonite Bible School, known as the Bienenberg, not too far from Basel. This school was established after the Second World War with the help of MCC and European Mennonites. Cornelius Wall, who together with his wife had spent many years working with refugees after the war, led in the establishment of this school. I had been at this school on at least six former occasions for ministers' courses, so we had a good idea of where we were going.

In Toronto we had to get a work permit from the Swiss embassy, and so on August 31 we boarded Swiss Air to fly across the Atlantic on our way to Zürich. Here we transferred for a flight to Basel, where Helmut Doerksen welcomed us. It didn't take long for us to settle into a small basement apartment of two rooms and a bath, known as the Waldhüsli.

After registering with the police, getting a chest X-ray, and opening a bank account, we settled into the routine of school life. I lectured on Genesis, the Revelation and, in the evening school, the Gospel of Mark. Because all my materials were in English and because I hadn't taught Old Testament for twenty years, I had to write or type new notes for all my classes.

The average age of the students was twenty-five. They came from very diverse backgrounds as far as training and experience was concerned. There is both a French and a German stream in the program of studies. I taught only in the German section. Besides Mennonite students from France, Germany and Switzerland, many came from state churches. This always led to questions when such matters as the concept of the church, or of baptism, came up for discussion.

Students were divided into small groups with faculty members in each of the groups. These groups met weekly for prayer, discussion or play. Tuesday nights the entire school family met for prayers. The faculty met for prayer and consultation every morning at 7:45. Classes began at 8:15. On Thursdays the entire staff met for coffee and a time of sharing.

When we were not otherwise engaged we regularly attended the Schänzli Mennonite Church, near Basel, where Paul Hofer, a graduate of MBBC, Winnipeg, was the pastor for many years. Paul and Heidi are known for their hospitality, which we also enjoyed.

Repeatedly they invited us to their home, and shortly after school began they took us to the Thuner See, where Hans Kasdorf, a good friend from MBBS, Fresno, was giving lectures on missions. The Helmut Doerksens also showed us great hospitality and took us to church regularly in their van and on several occasions we made short forays with them into the beautiful Swiss countryside.

Occasional visits from Canadian or American friends helped to break the tedium of the daily grind.

Before accepting the invitation to teach at the Bienenberg, I had promised to speak at the annual meeting of evangelical church leaders in Austria, and so on October 31 Lena and I took the train to Spital am Perm--a day's travel from Basel. About 175 church leaders and missionaries from various denominations had gathered for five days to grapple with the subject of Hermeneutics. It's a topic that can be rather divisive, since most church bodies are confident that they have understood the Scriptures correctly. Dr. Fritz Lippert, a judge from Vienna, chaired the meetings and set a good tone for the lectures and the intense questioning that was part of the conference. Besides giving three hours of lectures every day, we usually had an hour or two for questions. But the questioning continued even during meals and sometimes I quite literally had to escape to my room in the hotel, where all of us stayed, in order to catch my breath.

After an exhausting but exhilarating week we returned to Switzerland and to the classroom. The following weekend I had a series of Bible messages in the Schänzli Mennonite congregation.

December 19 marked the close of the fall semester, and so Lena and I took the train the following day and went to Paris. We got there shortly before lunch, learned how to ride the Metro, and began visiting places of interest. We began at the *Arc de Triumph*, walked along the *Champs Elysees*, and looked at ancient palaces. We had a hotel reservation, and after a night's rest we joined a guided tour that concentrated on the Louvre and the famous Notre Dame cathedral. On our own once again we walked to the Eiffel Tower, and upon Lena's insistence we took the elevators right to the top. That gave us a magnificent view of this historic metropolis. On our last morning we decided to walk the 700 steps leading up to the *Sacre Coeur* Church, and then made our way to the train station. Because of a mix-up in the reservations I had to stand in the aisle of our train car for a long time. When I finally got a seat it was over against an eight-year old boy, who did not particularly contribute to the peace of our compartment. We got back in time for Christmas which we spent with Helmut and Lydia Doerksen and their family.

On December 28 Walter and Christine Hofer took us for an all-day trip to Interlaken. Here we boarded a cog-wheel train, called the *Jungfrau* Railway, for the top of the mountain, from where one has breath-taking views of a number of mountain peaks. On December 30 Hans-Rudi and Irma, who lived on the floor above us and who are in charge of maintenance at the Bienenberg, took us to Berne, the capital of Switzerland. We had been there before, but now we had time to visit the city museum, the parliament buildings, and other sites of interest. For supper we drove to the Emmental, where Hans-Rudi's aging parents live. Although such trips were tiring, they were quite enjoyable.

Shortly after the second semester began, I travelled by train to Karlsruhe, Germany. A conference of Mennonite church leaders from southern Germany took place at the Thomashof and I had been asked to give six lectures on biblical subjects during a four-day gathering. Paul Hofer came up for the last day and I had an enjoyable trip home with him.

In February, Claude and Elizabeth Beecher took us, together with their family of four children, to Strasbourg on a weekend. Claude taught in the French division at the Bienenberg and was working on his doctorate at Strasbourg. We visited points of interest in this historic city, spent the night at Claude's brother's place, and drove back to Basel on Sunday afternoon, with a stop for coffee at Claude's parents in Mulhouse.

At the beginning of March we drove back and forth to the Mennonite Church at Birkenhoff in the Alsace three times. I had been asked to serve with Bible messages Friday through Sunday. Max Widmer, who had been a student at MBBC, had taken us to the Alsace on an earlier occasion and he faithfully chauffeured us on this weekend as well.

Classes are cancelled for a time at the Bienenberg in March in order to give the students an opportunity to do practical work in the churches. We made use of this lull to teach church leaders in Germany who had come from the Soviet Union. The Logos Mission had arranged for an intensive course in the book of Revelation at a retreat centre, in Willingen. Lena and I travelled to Bielefeld by train, and on Sunday I preached in one of the Mennonite Brethren churches in that city. In the afternoon we were taken to Willingen where we got acquainted with the students who had registered for the course. Most of those in attendance had been strongly influenced by the teachings of John Darby (although they had never heard of him), and several of those in attendance were rather taken aback to discover a non-dispensational interpretation of the last book of the Bible. However, the week went very well and on Saturday afternoon we returned to Bielefeld.

For supper we were invited to the home of Willie and Neta Peters. Neta is a cousin of mine. When the German armies invaded the Ukraine in World War II, they became separated and Neta, who came to Paraguay and then to Canada, did not see her husband for thirty-five years. More recently he came out of the Soviet Union and they are now together again. She had also invited Hans and Neta Neufeld, who had just recently come from the Soviet Union. Hans is a son of my father's sister. I had never seen this cousin of mine, who was eleven years old when we left for Canada in 1926 and who, as he told us, had been on the wagon when we were taken to the railway station. His life seems to have been one long tragedy: digging trenches for the Soviet army, later being inducted into the German army, being captured by the Americans, and then emigrating to Paraguay. In Paraguay he discovered that his family was in Siberia, and so he returned to the Soviet Union. After 17 years of separation he finally found his family again. That could have been my story--but for the inexplicable grace of God.

A few weeks later Lena and I were on our way to Germany

once again.   This time we travelled to Neuwied, where I had promised to give messages Thursday through Sunday.   Daniel Geiser, the pastor, took me to the train station at Coblenz on Sunday afternoon and I returned to Basel.   Lena travelled with Catherine Jantz to Gummersbach, where she wanted to visit relatives who had recently come out of Soviet Union.   (We had enjoyed the hospitality of MCC workers, Hugo and Catherine Jantz during our days in Neuwied.)

In April the Mennonite Brethren Church leaders and missionaries of Germany and Austria met for four days at the Thomashof and so Lena and I made our way there once again.   I had been asked to give several lectures.   It was a joy to meet so many friends and even former students who are now serving in Germany and Austria.

On Easter Sunday I preached once more in the Schänzli church and the following week the academic year at the Bienenberg came to an end.   I could not stay for the graduation exercises because I had committed myself to a ministry in the Soviet Union beginning May 3.   The Logos Mission had asked me to teach Russian Baptist church leaders, none of whom had had the opportunity to attend Bible school.   My tickets and my visa arrived on the last day of class and the following day I flew to West Berlin.   From here I took a taxi to the Tegel Airport and spent a night in a hotel in East Berlin. Next morning I took Aeroflot to Moscow.   Here I had to transfer to a different airport in order to fly to Riga, where I was to teach for one week.

Victor Reimer was to meet me at the airport in Riga and be my translator.   To my dismay there was no one at the airport to meet me.   I waited for a long time, hoping someone would come to pick me up, but in vain.   Finally I took a taxi to Hotel Latvia.   Because I didn't have a reservation they did not want me, but when I was willing to pay in dollars they allowed me to stay for one night.

No one knew where I was and I knew nobody in Riga.   I had the name of a Baptist pastor scribbled on a piece of paper and I had a telephone number (not his). Before I went to bed I called the number. A Russian-speaking woman answered. She knew no German or English so I simply said my name, Hotel Latvia, and the name of the pastor. With prayer I went to bed, thinking that I might have to return home next day. But before I fell asleep there was a knock at my door--there stood the pastor, Alexander Krupcheck, with a translator. The woman I had called was a member of his church and had alerted him to where I was. Students had come both from Lithuania and Latvia for the course and would have had to return had we not gotten together.

The next morning we drove to a retreat centre outside of Riga and here we studied, ate, prayed and went for walks together. However, unless a translator was present, we could only look at each other.

It was hard to find translators, and in the seven days of classes I had five different translators. They came from Riga for the day and then went home when classes were over and so both I and the students forfeited wonderful opportunities for dialogue and conversation.

The students were eager to learn and asked a great many questions. The facilities and the food left much to be desired, but this was overshadowed by the spirit of devotion to Christ and his kingdom on the part of the students. In the end they gave me a gift by which to remember them and then sang "Near the Cross" for me in Russian. Before we parted they asked me to bless them and with that the first week came to an end.

I was hesitant to continue my travels because Victor Reimer had not come, but Pastor Krupchek insisted that I fly to Krasnodar, where I was scheduled to have another week of classes. At 4:00 on Saturday morning he took me to the Riga airport for my return to Moscow. Here I had to change airports again and that always meant haggling with taxi drivers over the cost of the fare. I had to wait until later in the day before my plane left for Krasnodar--a large city on the Kuban River, in the Caucasus.

After a two-hour flight we arrived safely and I was greeted at the airport by a Baptist pastor, Michael Sibor. Unfortunately, without a translator we just looked at each other. With him was a young man who took us through the city at break-neck speed. I had no idea where we were going or why the rush. Suddenly we stopped before a church building and a man who knew German came out to welcome me. Russian Baptists have church services on Saturday evenings as well as on Sundays. It was eight o'clock in the evening by now and I was asked to come in and speak to the congregation. I explained that I had been on the way for sixteen hours and that I was totally exhausted. By then people began to leave, for the service was over and so I was spared.

Pastor Sibor and his wife, together with several others, including the German-speaking translator, all went to Vladimir's house, where I was to spend the next two nights. Vladimir and his wife had six children. I was given a room with a bed, but the room was scarcely big enough to accommodate me and my travel bag. I had had next to nothing to eat all day (one doesn't get meals on Soviet planes inland), and it wasn't until 10:00 that we had supper. Then I discovered that the pastor and his wife were also staying for the night. I didn't know where everyone would sleep, but I found out early next morning when I searched for the washroom. As I opened the door of my room I saw Michael and his wife sleeping on a couch. I slipped quietly into the next room and there lay Vladimir and his wife. Where all the children slept, I do not know.

There was no sink, no mirror, and no hot water, so I finally found a tap that yielded some cold water and tried to shave as best I could. I was to preach that morning, and my translator came for breakfast and went with us to church. There were four sermons altogether. With choirs, solos, recitations and testimonies the service lasted at least two-and-a-half hours. A woman who knew German got up in the audience and sang a song for me. At the close of the service I was asked to answer several questions.

I had been asked to speak in the evening service again but after lunch the pastor asked if I would be willing to answer questions all evening. What I didn't notice was that only the elders asked questions. Later I was told that the young people are afraid to ask questions lest they be disciplined. When the evening service was over and we were back at Vladimir's house, the pastor asked if he might invite the young people to the house so that they could also ask their questions. How he let them know, I never found out, but after a nine o'clock supper they arrived. Their questions were much more relevant than many of the questions that had been asked in church. I didn't want to be dragged into controversial issues, but one which I couldn't avoid was the question of the head-covering for women. I gave them my understanding of 1 Corinthians 11, and it seemed to me that they agreed that people living in other cultures need not imitate first-century dress. It had been a long day.

On Monday morning I was taken to the pastor's house, where I was to stay for the rest of the week. Classes started that day and students had come from as far as 1000 kilometres. We met in a large private home, where all thirty students and I also had our daily noon meal. (I ate breakfast and supper at the pastor's house.) A young girl who was studying English and French at the Kuban University translated for me the first day. She was a member of a Baptist church and was somewhat troubled, for she had been seen wearing slacks, and that was a serious offence in the eyes of church elders. Now that the church is free, young people are seeking higher education and the elders, many of whom suffered imprisonment for their faith, don't know how to handle these new freedoms. Nina asked many questions after the lectures were over.

Next day a young man, Sasha, who had travelled all night from Kiev, was my translator. One day, after several hours of class, a group of American churchmen suddenly arrived and asked whether they could speak to the class. Well, they took the rest of the day, including the evening. They filmed everything and would no doubt give glowing reports back home. Toward the end of the week Victor Reimer arrived. Evidently he had not received his visa in time. He now took over as translator and taught some classes himself.

Saturday was to be the last day of classes and I was to leave early Sunday morning. Victor encouraged me to come with him to Maikop, 150 kilometres away, to attend a wedding on Saturday night. It was a bad mistake, for I didn't get back till 1:00 AM and at 5:00 AM I had to leave for the airport.

The flight back to Moscow was uneventful. As we flew over the Ukraine I had to think of my birthplace and of our forebears who had at one time lived in prosperous colonies, but had lost their lives in the Stalin era. By contrast, I was a free man and had enjoyed the undeserved good things of life.

For the third time I had to switch airports in Moscow in order to fly back to Berlin. Fortunately this time I left from the international airport where things are done in more or less standard fashion. Late in the afternoon we arrived in East Berlin. Once again I had to pay for a visa to cross to the West (something that is now a thing of the past) where I booked into a hotel and enjoyed the luxury of a hot bath. Next day I flew to Basel and home to the Bienenberg.

We were getting ready to wrap up our year in Europe. However, I had promised to lecture at a church workers' course that met the last week of May. Just prior to that I spoke at Max and Astrid Widmer's wedding in France. It was a twelve-hour marathon and we returned at two in the morning.

On June 2 Bernhard Ott of the Bienenberg took us to the Basel airport from where we flew home via Zürich. I felt so depleted after all this that I suffered from exhaustion that first week in Winnipeg in the home of our children.

We now faced the move from Winnipeg to Abbotsford. I had rented a Ryder truck onto which we loaded all our belongings and set out for the west coast. When we came to the B.C. border we were told that the Trans-Canada was closed because of mud-slides and that we would have to make a long detour through Cranbrook, adding considerably to the length of our trip. Finally, however, we did arrive in Abbotsford and with the help of our children, who had come from Vancouver, we moved into our new condominium on Trafalgar Street. The next few weeks were spent in purchasing appliances and furniture and just getting settled. On Sundays we visited different churches in the area to get to know them. At the end of July we flew back to Winnipeg for a week to attend the Mennonite World Conference. After purchasing a car and packing the necessary things, we made our way to Fresno, where I had been asked to serve as visiting professor of New Testament.

31

Three-score Years and Ten

We had left Fresno in 1982 to assume the leadership of our college in Winnipeg. It never crossed our mind that we would some day return to Fresno. However, Tim Geddert, Professor of New Testament at our seminary (and our nephew), was taking a three-year leave of absence with his family to minister in Germany. As a result, we were asked to return to the seminary and to fill in for him. The seminary assumed responsibility for finding an apartment for us. We took only what could get into our car and by mid-August we made our way south. Seminary classes did not begin until September, but since we had been away for eight years, we chose to come early and to share in the annual faculty retreat.

On our way back from the Mennonite World Conference in Winnipeg, Lena, who had always enjoyed good health, developed severe back pains. They became even more severe after we arrived in Fresno. Eventually we discovered that she had a severe case of osteoporosis. Besides causing her much pain, her bodily posture was severely affected. Medications gave her some relief, but we had to accept this disability as something she would probably have to live with.

Before classes began, our daughter Grace from Long Beach, and our youngest daughter Doreen and her two boys, came to visit us. Doreen, with her husband and children, were about to leave for Cracow, Poland, where Sam, our son-in-law, was to do research for his doctoral dissertation in East-European Studies.

Since we had been away from Fresno so long, and most of the students were new to me (except former MBBC students), I began my classes with some trepidation. However, once we got into the stream of things, it went quite well.

The General Conference of Mennonite Brethren Churches had

its meetings in Kansas in November 1990, and because I was still a member of the Board of Reference and Counsel I attended the sessions. The most contentious item that surfaced at that conference was our peace position.

During the course of the year we were invited to participate in several Bible conferences. We had a three-day Bible conference in the Bakerview Church, Clearbrook, in January. At Easter we motored to Pasedena, where I had been asked to speak at a four-day Bible conference in a German Baptist church.

Before the semester ended, I flew to Harrisonburg, Virginia, to speak at the graduation ceremony of Eastern Mennonite Seminary. Although the trip was arduous (flight delays and missed connections), I was warmly received in the home of George Brunk III, Dean of the seminary, and his wife. I had not been back to Harrisonburg since 1975, and it was, in one sense, a homecoming. It was good to know that we had so many friends in Virginia--former colleagues, students and neighbours.

I returned to Fresno just in time to attend the graduation service of our own seminary. It was our joy to have Lena's brother, Peter Hamm, and his wife Betty, with us for a few days. They had come for the graduation of their son-in-law, Greg Bright.

For the summer we motored back to Abbotsford to be close to our children, grandchildren and other family members. Lena found the trip difficult because shortly before graduation she had fallen and broken her right elbow. As soon as we got home she began physiotherapy in an effort to restore the function of her arm.

Shortly after our return I flew to Edmonton to attend the conference of the German Baptists. They had asked me to expound the book of Revelation. I stayed with a delightful elderly couple, met some former students, and enjoyed my ministry among these German-speaking people very much.

I had not been to the Canadian Conference of Mennonite Brethren during the two years that we were abroad and so I looked forward to attending the sessions in Saskatoon at the beginning of

July. Lena thought she would find it hard to sit through the long sessions and chose rather to stay at home. I was not very impressed by the way the Conference was handled. There was very little discussion of issues facing the church and I felt we had lost something very valuable. Nevertheless, it was good to meet with numerous friends from all across Canada.

During the summer I worked ahead on my courses for the coming year. We had been asked to return to Fresno for a second year as Visiting Professor. Friends from other parts of the country dropped in occasionally. Family get-togethers made our summer interesting. All of my family and most of Lena's family live in the Fraser Valley. Since we had not lived in B.C. for forty years (not since I was a student at the University of British Columbia), it was a joy to be close to so many of our family and friends--not to mention our children and grandchildren in Vancouver.

In the middle of August, Ray and Eleanor, our children from Winnipeg, came to see us with two of their children. Their eldest son, Jonathan, had left for Chad, Africa, on an MCC assignment. Before we fully realized it, the summer was gone and we were on our way to Fresno once again.

On May 17, 1992, forty seniors graduated from seminary and we were glad that we could have a small share in the training of some of them. We wish them well in their future ministry.

We had now been away from home for four years following retirement from MBBC in 1988, and we looked forward to a more settled life. We were still members of the Elmwood Mennonite Brethren Church, Winnipeg, and it was time for us to find a new church home in Abbotsford. During the two years that we taught in Fresno as visiting professor we attended the Butler MB Church, where we had been members during the years when we lived in Fresno. As soon as we returned to Abbotsford we became members of the Bakerview MB Church, Clearbrook. We knew many of the members of this church from earlier years. Moreover, Lena had a brother and I had a sister in this congregation.

Had we anticipated that the seminary would invite us back for a third year, we might very well have considered such an assignment. However, Wally Unger, president of Columbia Bible College, had asked us earlier if we would consider teaching some classes in the 1992-93 school year, and I had declared my willingness to do so. This would allow us to remain in Abbotsford. With this in view I spent part of the summer of 1992 preparing lectures for classes in New Testament subjects. So, after my seventieth birthday, I find myself in and out of the classroom and ministering in various congregations in the Fraser Valley. As I reflect on the seventy years that God has allowed me to live on his good earth, I am constantly overwhelmed by the grace of God that has come to be so undeservedly. Early in childhood Christ drew me to himself, and whatever I have been able to accomplish in life is but a footnote to that encounter with the living Christ. God, in his mercy, has sustained me in the faith in spite of intellectual challenges on university campuses and ridicule by secular humanists, whom John in the Revelation calls "earthdwellers." Moreover, I have had the great privilege for most of my life of being a participant in the ongoing work of Christ's kingdom. Teaching in Bible schools, colleges and seminaries at home and abroad, preaching in churches at home and in other countries--it all fell into my lap as a gift of God's unbounded favour.

I always get a bit nervous when fellow-believers report on their close walk with God: their victories, healings, and so forth. Since we are still in this age, in which the flesh and the Spirit are at war with one another, and since we have only the firstfruits of the Spirit, we should be a bit cautious about overstating our spiritual attainments. But let me give you just a glimpse into my life and thought.

In my late teens I resolved to have daily devotions. With a bit of discipline, this is a habit not too difficult to acquire, and once it is established, just like other good customs, it becomes a liberating experience. Customs, writes Eduard Schweizer of Zürich, are like railings along a stairway: they don't hinder you from going up and down, but they protect you from falling over the edge. In my devotions, usually in a morning hour, I read God's Word, listening for his voice. Just as you do not analyze the words of someone you love, writes Dietrich Bonhoeffer, but accept them as they are said to you, so we should accept God's Word and ponder it in our hearts. That is meditation. Sometimes I use other devotional helps, such as hymns, prayer books, or readings. My prayers, as one might expect, embrace my extended family, my daily tasks, my fears and failures, my hopes and dreams, and much intercession for our schools, our churches, my present and past colleagues, my friends and sometimes even my enemies.

God has graciously given me a deep confidence in his Word, the Scriptures. It has been my life's quest to understand the Scriptures and to ask how they apply to the ever-changing life situations in which believers find themselves. To the end of my days I shall be grateful to God for allowing me to acquire a knowledge of the biblical languages. Although they are no guarantee against failures in hermeneutics, they are indispensable tools for the study of the Scriptures. The Danish theologian, Kiergegaard, chided the theologians of his day for acting like school boys who knew they were going to be punished and so, to minimize the hurt, stuffed their back pockets full of lexicons and grammars. By contrast, I have found that one can bury one's head in a lexicon and come out with the glory of God.

It didn't happen over night, but I see it more clearly now than in my younger years, that intense academic efforts do not endanger a person's devotion to God. In fact, I have found the opposite to be true. When one offers one's academic activities up to God as a daily sacrifice, they become a means of grace. My patience tends to wear thin when I encounter students who in the name of piety shy away from the rigors of study.

My life has not been lived on cloud nine. John Newton's confession, "Through many dangers, toils and snares, I have already come," is also my story. There have been high points of elation, to be sure, but there has also been sorrow and grief. My late teens were overshadowed by my deep desire to live a godly life and my inability to attain to what I thought were the biblical standards. The tragic death of my twenty-one year-old brother plunged me into unspeakable depths of grief. Then, as I began to teach and to enjoy the friendship of wonderful colleagues, I had to discover that some of them had feet of clay (as do I). Sins of the spirit--jealousy, greed, slander--can be so destructive to cooperative efforts in the work of the kingdom!

Another deep disappointment to me was to discover that liberal theologians can be so prejudiced, narrow and defensive, that they will not tolerate a more conservative approach to Scripture. I had completed my course work, met all my language requirements, and passed my comprehensive exams for my doctorate in Chicago when my thesis advisor insisted that I accept his view of Scripture or drop the subject. To drop everything and start over again at another university was probably one of the low points of my life.

As for my family life, all I can say is that I have been greatly blessed. In Lena I have found a constant support these past forty-nine years. She is the mother of our five children and skimped and saved for many years so that we could send them to private school, pay for music lessons, and keep them dressed and nourished. Her prayers for the family and her concern that all of them should become followers or Jesus have been constant. She has spent many months alone with the children when I was away, either in studies or on service assignments in other lands. I can never repay her for all she has done for me and our children.

With respect to church-life, Lena and I have been members of the Mennonite Brethren Church all our married life and we retained membership in our church even when we lived in places where there was no MB church. My contribution to the local churches of which we have been members has been primarily in preaching the Word. This I have done gratis and with joy. Also, I have served many years on church councils and from time to time as pastoral assistant. Lena has served in more practical ways. We have kept up the practice of tithing throughout our married life and have tried to support the church through our prayers.

My life has been greatly enriched by the many contacts I have had with other Mennonite bodies over the years (not to speak of Baptists, Christian and Missionary Alliance, and others). In my growing-up years the lines between Mennonite Brethren and General Conference Mennonites were rather clearly defined. My parents had both left the *Kirchengemeinde* in Russia and threw in their lot with Mennonite Brethren. Naturally they set the selves off from their past rather sharply and that attitude influenced us as children. As a result we had little to do with non-Mennonite Brethren.

All this changed, however, when we came to Winnipeg. Here we were frequently invited to serve in Evangelical Mennonite Conference, Evangelical Mennonite Mission Conference, and General Conference Mennonite churches. In the case of the latter we served at various conferences in Manitoba, Saskatchewan, Alberta and British Columbia. Also, we had a friendly relationship with the faculties of the Canadian Mennonite Bible College, the Steinbach Bible College, and also with the seminary in Elkhart.

When we joined the faculty of Eastern Mennonite Seminary, where Myron Augsburger was the president, and George Brunk was the dean a whole new world opened up to us. The Mennonite Church has travelled a different road, historically, than those Mennonite bodies which have a Russian background. We were overwhelmed by the kindness and the acceptance these people showed us. Not only did we serve at the seminary, but we were frequently invited for preaching and teaching services in Virginia, Pennsylvania and Ohio.

Moreover, we were invited repeatedly to serve the Mennonite community in Switzerland--always a delightful experience. And while in Europe we were able also to serve in Mennonite churches of Germany and France.

As I write this I am lecturing at Columbia Bible College, which has become an inter-Mennonite school. These contacts with God's people from other Mennonite persuasions have led to deep friendships and to a widening of horizons which I shall cherish to the end of my days.

Many things have changed in the MB Church over the years. When we became members of the MB church we had as yet no salaried pastors. Also, the entire congregation participated in decision-making, although the church council prepared the agenda. The current trend to turn over the decision-making process to a group of elders is in my view, a rather mixed blessing. What I find amusing is that the new model is sometimes advocated as being the "biblical" model. One doesn't need to know too much church history to know that churches have derived a great variety of church structures from the Scriptures, and certainly no single model guarantees the spiritual vitality of a congregation.

Worship styles have also changed considerably in our life-time-- some no doubt for the better, others not. Although we have better trained preachers today, I am not terribly impressed (with exceptions) with the level of preaching in our churches. The music-making in our churches today is generally at a higher level than it was in the days of our youth. However, I fail to see how choruses sung with the accompaniment of electronic gear is supposed to be an improvement over the rich hymnody of our past. Nor does one have to "dance before the Lord," as David did, in order to be edified.

Perhaps one area in which I have witnessed a profound shift in my life-time is that of Christian ethics. Many of the things the church struggled with fifty years ago have become non-issues. Until the outbreak of the War, in 1939, only the *avant garde* had radios, and not with the blessing of the church. The argument was that it allowed the world to enter the living room. However, when war broke and people were anxious to know how the battle was going, the radio was soon found in most of our homes. Even more critical was the advent of television. For some time it was too sensitive a topic for the Board of Reference and Counsel to put on its agenda for discussion. When it finally did come to the floor of the Canadian Conference, it was basically to warn against its dangers. Some churches even disciplined members who purchased TV's. Today we hardly talk about such items, although everyone agrees that the mass media have had a profound influence on the thinking of our society--Christians included.

If any one of us had attended a movie theatre in our youth, we would certainly have come under the discipline of the church. It was part of our baptismal vow that we would not attend movies. Also, it was still a rule at MBBC when I came on staff that students not frequent the theatres. That, too, is a question that has receded into the background. Our church in the past probably assumed too much responsibility in overseeing the daily lives of its members. Today, however, there is a great lack of accountability on the part of individual members to the local congregation.

Much time and energy was wasted, I believe, in trying to determine what was right or wrong in areas where it was difficult to find guidance from the Bible. It was not considered proper for Christian young people to go bowling, play pool, or go roller skating, for that meant associating with the world. Today such activities are generally considered innocent past-times, but as late as twenty-five years ago they created a lot of tensions. No doubt some of these issues arose out of our acculturation to a new society; they conflicted with ethical values brought over from Europe. And, when one looks at some of the current evils such as sexual promiscuity, drugs, abortion, wide-spread divorce, and the like even among Christian people, our struggles with ethical issues that lay in grey areas were child's play in comparison. However, there was in the past a great concern that individual believers should not offend others by their behaviour, and that concern has unfortunately been pushed into the background by our individualism today.

Theologically, too, there has been a shift in the last half of this century. The first paper that I ever presented at a study conference dealt with the question of "The Perseverance of the Saints." The teaching of eternal security was seen as dangerous by most of our church leaders. Accordingly, we grappled with the warnings of Scripture against "falling away from the faith," and the assurances that Christ would keep us safe to the end. Today I don't hear either college or seminary students discussing this issue, even though they know more about Calvinism and Arminianism than we did.

Another question that made people nervous a generation ago was how to harmonize the Scriptures with the discoveries of modern science. Since I taught the book of Genesis at MBBC in the fifties, I had to come to terms with this question. I was greatly helped by Bernard Ramm's book *The Christian View of Science and Scripture,* and by his later volume on hermeneutics, *Protestant Biblical Interpretation.* When I was asked to give five lectures on creation at a study conference held at Tabor College, I disappointed some church leaders for not "hammering" godless scientists. There was a general feeling at the time that one had to decide between holding firmly to biblical teaching or to the discoveries of science. It was my conviction, however, that the God of the Bible was also the God of creation, and that we could rejoice in discoveries made in both of these fields. (The enormous ethical problems that some scientific discoveries have created were not in focus at that time.)

When the charismatic movement burst upon the scene and made inroads into some of our churches, our biblical scholars were forced to study the relevant New Testament texts with greater intensity. At a study conference in Denver, sponsored by the Board of Reference and Counsel of the General Conference, I presented a paper on the baptism of the Spirit. Although I argued against a two-stage salvation experience (conversion and baptism of the Spirit), there were those who thought I was too sympathetic to the movement. In light of the fact that the Alberta MB Conference had gone on record (when we still lived in Alberta) condemning Pentecostalism as a heresy, I can understand the hesitancy to see any good in this movement. We cannot deny that many people in our own churches have found spiritual renewal through the charismatic movement, but that doesn't mean that the theological problems have disappeared; they are still with us.

Since I was a member of the Board of Reference and Counsel of the General Conference for eighteen years, I was involved in many theological issues that surfaced during that time. Many of them arose out of different ways of reading the Bible. I recall giving lectures on hermeneutics at Tabor College which some listeners found unsettling. When we were invited to join our seminary faculty in 1975, I was asked what I thought might be the most critical issue facing our churches. I answered: hermeneutics. Although I claim no gifts of prophecy, that prediction was clearly fulfilled.

The teachers in our colleges and in our seminary by and large had moved away from the dispensational approach to the Bible. I, too, had long come to the conviction that the teachings of John Darby "divided the word of truth" in such a way that the unity of the Bible was undermined. The matter became rather acute when some church leaders insisted that I must follow the hermeneutics made popular in America by the Scofield Bible. Although I tried to accommodate our church leaders in other areas, on this issue I was unyielding. We then decided to have a conference on hermeneutics to which all the Bible teachers of our schools were invited. We met in Fresno and had a very meaningful consultation on how to interpret the Bible.

Through the publication of Harold Lindsell's books *The Battle for the Bible* and *The Bible in the Balance,* some church leaders were sure that our colleges and seminary no longer held to the "inerrancy" of the Scriptures. I was particularly embarrassed by Lindsell's second volume, in which he devoted a chapter to the departure of the Mennonite Brethren from the faith . He mentioned me, together with two other teachers, as representative of those who had lost their high view of the Bible. I had not reviewed Lindsell's first book favourably, because of its belligerent spirit, and so he inferred that I had a lower view of Scripture than he did. When this question was finally resolved at the General Conference in 1987, held in Abbotsford, I had the joy of writing the resolution that was accepted by the Conference. It is not a very edifying spectacle when some of those who make slogans (such as "inerrancy") the litmus test of a person's view of the Bible do not take the authority of the Word of God seriously in some important areas of the church's life.

However, no question caused so much controversy in my experience as teacher and preacher as the question of eschatology. Having discovered the wonderful continuity of God's saving plan for humankind in the Bible, I lost interest in the eschatological intricacies of the dispensational school. I had disposed of Larkin's eschatological charts long ago. Questions such as "Will Christ come before or after the tribulation?" became irrelevant for me, for Jesus and the apostles clearly taught that the saints must enter the eternal kingdom through much tribulation. Since I found no evidence from the New Testament for dividing up the return of Christ into two "comings" (the rapture and the Day of the Lord), and that, in fact, the "last days" had begun in the first century, I was spared speculating about which current events might be signs of the imminent return of our Lord. As far as I was concerned, the establishment of the state of Israel in 1948 had nothing to do with the blessed hope of the believer. However, for such views I was called interesting names. I still have a folder full of letters denouncing my "heretical" views on eschatology. My book *And Then Comes the End* allayed some of these criticisms, when it was discovered that I held to every fundamental teaching of the New Testament on eschatology. What was missing was the nonsense that goes under the guise of "prophecy" (such as date-setting, or determining from political, sociological and economic developments how close we are to the end).

I must admit that there are aspects of current church-life that are not to my liking. Vice versa, there were practices in our churches fifty years ago that I am glad we have left behind. The many changes that have taken place in my relatively short life shall not affect my loyalty to the church. Having worshipped in so many different churches and in other cultures, I can overlook some of the innovations that strike me as trite and absurd.

Seven decades have come and gone. Inevitably the question of the Chronicler comes to mind: "Who am I, Lord God, and what is my house, that you have brought me thus far?" (1 Chronicles 17:16). How many more years he will allow us to continue this earthly pilgrimage we cannot tell. Whether he will call us by death or by his glorious coming is not for us to determine. He has promised to be at our side even if we should have to walk through the valley of the shadow of death. As long as we live, we want to serve the Christ who loved us and gave himself for us.

IT IS NOT FINISHED

It is not finished, Lord.
There is not one thing done;
There is no battle of my life
That I have really won.

And now I come to tell Thee
How I fought to fail.
My human, all too human, tale
Of weakness and futility.

And yet there is a faith in me
That Thou wilt find in it
One word that Thou canst take
And make
The centre of a sentence
In Thy book of poetry.

I cannot read the writing of the years,
My eyes are full of fears,
It gets all blurred and won't make sense;
It's full of contradictions
Like the scribblings of a child.

I can but hand it in, and hope
That Thy great mind, which reads
The writings of so many lives,
Wilt understand this scrawl
And what it strives to say - but leaves unsaid.
I cannot write it over, the stars are coming out,
My body needs its bed.
I have no strength for more,
So it must stand or fall - dear Lord,
That's all.

> G. A. Studdert Kennedy.